RUNNER'S WORLD.

GUIDE TO

ADVENTURE RACING

RUNNER'S WORLD.
GUIDE TO
ADVENTURE RACING

HOW TO BECOME A SUCCESSFUL RACER AND ADVENTURE ATHLETE

IAN ADAMSON
THE WORLD'S GREATEST ADVENTURE RACER

PHOTOGRAPHY BY **TONY DI ZINNO**

RODALE

Notice

The information in this book is meant to supplement, not replace, proper exercise training. All forms of exercise pose some inherent risks. The editors and publisher advise readers to take full responsibility for their safety and know their limits. Before practicing the exercises in this book, be sure that your equipment is well-maintained, and do not take risks beyond your level of experience, aptitude, training, and fitness. The exercise and dietary programs in this book are not intended as a substitute for any exercise routine or treatment or dietary regimen that may have been prescribed by your doctor. As with all exercise and dietary programs, you should get your doctor's approval before beginning.

Mention of specific companies, organizations, or authorities in this book does not imply endorsement by the publisher, nor does mention of specific companies, organizations, or authorities imply that they endorse this book.

Internet addresses and telephone numbers given in this book were accurate at the time it went to press.

Printed in the United States of America

Rodale Inc. makes every effort to use acid-free ∞, recycled paper ♻.

Photographs by Tony Di Zinno, except: Ian Adamson, pp. xx and 13

Book design by Drew Frantzen

Library of Congress Cataloging-in-Publication Data

Adamson, Ian, date.
    Runner's world guide to adventure racing : how to become a successful racer and adventure athlete / Ian Adamson.
        p.   cm.
    Includes index.
    ISBN 1–57954–836–9 paperback
    1. Adventure racing.   I. Title: Guide to adventure racing.
    II. Runner's world.   III. Title.
GV1038.A33   2004
796.5—dc22   2003025401

Distributed to the book trade by St. Martin's Press

2 4 6 8 10 9 7 5 3 1 paperback

 **RODALE**

WE **INSPIRE** AND **ENABLE** PEOPLE TO IMPROVE
THEIR LIVES AND THE WORLD AROUND THEM

FOR MORE OF OUR PRODUCTS
WWW.RODALESTORE.COM
(800) 848-4735

FOR HEATHER AND DON,

WHO PROVIDED ME WITH THE ENCOURAGEMENT AND
OPPORTUNITIES TO PURSUE AN UNCONVENTIONAL LIFE.

"Don't be too timid and squeamish about your actions. All life is an experiment. The more experiments you make the better."

—Ralph Waldo Emerson

CONTENTS

Part 3

Part 4

Adventure-Racing Resources

FOREWORD

EXPERIENCING A WEE BIT OF ADVENTURE, COMPETITION, AND INSIGHT WITH THE TOUGHEST MAN ON THE PLANET

by Bill Katovsky

You won't find him swapping spittle and broken chairs with loutish, muscle-bound pro wrestlers. Nor will you ever see him lifting a midsize Japanese car in one of those televised "Strongman" competitions. But if there ever comes a time when some organization gives out an award for "Toughest Man on the Planet," that honor should go to Ian Adamson. He is the best all-around athlete I have ever known. And I have followed the multisport scene since the early 1980s, and have written extensively on all the triathlete legends. Ian is the Little Giant.

I first met Ian during the spring of 1996 when I attended a 4-day class at the Presidio Adventure Racing Academy in San Francisco. He was an instructor. At the school, we learned the basics of rope climbing and descending, kayaking, horseback riding, and navigation by compass.

Graduation was marked by a 24-hour adventure race in San Francisco Bay and throughout Golden Gate National Recreational Area. We were divided into two teams of five each. It was Ian's job to travel with my team, giving us advice and pointers along the way.

The day began with a 2-hour hilly trail run, followed by 6 hours of kayaking. It was my good luck (or misfortune) to be paired with one of the strongest female kayakers in the world, Andrea Spitzer, part-time model and world-champion ultradistance paddler from Germany. My

Ian Adamson

arms were limp noodles by the time we reached the Sausalito Beach. But we were in first place. We jumped on our mountain bikes for a hill-filled 10-mile ride. Then the real fun began: 25 miles of hiking steep fire roads in the mountains of the Golden Gate National Recreation Area. Up and down we went, as if we were on some out-of-service giant escalator to fatigue.

By late afternoon, I was feeling beat. In adventure racing, all members of a team must stay together. A team is only as fast as the slowest member—and this time I was the one. During an ascent of a steep hill, I felt a hand pressing on my back. I turned around—it was Ian. Hey, I didn't mind the assistance, but I outweighed Ian by 30 pounds. He's pushing *me* up the hill? He flashed me a big Aussie grin, looking like he had just stepped out of one of San Francisco's best restaurants.

As dawn was breaking, our team collapsed in a tired, dirty heap at the final race checkpoint: American Youth Hostel. We won; the other team wouldn't arrive for several hours. They had taken an extended rest during the night.

Ian and I became close friends after that race. Back then, he was well-liked on the global adventure-racing circuit, but he was hardly a household name. Today, he's widely recognized as one of the world's foremost adventure racers.

Ian is hewed from a most remarkable slice of DNA, a perfect strain of brains with brawn, equally at home in the jungles of Borneo or Fiji and in the science lab, where he applied his advanced college degree in mechanical engineering to create a patented medical device for CPR. He earned a berth in *Guinness Book of World Records* for setting the world record in marathon kayaking—217 miles in 24 hours along the Yukon River. He also spends a lot of time in the kitchen, where he is a gourmet chef. He's been cohost of *Men's Journal Adventure Team* on Outdoor Life Network. And he's a motivational speaker and instructor at adventure-racing schools. He's also a Cessna pilot and trained concert flautist.

With consistent victories in all the major adventure races (Raid, Eco-Challenge, X-Games, and Southern Traverse), Ian is the sport's Tiger Woods. He has the same toothy, incandescent smile. And like the golf phenom, Adamson's biological parents come from different racial backgrounds: His mother is English and his father is from Singapore. While Ian has achieved deity status among adventure racers, this supremely talented multisport athlete goes about his daily training and activities in Boulder, Colorado, with all the reserve and quiet anonymity of a Zen monk. The physical muse that motivates this Mighty Mite is a childlike curiosity to visit new worlds. He embodies the playful restlessness of a young child.

I once traveled with Ian to Costa Rica for a jungle-man-style adventure vacation. We were on a landmark pioneering odyssey, a do-it-yourself weeklong fitness vacation that was more adventure pacing than adventure racing. The goal was simple: get athletically trashed by running up the 10,000-foot Turiabla volcano, mountain biking down it, whitewater rafting down the Picuare River, kayaking in the Gulf of Nicoya, running along its rocky coastline, horseback riding on a flat, sandy beach, and then surfing. But unlike real adventure-racing McCoys, who might go 3 consecutive days without sleep, we would be bedding down at night in lodgings, homes, and even a four-star hotel along the way. No sharing of tooth-brushes, living out of smelly packs, or hobbling around with trashed, blis-tering, duct tape—encased feet.

Our third day in Costa Rica began with a 30-minute ferry ride from Punteranas, a decrepit port on the Pacific lifted right out of a Graham Greene novel, to the Nicoya Peninsula. Once we docked, we headed di-rectly for the sole restaurant on the deserted shore, a thatched-palm-roof affair, where we scarfed down a big breakfast of Cokes, scrambled eggs, black beans, and rice. With the meal still rumbling through our systems, we got on our mountain bikes for a several-hour ride over sandy farm roads. The going was hot and tough. Being the slowest rider, I cycled alone. Everyone else was about a half-hour ahead. The occasional farmer would politely point out the right direction when I would haltingly ask, "Dónde es amigos?" I finally caught up with the gang at another restau-rant right on the coast. Everyone was finishing a big lunch of seviche (fish marinated in lime). Preparations were under way for the next leg: a 20-mile kayak trip through the island-dotted Gulf of Nicoya. We each had a solo kayak.

By the third or fourth hour of paddling, I could barely raise my arms. Once again, I was all alone, this time in the calm Pacific waters, knifing the paddle blade into the water like an irregularly paced metronome, Left, right, left, right. All the others were far, far ahead. I couldn't even see them. I only caught up with everyone because they had taken a long rest on the shore of a nearby deserted island. We still faced several more hours of kayaking before reaching our destination: a campground/restau-rant in a tiny village near the Barcelo resort. Night was soon approaching and we would have to be paddling in the dark—a recipe for disaster. None of us had brought lights. So we decided to stay together as a pack.

Except I had trouble keeping pace. So we did what all good adventure-racing teammates should do: We employed teamwork. Using bungee cords, Ian attached the back end of his kayak to the front end of mine, and began towing me.

Because kayaks are designed to skim along the surface and not displace water like, say, a tugboat, it took Ian double the effort to paddle half as far. I would have been eager to lend assistance, but my lactic acid—engorged biceps were spasming with muscle cramps. So with twilight coloring the sky a brilliant shade of reddish purple, I leaned back in the cockpit and relaxed while Ian zigged and zagged in his attempt to move both our kayaks forward.

"So, Ian, how are you doing up there?" I asked with affected nonchalance.

"No problem at all, mate," he warmly responded.

"Aren't you getting tired?"

"No.

"Are you sure?"

"Oh, it's a wee bit difficult, so I'm just treating this as an extra-hard workout."

Never once did he ask me to paddle. After about an hour, my biceps stopped cramping, and I could resume paddling. The shore lights twinkled about 2 miles off in the distance. Pride and determination kicked in. I unfastened the bungee cords, thanked my tower, and began to paddle. My upper arms were functional again after the rest, but without Ian's generous assistance, I would have been a bobbing cork on the gulf waters until daybreak.

The fourth day's destination was the Cabo Blanco nature reserve on the southern tip of the Nicoya Peninsula. For much of the morning, we had bombed and bumbled through thick jungle undergrowth. We had long ago left the marked trail because we had a paranoid aversion to the local ranger, whose job (apart from resting cozily in the shade in his hammock) was ostensibly to keep people out of the reserve. We followed a streambed uphill that petered out the way all false trails do. The forest grew thicker, the terrain steeper, the thorn bushes thornier, the day hotter, and our nerves tauter. Yet Ian was having a grand time. "Let's just climb to the tallest hill and we'll be fine," he extolled in his calm, Tony Robbins—positive voice laced with his Australian accent. "We'll see the ocean," he continued, "and we'll take it from there." We were carrying no compasses, little water, and only a few energy bars.

When we summited, Ian paused to take a bearing, using the sun and his own shadow as part of some private trigonometric calculation, then charged off to the east, to the Pacific. The group followed our intrepid pathfinder. But our path was a long, steep embankment covered with plant life. We pinballed off trees, holding on to breakaway vines to slow our descent. After another hour of scrambling over boulders and limbo dancing under fallen trees, we reached the beach. We were all safe, though scratched and nicked. We had been in the jungle for less than 4 hours.

We still had a 5-mile run/hike ahead of us to the Mal Pais Surf Camp, but we would take a lunch break there and dawdle in the swimming pool. We needed that hour of reprieve before being set up on horses for our 4-hour horseback ride along the deserted beach to a sprawling cattle ranch. As we trotted and walked on horseback along the empty beach, the sky turning salmon-colored in the twilight, we stopped once for a fresh-coconut break. They were watery and delicious.

The sun dropped lower, its luminous disk a fiery orange ball propped on the flat silvery water. I looked over at Ian, who was having fun coaxing his horse to gallop in the surf. "Ian," I yelled over, "if I asked you right now—I mean, right this very instant—to go back and run along the beach all the way back to where we got lost in Cabo Blanco, and have them meet us at the ranch at the end, would you? Could you?"

Without hesitating, Ian replied, "Sure. It might take me a while since it will be at night, but I'll do it."

—Bill Katovsky founded *Tri-Athlete* magazine (renamed *Triathlete*) and is the founding editor-in-chief of *Inside Triathlon*.

ACKNOWLEDGMENTS

Many thanks to my good friends and teammates over the years, especially John Howard, Robert Nagle, Steve Gurney, Keith and Andrea Murray, and Jane Hall, who have inspired and taught me a great deal about racing, teamwork, and life in general.

I am also grateful to my teammates Danelle Ballangee, Sara Ballantyne, Mike Kloser, Michael Tobin, and Dan Weiland, who continue to push the limits of human performance and challenge me to keep up with them when we race. And to Isaac Wilson, who has kept us all laughing, even when sick, tired, dirty, crabby, and covered from head to toe in wasp bites.

Thanks to Novak Thompson, Rebecca Rusch, and John Jacoby from team Montrail, and my teammates on team Nike ACG/Balance Bar, Danelle, Mike, and Michael, who kindly shared their expertise in "Tips from the Top."

Special thanks to Bill Katovsky, without whom this book would still be rattling inside my head, and to Andrea Pedolsky, my patient and good-humored agent.

Thanks also to Jeremy Katz and the staff at Rodale Inc., and to Alisa Bauman, who did a fine job deciphering and simplifying the technical jargon that crept into the text.

I am indebted to Tony Di Zinno for providing the wonderful images captured over the last 10 years as he suffered through the same filth and privations in races as the rest of us, but without the lure of a prize check at the finish.

I have been fortunate to have had the support of many wonderful sponsors over the years, all of whom have believed in the sport of adventure racing and have helped grow it to the level it is at today. Special thanks to the folks at Nike ACG, Balance Bar, Oakley, Giro, Giant Bicycles, Petzl, SoBe, Watchful Eye Designs (Splash Cady/TitanSac), Simon River Sports, Sterling Ropes, Suunto USA, Kahtoola, Prijon, Cross Skate,

JetLites, TriAll3Sports, RailRiders, GoLite, Salomon, Futura Surf Skis, Ultimate Direction, Princeton Tec, Stolquist, Lotus Designs, and Dana Designs.

Almost finally, thanks to everyone I forgot to thank, which is a remarkable feat for me to remember, now that I have lost so many brain cells racing.

Finally, extra special thanks to Carla, whose patience, understanding, and support helped make the process of writing this book a pleasure, and to Bruce and Jackie Ross, whose patience, understanding, and support of both of us made Carla's patience, understanding, and support bearable for her. Please take a Tylenol and call me in the morning if pain persists.

For me, adventure was part of my upbringing. Here is what one of our family vacations looked like.

INTRODUCTION

THE JOYS OF ADVENTURE

Adventure racing is an unusual sport, part adventure, part race, part human experience. The sport has helped me to live a little more poignantly and to taste more of life's abundant fruits. Each race has expanded my experience of different cultures and lands, challenged my ideas, and pushed me further than I thought I could go. During an adventure race all of life's most basic components are compressed and amplified. It's as if a year's worth of physical, mental, emotional, cultural, and spiritual experiences have been scooped up and squashed together into a week's time.

Successful adventure athletes quickly figure out how to communicate, avoid conflict, work as a team, and develop synergy. Character traits that most people value highly—honesty, integrity, kindness, selflessness, generosity, and sensitivity—are all central to a successful adventure racer's nature. People who don't embrace these values can succeed for a while on strength, charm, and charisma, but they don't tend to last long.

As I approach my late thirties with almost 20 years of adventure racing experience, I feel I am only halfway to my destination. I think of adventure racing as a postdoctoral degree in living. I take the lessons learned from racing and apply them to my family life, my professional life, and my personal life.

I was introduced to the sport of adventure racing—or more accurately "multisport," as it was then known in Australia and New Zealand—in 1984. Some crazed friends who insisted that beating themselves up and getting lost in the Australian bush was "fun" tried to talk me into competing in my first multisport race. I thought they were more than a few sausages short of the barbie, and I wanted nothing to do with the pain, hunger, confusion, and ultimate suffering involved.

Anyone who raced vast distances on bad food, in ugly conditions, and on little sleep was clearly a spoke or two short of a wheel.

My masochistic tendencies somehow got the better of me, however, and I agreed to be a support crew for some mates doing WildTrek, a 2-day winter race in the Southern Alps of Australia. The event included Nordic skiing, orienteering, cyclocross, and whitewater kayaking. Sometime later, a combination of peer pressure ("Are you a wimp, or what?") and a state of mild inebriation caused me to reluctantly agree to compete in the race. I consequently embarked on a largely ineffective, but thoroughly enjoyable, training program that consisted of social weekend paddling expeditions with the Sydney University Canoe Club and a handful of triathlons. A year later, my teammate Keith Tuffley and I donned our delightful rainbow-colored Lycra body suits and launched into our first, painfully satisfying adventure-racing experience. As we shivered in the predawn of day 2, scraping ice out of our kayaks and barely able to fold our stiffened limbs into their claustrophobic cockpits, I swore black and blue never to suffer this much again. Twelve hours later at the awards ceremony, after I wolfed down a full meal and with libations in hand, the joy set in. We had finished third, but our placing seemed irrelevant. Just finishing provided an amazing feeling. I was hooked.

A Short History of Adventure

Humans have been involved in adventure for as long as history itself. The drive to discover has led people to establish new civilizations, explore new countries, and discover new lands. Adventure is a personal journey of discovery, and many have lived this dream, from Homer's Odysseus to Marco Polo to Captain James Cook, from Lewis and Clark to Shackleton to Earhart, from Neil Armstrong to Buckminster Fuller. In the last 100 years, people have raced to claim firsts to both geographic poles and all the 8,000-meter peaks.

In the late 1400s a flood of European explorers raced to discover the untold wealth of the ancient and the New World and bring back the

Team Eco-Internet leads the 1996 Eco-Challenge in British Columbia.

riches to their homelands. Within a period of only 11 years, Bartholomeu Dias, Christopher Columbus, John Cabot, Vasco da Gama, and Amerigo Vespucci had thrown together a bunch of motley crews and raced off across the high seas in their improbably tiny craft. Many of the explorers and their followers discovered fabulous treasures during their bold, exciting, and somewhat dangerous undertakings.

During the next 300 years or so, most of the New World was "discovered" by Europeans as merchants and traders bounded around the planet to secure their wealth. As countries were conquered and Empires built, less and less was left to discover, and by the late 19th century the only adventurers left were those who wanted to secure bragging rights. James Clark Ross risked hypothermia nosing around Antarctica. Stanley, Livingstone, and Richard Burton trudged around Africa and succeeded in hosting an impressive array of nasty tropical diseases. Several deranged individuals whose brains were baked by the relentless sun of Australia's vast and inhospitable interior tried to find an inland sea in the desert.

By 1900 racing to very cold, very high, and otherwise inaccessible places that were unfriendly to humans became the reckless pursuit of the rich and foolish. Watching these often irresponsible dramas unfold became a slow-motion spectator sport for whole nations, while national newspapers sponsored these races of adventure. In 1909 American Robert E. Perry won a hard-fought battle with Norwegian Fridtjof Nansen to reach the North Pole. Then in 1911, another Norwegian, Roald Amundsen, squeaked by Englishman Robert Falcon Scott to win a close race to the South Pole. Unfortunately for Scott, he not only lost the race by a few weeks, but lost his life by a few miles, unwittingly succumbing to the cold in his tent just 11 miles from a food and fuel cache.

In 1953, Edmund Hillary, a gangly sheep farmer from New Zealand, and his trusty Sherpa guide, Tensing Norgay, became the first humans to summit Mount Everest, ending a race to the top of the world that had lasted almost a century.

Ultra-Endurance Competitions

As the privileged and well-to-do sallied forth on their adventures of exploration around the world, other less well-heeled individuals started turning to similarly difficult endeavors. This opportunity arose with the Industrial Revolution as people found they no longer had to work 12 hours a day, 6 days a week, to make ends meet. With all the extra leisure time and few places left to explore, people began to wonder about the outer edges of their abilities. Ultrarunning and ultradistance cycling became quite popular.

In 1762 John Hague of Britain won the first 100-mile foot race in a time of 23 hours, 15 minutes, which isn't too shabby even by today's standards. Another Englishman, by the name of Foster Powell, became the first ultrarunning star in 1773 when he walked the 396 miles from London to York and back in 6 days on a wager for 100 guineas (over $100,000 in today's money). Six-day races (known as pedestrianism) subsequently became popular because they were the longest events that could be held without competing on Sunday. Typically, 6-day races started at the stroke of midnight on Sunday and concluded at the same time the following Saturday.

American Edward Payson Weston grabbed the broader public's attention in 1874 by covering 500 miles in 6 days. Another Englishman, Charlie

Rowell, set the standard for ultra-endurance events by running hard for the first 3 days of a 6-day race and dominating the field to the finish. In February 1882 he set out to produce the ultimate 6-day performance and covered the first 100 miles in 13:26, 150 miles in 24 hours, and 258 miles in 48 hours. These remarkable records lasted almost 50 years.

In 1884 yet another Englishman, Thomas Stevens, rode from Oakland to Boston in 104 days, 6 hours, on a penny-farthing cycle, a feat not bettered on a "standard" bicycle for almost 60 years and never repeated on a penny-farthing. In 1943 American Jack Russell rode a bicycle from Miami to San Diego in 27 days, 17 hours. Since then there have been many attempts at the record, and in 1982 the competition became an organized race called RAAM (Race Across America), where the winners finish in around 8 days.

Running and cycling were not the only sports lending themselves to challenges of extraordinary distance. In the 1960s, two canoe races of over 250 miles started, one in Australia and one in Texas. In 1962 Frank Brown and Bill George decided to make a "safari" out of paddling the 375 miles of the San Marcos and Guadalupe rivers in a large rowboat from Aquarena Springs all the way to Corpus Christi on the Gulf of Mexico. Over the years this, too, developed into a race, and today the official distance is 261 miles from San Marcos to Seadrift, including dozens of portages, logjams, bridges, mazelike swamps, venomous snakes, and ferocious reptilelike garfish that ram boats and people alike with alarming frequency.

Another dimension was added to ultradistance endurance sports in 1974 when Gordie Ainsleigh decided he'd run the trails of an annual horse race from Lake Tahoe to Auburn in California because he didn't have a mount. This route became the Western States Trail 100 and spawned the development of trail running (as opposed to road running) in the United States.

The Modern Era of Adventure Racing

With nothing much left to explore in the geographic world and few bona fide adventures to pursue, people began combining sports and creating their own outdoor escapades. Troops of hippies invaded places like

Nepal, Casablanca, and Thailand in the 1960s and '70s, and when there were no places left to fill with funny-smelling smoke, they started getting really creative. Adventure travel was born and an industry grew up with it.

The Iditarod Trail, from Anchorage in south-central Alaska to Nome on the western Bering Sea coast, is home to a whole family of wilderness races, all of which started with the original Iditarod Sled Dog Race in 1973. Although this race is not strictly human-powered, the Iditarod requires a high level of skill, teamwork, and exceptional endurance. This event covers the length of the Iditarod Trail, with each team of 12 to 16 dogs and their musher covering the 1,150 miles in 10 to 17 days. Since 1983 a host of "nondog" races developed—on foot, snowshoes, skis, bike, or a combination of these. In 1984 the Iditaski was created, and 3 years later the Iditashoe. The Iditabike was added in 1989 (won by mountain bike world champion Mike Kloser, another athlete who features prominently in adventure sports later on). And in 1991 the sports were combined as a small festival of suffering and renamed the Iditasport. The Iditasport Extreme was created in 1997 as the adventure-racing wave washed up to Alaska (350 miles, anything goes) and in 2000 race director Dan Bull added the Iditasport Impossible, traversing the entire Iditarod Trail.

Triathlon is another parent to adventure racing. The first recognized race combining three sports took place September 4, 1921, in Marseilles, France, by the Petit Perillon swim club. It was called Course des Trois Sports, or the Race of Three Sports. The race consisted of a bicycle leg of about 4.2 miles, a run of 3.1 miles, and a 200-meter swim. Two races in California ushered the modern era of triathlon in 1974: Eppies Great Race in Sacramento, the longest continuously running three-sport event (run-bike-paddle), and the Mission Bay Triathlon in San Diego, which was the first to use the currently accepted standard format of swim-bike-run.

The more extreme version of triathlon started in 1978 on the island of Oahu, Hawaii, inspired by a debate among competitors about who was fittest: swimmers, runners, or other athletes. One of the participants, Navy Commander John Collins, proposed an event to settle the argument. He suggested combining three existing races, the Waikiki Rough-water Swim (2.4 miles), the Around-Oahu Bike Race (112 miles), and the Honolulu Marathon (26.2 miles). Gordon Haller, a runner, won the inaugural race, dubbed the Ironman, in 11:46:58. Triathlon really hit the scene in 1982 when ABC *Wide World of Sports* televised the dramatic race to the finish between Kathleen McCartney and Julie Moss in the Hawaii Ironman (which had moved to Kona in 1981). Moss was leading the race when she collapsed yards from the finish line. As she crawled to the end, McCartney passed her.

The Kiwis got in on the act in 1980, when an eccentric Kiwi promoter named Robin Judkins dreamed up the Alpine Ironman, based loosely on Hawaii's Ironman. The Alpine Ironman was only a couple of hours long, but it combined the sports of Alpine skiing, trail running, cycling, and whitewater kayaking. This was probably the first event in New Zealand of a genre that is now called multisport, and it set the stage for the country to become a hotbed of world-class adventure athletes, including John Howard, who won all seven Alpine Ironman events. Judkins quickly moved on to bigger and better things and, in 1983, staged the first coast-to-coast race across the New Zealand's South Island, one of the proving grounds for today's adventure racers.

Back in the United States, in 1981 George Ripley dreamed up the Alaskan Mountain Wilderness Classic, which involved crossing 155 miles of Alaskan wilderness from Hope to Homer. He coined the name Wilderness Racing in the process. The event was the first to be self-supported and the first to incorporate wilderness navigation, now a defining factor in all long adventure races.

Eric Ward, a rafting guide from the state of Victoria in Australia, saw the Alpine Ironman and decided to build on the idea by incorporating orienteering, Nordic skiing, mountain biking, and whitewater kayaking into a race with teams of two competing over 2 days. This race, which first ran in 1982 as WildTrek, is now known as the Winter Classic (www.canoevic.org.au/events/calendar.html). In its heyday in the late 1980s, it was one of a series of three races, including the Spring Classic and Summer Classic. The series winner took home a new Subaru sport-utility vehicle.

Why I Love Adventure Racing, and Why You Will, Too

Most people wouldn't classify adventure as a sport, and, similarly, racing isn't typically associated with adventure. Put the two together, however, and it's an amazingly comfortable marriage.

Adventure racing is the surprisingly well-balanced grandchild of triathlon, backpacking, exploration, and adventure travel. It's a sport that accommodates the wanderlust of the most ardent traveler, the competitive urges of a hard-core athlete, and the spiritual desires of a wilderness devotee.

Now, 18 years after it heralded my introduction to the sport, the WildTrek is still running. I suffered like a bad dog in that first race in 1985, but as the saying goes, the more you suffer, the greater the retrospective enjoyment. Unfortunately, suffering tends to decrease with experience and one has to go longer and harder to get the same wonderful postrace effects, something akin to an addiction to misery.

Eighteen years on, I am still in pursuit of pain, and these days it takes quite a harsh environment to get there. I have been in 210-degree ground temperatures (ESPN X-Games, Baja, Mexico, June 1997), on 20,000-foot peaks with a wind chill of 80 degrees below freezing (Raid Gauloises, Ecuador, October 1998), and caught in a typhoon during a military incursion (Elf Authentic Adventure, Philippines, May 1999). I have crossed countless countries, the Andes, the Himalayas, deserts, and tropical islands. I've been over, under, and in the water, ground, and air. I've traveled through every climate zone (often in one race) and on every continent. I've ridden all manner of large and small animals, some cantankerous, others impossibly stubborn.

The reality is that adventure racing gives me the opportunity to experience wild and wonderful places, to share them with close friends, and, frequently, to exceed my known limits. Ultimately, my love for adventure racing is a love for life.

PARTONE

Athletes take off at the start of the 2002 Outdoor Quest in Borneo, Malaysia.

No pessimist ever discovered the secrets of the stars,
or sailed to an uncharted land, or opened a new heaven
to the human spirit.

—Helen Keller

 # OVERVIEW OF THE SPORT

FROM SHORT SPRINTS TO FULL EXPEDITIONS, AND EVERYTHING IN BETWEEN

Adventure races come in all shapes, sizes, and formats, ranging from 2- to 3-hour sprints involving several outdoor sports to expedition-length odysseys that require months of planning and preparation and several weeks to finish. Although some races can be extremely complex, their basic tenets remain the same: a start line, a finish line, and a few checkpoints in between that you must hit. After the start, teams navigate their way through the wilderness by foot, boat, bike, rope, and many other means, continuing nonstop until they reach the finish. They must stay together at all times. The first team across the finish line is the winner.

In this chapter, you'll learn about the six main types of adventure races.

Sprint Races

These races, lasting 6 or fewer hours, cater to the weekend warrior. Most sprint races require only basic skills in paddling, mountain biking, and trail running, and the ability to work together as a team.

A typical sprint race involves running, mountain biking, canoeing or kayaking, and some form of adventure skill, often with ropes, obstacles, or more cognitive challenges. The HiTec adventure race series has defined sprint racing in the United States. In this race series, up to 300 coed teams of three compete on a semiurban "wilderness" course. The races include four basic elements: trail/road running, mountain biking, kayaking, and test taking. To draw the maximum number of participants, races are held in large city parks or other open areas in or near large population centers.

The HiTec special tests include a delightful array of torturous obstacles borrowed from military boot camps or dreamed up over a few refreshing drinks by the course directors. Some involve scaling 12-foot walls, navigating oil-covered slopes, and traversing high wires. Mud pits, mazes, archery, hand lines, orienteering—you name it, a HiTec race has had it. One particularly devious test involved one person removing a shoelace and tying it to a high wire. To get to the wire, the team member had to climb a smooth pole while his or her teammates steadied it. Once he or she successfully tied the shoelace, the teammate came down the pole. Then the entire team threw their shoes in a pile with (eventually) 299 other shoes. After completing another leg of the race, the team returned to the shoe pile and had to find their shoes and retrieve the lace, or go without. The fastest strategy was the latter, but it resulted in quite a few sore feet by the end of the race.

The Action Asia Challenge series is another large sprint event held throughout Southeast Asia. The main difference between Action Asia and HiTec is in the special test (or adventure skill). The Asian races include large ropes courses—rappelling (controlled rope descent), zip lines (flying fox), or Tyrolean traversing (a climbing technique using a horizontal rope to cross chasms), and the courses are somewhat longer than HiTec (about 4 hours for the winners).

Keith Tuffley (right) and Ian Adamson (left) get ready to start the 2-day 1987 Winter Classic in Victoria, Australia.

Day Races

Day races often incorporate wilderness navigation and may last into darkness, despite their somewhat misleading name. A typical day race is geared to the serious endurance multisport junkie and often takes a good deal of physical preparation and technical savvy to complete. An athlete in a day race will probably enter the realm of good suffering at some point in the event. The retrospective enjoyment factor increases over that obligatory postrace beverage and postmortem.

Day races often include navigation challenges. Usually, that will mean the entire course is unmarked and competitors must use a map and compass to find each checkpoint. Such races require a higher level of skill than sprints, since racing in the dark is more difficult and potentially more dangerous than daylight racing.

24-Hour Races

So-called 24-hour races are for the truly committed, or more aptly those who truly should be committed. These events inevitably last an entire weekend and require months of training and countless spousal accommodations.

There is some overlap between day races and 24-hour races, as the definition of each is very loose. Day races may have a 16-hour cutoff and extend into the night, but winners of a "24-hour" race may cross the line in under 16 hours. Typically, a day race starts and finishes on the same calendar day, whereas 24-hour races extend into the hours of 2 calendar days. One of the reasons for the overlap between the two formats is the spread of finishing times. The tail-end teams typically take three times as long as the winners, so that a 12-hour winning time translates into a 36-hour end time.

Twenty-four-hour races are a good starting point for anyone wanting to move up from sprint races to multiday races. You will experience some real sleep deprivation in a 24-hour race, and the distances involved become significant even for experienced ultradistance athletes. Fatigue and lack of sleep result in some interesting challenges to mental acuity, focus, enthusiasm, and physical performance. Decisions become more difficult, thinking becomes hazy, communication between teammates can be strained, and everything takes a lot more effort than usual.

Weekend Races

Most weekend races actually require about 4 days to complete, since the prerace preparations and postrace cleanup become significant. Such races often include a broader range of sports, with more obscure events (see the glossary on page 240 for definitions of any unfamiliar sports and terms), such as inline skating, rock climbing, cyclocross, coastaleering, canyoneering, and scootering, making appearances. Personal relationships are tested before, during, and after the race, and retrospective enjoyment takes on a whole new dimension. At this level, participants find themselves molding their lives around the event, and the family car often gets relegated to the street as race gear takes over the garage.

The Wild Onion urban adventure races are weekend affairs that provide a perfect forum for the adventurely committed. The races usually start on a Friday around midday, and the fastest teams finish sometime after noon the following day. The timing of the race requires a Thursday-evening arrival at the race site for check-in and registration, but gives everyone the opportunity to celebrate and then sleep on Saturday night. This schedule allows participants to get to work on Monday with some semblance of consciousness and minimal nodding and drooling in their weekly planning meetings.

Expedition-Length Races

Continuous multiday races test even the most dedicated pundits. The level of skill required for athletes to stay safe becomes proportionally more challenging. Teams will generally have to be competent negotiating class IV whitewater rivers, high alpine mountaineering, highly technical mountain bike trails, and open ocean. They must also navigate remote wilderness using only map and compass. Racecourses are typically so inaccessible, and distances so vast, that any rescue may take several days, if one is even possible.

People who attempt expedition-type races find that their lives revolve around the training, preparation, and organization of the sport. Personal relationships either adapt or perish, disposable income gets diverted to the cause, and additions are made to the garage to accommodate the accumulation of crampons, climbing harnesses, bikes, canoes, kayaks, pack rafts, wing paddles, canoe paddles, breakdown paddles, kites, sails, hiking poles, ski poles, skis, ski boots, ski wax, wax tables, snowshoes, avalanche beacons, avalanche probes, snow shovels, running shoes, trail shoes, water shoes, bike shoes, mountain boots, gloves, hats, jackets, overpants, base layers, midlayers, fleece, socks, oversocks, gaiters, altimeters, compasses, maps, map cases, sleeping bags, bivouac bags, sleeping mats, tents, stoves, water bottles, water purifiers, mountaineering packs, race packs, day packs, gear boxes, bike boxes, duffel bags, bags to hold bags, and the thousand other associated pieces of endurance detritus.

BETWEEN YOU & ME

I encountered my most memorable life experience ever during the first mountain bike ride in the 2000 Eco-Challenge in Sabah, Borneo. We were somewhat sleep-deprived and couldn't figure out why there were large piles of steaming vegetable matter all over the trail. Buried in the cacophony of sound around us were deep-throated grunts, gurgles, and trumpeting, which made us increasingly nervous. As we wound our way along the trail, the large green piles got steamier and moister and the strange sounds were accompanied by random crashing and rustling. Finally, we rounded a corner and stopped dead in our tracks, facing a similarly dismayed pachyderm, jaw frozen in surprise and with a mouthful of half-eaten bamboo draping to the ground. Everyone, including 20 large gray animals, was startled into action as Mike, always the motivator, yelled, "ELEPHANT!" A small stampede followed, luckily in a direction other than ours, and we continued on our way with new vigor.

Expeditionally insane athletes are the common animals found in long multiday races, although regular Joes and Janes can be spotted in the herd if you look closely. Following Pareto's Principle (Pareto was an Italian economist who proposed that 20 percent of the people won 80 percent of the wealth), more than 80 percent of the time put into these races is not actually spent racing. To compete in one of these events, you must spend a month at the race site in prerace, race, and postrace activities, and a minimum of 4 months in preparation prior to the event. Most athletes need a year to prepare. Despite the significant material and time costs and personal sacrifices, the vast majority of people become addicted to expedition-length races after just a taste. Long races provide a rare opportunity to experience extremes in nature and human interaction that are simply unachievable in everyday life.

Stage Races

Stage racing is becoming increasingly popular. Stage races provide a break between sections, lasting as little as 20 minutes (Salomon

X-Adventure) to as long as an entire night (Mild Seven Outdoor Quest). As a result, stage races tend to require athletes to carry considerably less, and lighter, equipment than continuous races, and the pace and intensity are much higher.

Another format that has become popular is the "mixed" stage race consisting of several stages of different lengths. Extreme Adventure Hidalgo and CAMDEX in Mexico, and International Bimbache Extrem Raid in the Canary Islands have three stages of 6, 12, and 24 hours over 4 days. This stage system allows long-course and sprint specialists to mix it up on an even field.

Various teams trek at high altitude in the Valley of the Volcanoes in the 1998 Raid Gauloises in Ecuador.

"Wherever you go, go with all your heart."

—Confucius

---

2 BIG RACES, SCENIC PLACES

EVERYTHING YOU NEED TO KNOW TO CHOOSE YOUR EVENT

As of 2003 you have more than 800 adventure races to choose from, almost half of them in the United States. These events take place everywhere from the desolate high plateau of Tibet to the lowlands of Europe to the frozen wastelands above the Arctic Circle. Below, you'll find detailed information about some of the most important international adventure races, from the oldest to the newest.

Raid Gauloises

The original multiday adventure team competition, Raid Gauloises (now called the Raid World Championships) has defined modern-day adventure racing much as Hawaii's Ironman has defined the triathlon. The Raid is a contest between coed teams of four (originally five with a support crew of two) that race 24 hours a day between a start and a finish line on an unmarked course, using only map and compass and nonmotorized transport. The first complete team to cross the finish line wins.

Compared with other major international adventure races, the Raid is quite a long event distancewise, usually covering about 600 miles. The winning team finishes in about a week. The cutoff (last official finish time) is 10 days. Race organizers encourage and assist teams in finishing, allowing slower teams to cross the finish line on a shortened route. This generally entails a bus or truck that shuttles teams forward through the course, skipping one or more sections.

Since 1989 the event has traversed New Zealand (South Island), Costa Rica, New Caledonia, Oman, Madagascar, Malaysia (Sarawak, Borneo), Argentina (Patagonia), South Africa (Lesotho), Ecuador, Tibet, Nepal, Vietnam, Kyrgyzstan, and Peru. The race organizers encourage interaction with local indigenous inhabitants and design their courses so that competitors get a real sense of a country's geography, history, and culture.

The rules ensuring compliance are quite complicated, and enforcement is somewhat laissez-faire and extremely subjective. As the first and longest-running of the major international adventure races, the Raid is something of a law unto itself. To be successful at the Raid, you need someone who is fluent in the French language, and preferably a native of that country. Since the vast majority of the race staff are French, they naturally provide more information and assistance to French teams. Many foreign competitors claim that this is taken to an extreme level, even accusing the race organization of being uneven in their treatment of the rules and of non-French teams.

Southern Traverse

The Southern Traverse remains one of the few major international races to maintain a grassroots feel, due in part to the lack of prize money and international media. As a result the event is mostly about the race—and with a very deep pool of high-level adventure athletes on hand, it is extremely competitive. The format is similar to Raid Gauloises, except that unlimited support crew are allowed, and personal boats and vehicles must be used. As a result the race heavily favors the home team (New Zealanders). In fact, no international team has ever won the race, although teams from Finland and the United States placed second and third in 2000. That year, the local favorites had an enormous support crew—including a catering van, cook, mobile bike shop, mechanic, local wilderness expert, and a camper to sleep in. The international teams had to rent minivans and borrow gear to try to match the Kiwis' custom-made racing kayaks. They also had to spend a lot of time deciphering maps in areas the Kiwis knew as well as their backyards.

The Southern Traverse is a true racer's race, designed for and by athletes. It embodies the spirit of adventure racing as it was originally intended. The course is always highly varied and the navigation extremely challenging. The terrain incorporates deep wilderness, and the weather is suitably ferocious. Hot, sunny conditions can change to 60-mile-per-hour blizzards in a matter of hours at virtually any time of year. The Southern Alps of New Zealand are a true paradise for staging an expedition-style race, with abundant high-alpine wilderness, glaciers, endless fjords and lakes, whitewater rivers, and vast areas of completely untracked wilderness.

BETWEEN YOU & ME

Up until 2000 the Southern Traverse allowed three- or five-person teams, and teams of all one gender. As you might expect, the all-male teams tended to outperform all-women or mixed-gender teams, as men are physically stronger than women.

You may or may not have expected that the three-person teams tended to outperform the five-person teams. The larger the team, the greater the likelihood of someone becoming sick or injured, or of equipment being lost or broken.

Indeed, the cards were stacked against us in 1996, when I competed on a team with John Howard, Keith Murray, Cathy Lynch, and Robert Nagle. In a race with Team Outside Sports (a three-man team), we embarked on one of the all-time classic battles to the finish, racing our kayaks across Lake Wanaka to Queenstown. We edged out Outside Sports by barely 2 minutes—equivalent to about a 3-second margin in a competitive marathon foot race—and became the only five-person, mixed-gender team in the history of the Southern Traverse to win overall.

John Howard ascends Blenco Falls during the 1997 Eco-Challenge in Queensland, Australia.

Eco-Challenge

The Eco-Challenge is the best known of the major international expedition races in the United States. Although it is by no means the largest, richest, or most competitive event, it draws by far more interest and more media exposure in the Americas than most of the other races put together.

From an athlete's perspective, the race is quite straightforward and well-orchestrated. Pre- and postevent functions are impressive, and the professionalism of the event staff is unparalleled among the major events. You don't need as much equipment as in the Raid, and the race shows relatively limited bias toward the local teams. Nonetheless, the event is still very expensive. Raid can cost up to US$50,000 to be competitive, Southern Traverse about $20,000, and Eco-Challenge in the $30,000 range, depending on its location.

Securing an entry into the Eco-Challenge is quite difficult. Any complete previous winning team gets an automatic invitation, as do the top 15 teams from the previous year. Teams can also win entry at one of the regional qualifying races in North America, or in the Armed Forces Eco-Challenge, which is held in the United States. The rest of the teams rely on a "lottery" after submitting an entry online on a certain day, generally in February each year. Teams are then selected according to their country of origin (Eco-Challenge has strict nationality rules in that teams must consist of athletes representing only one country), ability, and television appeal.

Regarding the latter, as in most high-dollar events, there is a balance between media requirements, sponsor constraints, and the event itself. In the case of the Eco-Challenge, the television show is extremely important, since it is the vehicle that keeps sponsors interested (through TV ratings). To meet ratings requirements, the producers juggle the competition, TV appeal, and event location in deciding the combination that will work best (see "Inside Facts").

Eco-Challenge races have been held in southeasten Utah (1995), the coastal range of British Columbia (1996); far north Queensland, Australia (1997); Morocco (1998); Patagonian Argentina (1999); East Borneo, Malaysia (2000); South Island of New Zealand (2001); and Fiji (2002). No race was held in 2003.

INSIDE FACTS

MTV aired the 1995 Eco-Challenge in Utah, ESPN the 1995 race in Maine, and the Discovery Channel each race from 1996 through 1999. In 2000 the USA Network picked up the show for a 3-year stint, and changed the format from a documentary style to a more popular "reality" style. This caused a paradigm shift in the way the event was portrayed and in turn affected the team selection. In 2000, celebrity teams earned acceptance into the race, including a group of former *Playboy* centerfolds. In 2001, the first *Survivor* contestant, from the reality television show of the same name, got an entry. By 2002 the race started to attract some big-name celebrities, with a team that included Hayden Christensen, the young Anakin Skywalker from the movie *Star Wars: Attack of the Clones*.

Outdoor Quest

In 1997 event producer Nick Freyer from International Management Group (IMG), Hong Kong, joined forces with San Diego—based triathlon race director and sports agent Murphy Reinschreiber and came up with the Outdoor Quest. This race successfully melded Ironman triathlon with adventure racing in a 4-day stage race totaling about 30 race hours.

The format of the Outdoor Quest incorporates seven sports: trail running, mountain biking, adventure skills (mainly on climbing ropes), sea kayaking, river kayaking, native-boat paddling, and inline skating. The races are fast and furious, as mixed-gender teams of four vie for $200,000 in prize money. Since the field is limited to 32 teams, and the format doesn't favor athletes from any particular sport, the event's alumni include an impressive list of world-champion and Olympic athletes from triathlon, Nordic skiing, trail running, snowshoeing, mountain running, kayaking, canoeing, gymnastics, and orienteering. Despite the skill depth of the field, serious amateurs can compete, although they generally find they have a hard time making the time cutoffs, which are set about 50 percent longer than the finish times for the top teams.

The Outdoor Quest has been held in the Sichuan and Yunnan provinces of China and the state of Sabah on the island of Borneo, Malaysia. Navigation skills are not a big factor in deciding the race results, and teams get to sleep each night in a five-star resort hotel, so the race often comes down to the wire. On several occasions only seconds have separated the top teams at the conclusion of the 4 days.

Salomon X-Adventure World Cup

The Salomon X-Adventure (pronounced "cross adventure") is a qualifying series for the Raid Gauloises. The X-Adventure series holds five or six races each year in various countries in Europe, Asia, Africa, North America, and the South Pacific. Each race lasts 2 days, with a winning time of around 30 hours. Officials award points to all finishing teams in each race and declare a series winner after the final race. The top 30 teams in the points series receive an entry into the Raid Gauloises, with up to six more invitation-only slots allotted by the race organization.

INSIDE FACTS

The Raid Gauloises, Eco-Challenge, and Discovery Channel Adventure Race all claim to be world titles, although the best teams tend to head to the races with the most prize money, currently Primal Quest and the Outdoor Quest. Over the years, different races have had a more genuine claim to being the championships, but no single event can claim it consistently. Race dates often clash, and the top teams will weigh their chances and the prize money and choose competitions that will maximize their earnings. A good example: In 1998 Eco-Internet and most of the European teams raced the Raid Gauloises in Ecuador, while the majority of teams from the Americas went to the Eco-Challenge in Morocco. In this particular case, it was logistically possible to do both events, but Eco-Challenge prohibited entry to any person who had raced in Raid to race in Eco-Challenge a few weeks later.

The first race of the series is usually a "winter" race, held early in the calendar year in a northern European country. Sports may include backcountry skiing, snowshoeing, ice-skating, ice climbing, kayaking, and orienteering. The rest of the race series uses summer sports, which may include mountain biking, canoeing in three-person inflatables, abseiling (rappelling), via ferrata (literally "the Iron Way," a big-wall climbing sport on fixed metal ladders, using safety harnesses and specialized slings), canyoneering (climbing, scrambling, and swimming through deep canyons), mountaineering, inline skating, and orienteering.

Teams consist of four athletes, at least one of whom must be a woman. Only three of the four teammates compete on the course at any one time. The athlete not racing any given leg accompanies the two support crew as they drive between transition areas with the equipment, apparel, and food. A female athlete from each team must be on the course for a minimum number of legs, usually 15 out of 20. This leads to some interesting race strategies. Race tactics must be flexible, depending on the strengths and weaknesses of team members, their physical and mental condition, and the length and difficulty of the legs.

Another twist to the race is the mandatory rest time between legs. This is generally 20 minutes, but varies according to the speed of the team. For each leg there is a first departure and a last departure time to the next leg. If a team arrives more than 20 minutes before the first departure time for the next leg, it rests an additional amount of time before departing again. If a team arrives less than 20 minutes before the last departure time, it gets less rest. Consequently, timing becomes quite complex, and faster teams tend to get additional rest, whereas slower teams often become increasingly exhausted as they race to beat the last departure times.

Raid the North Extreme

Raid the North Extreme is impeccably organized by elite adventure athlete Dave Zeitsma, and manages to tie up a well-crafted race package for a price unheard of in the Lower Forty-Eight. "The Extreme" is a true expedition-length odyssey, covering immense distances through absolutely pristine wilderness in the wilds of Canada. The well-balanced event incorporates the natural terrain, culture, and a healthy dose of true wilderness navigation—enough to challenge the elite and bamboozle even solid navigators, at least for a while. Past races have been held in really imaginative locations, including the Yukon, Newfoundland, and Labrador.

Prize money for the Extreme has been sufficient to attract big-name teams over the years, and royal battles have ensued between Canadian, Finnish, Spanish, Kiwi, and U.S. champions. This is a race worth serious consideration regardless of your budget, and will give you an experience equal to that of Raid, Eco, or Primal Quest. Another big plus is that you will be racing in a country where everyone speaks and understands English, even if you can't quite understand their often outlandish accents. The "Newfies," for example, have a dialect with a heavy brogue and peculiar colloquialisms reminiscent of 18th-century Ireland.

Primal Quest

Primal Quest made a huge splash on the adventure-racing scene in 2002 by offering the most prize money in the history of the sport (a

$250,000 prize pool, $100,000 for first place) and by paying 12 of the top athletes from around the world to bring their teams to compete. The event has made huge strides in professionalizing the sport, with big prize money, an athlete advisory board, and solid financial backing from Seagate CEO Bill Watkins, who is an adventure-racing enthusiast.

Primal Quest provides an expedition-style race for mixed-gender teams of four competitors and four support mates, on a course designed to take 5 to 7 days for the winners. The sports include mountain biking, river and lake kayaking, orienteering, fixed ropes, and mountaineering. Past events have all been held in mountainous regions of the United States, such as Colorado's San Juan Mountains and California's Lake Tahoe district.

As with the Southern Traverse, local teams have a huge advantage in Primal Quest since they have local resources and knowledge of local geography, topography, flora, fauna, and customs. Local advantages notwithstanding, the Primal Quest organization has made an honest effort to create a high-profile, well-organized event. The courses are checked by experienced athletes, such as John Howard, the rules are vetted by the athlete advisory board, and most of the race staff have experience with other events.

Exotica

The following is a short list of weird, wonderful, and exotic races from around the world.

Arctic Team Challenge, Greenland. This event is held in the very short window of time when Greenland is hospitable to human existence. It includes canoeing between icebergs, mountain biking, glacier trekking, and lots of local color. Four-person coed teams compete over 4 to 5 days. For more information, go to www.atc.gl.

Reunion de Aventures, Reunion Islands. Coed teams of four with a three-person coed support crew compete in this 6-day stage race that takes place in the exotic Reunion Islands in the Indian Ocean. The event includes ropes, canoeing, paragliding, jungle trekking, mountain biking, swimming, and caving. For more information, go to http://authentique.aventure.free.fr.

Raid Ukatak, Quebec, Canada. This race is a true expedition through midwinter in arctic conditions. Coed teams of four navigate 300 miles of forests, fjords, and tundra over 4 to 7 days. It includes Nordic skiing, snowshoeing, mountain biking, orienteering, and ropes. For more information, go to www.ukatak.com.

Length of New Zealand Race, New Zealand. This 28-day stage race covers 1,860 miles from the bottom to the top of the entire country. Solos and teams of three compete by mountain and road biking, kayaking, orienteering, and mountaineering. This is the best way to experience New Zealand. For more information, point your browser to www.nzwildplaces.com/introduction.cfm.

Volcanoes Challenge, Chile/Argentina. This mountain race through the Andes and pampas is replete with gauchos, wild stallions, and steaming volcanoes. It's worth the effort, especially after some delicious local red wines and legendary steak you can cut with a spoon. (Tofu is optional and available.) Coed teams of four hike, bike, and canoe over 250 miles around the rugged and spectacular "Volcanoes Road" of Patagonia. For more information, check out www.desafiovolcanes.com.

Cradle to the Coast, Tasmania, Australia. This 3-day off-road canoe triathlon begins in a world-heritage wilderness in Cradle Mountain National Park and finishes on Tasmania's east coast. Solos and teams of three may compete. For more information, check out www.threepeaks.org.au/tasultra/ctc.

Extreme Adventure Hidalgo, Hidalgo, Mexico. A 4-day race that has 6-, 12-, and 24-hour stages, the Extreme Adventure Hidalgo allows coed teams of three to canoe, kayak, mountain bike, spelunk, rope course, canyoneer, and orienteer. For more information, check out www.esmas.com/eah2003.

Guilin Challenge, China. This race offers a chance to experience the bizarre limestone towers of Guilin in southeastern China, and race around rice paddies tended by local farmers with funny straw hats and buffalo-powered plows. Teams of two in any gender combination run, bike, raft, clamber through caves, and rappel off cliffs through 40 miles of some of the world's most stunning scenery and remote villages. For more information, check out www.seyonasia.com/guilin/guilin.html.

International Bimbache Extrem Raid, Canary Islands. This event is the European adventure-racing championships, with trekking, coastal orienteering, canyoneering, rappelling, sea kayaking, scuba diving, inline skating, mountain biking, caving, and cultural activities. The race is open to 4-person coed teams and is staged over 4 days with 24-hour, 12- hour, and 6-hour legs. The team with the lowest combined time over the three stages wins. For more information, point your browser to www.meridianoraid.com/ingles/bimbacheing.html.

Tour d'Afrique, Cairo to Capetown. This involves 100 days of butt-bruising bicycling over 6,600 miles—the length of Africa. If you feel like tenderizing your tush to raise funds for educational, environmental, and ecological programs, then sign up! For more information, check out www.tourdafrique.com.

Various races, South Africa. A whole world of races exist among the elephants and zebra on the big, dry continent, from Lesotho to the Zambezi, and the athletes are not too shabby either. The local studs were fourth in Eco-Challenge 2002 on their first foray beyond their home turf. There is a veritable smorgasbord of choices for adventure-racing athletes in South Africa, from solo participants to coed teams of four, in events held every weekend. Races vary in length from a few hours to several days, including 250-mile, expedition-length events. For more information, check out www.ar.co.za.

Adrenalin Rush, Ireland. One of Europe's premier adventure races, the event includes ropes, navigation, trekking, kayaking, swimming, and

Ian's Adventure-Racing Wisdom

You lose brain cells each time you race. Thanks to those lost brain cells, a type of amnesia sets in after each race, allowing you to forget how much you suffered. The more races you compete in, the more brain cells you lose, until each race melds into the next. At this point your life becomes adventure racing. If you have any interests outside the sport, you should give them up right now or go and hit your head repeatedly with a large hammer until you forget about them.

mountain biking. Interestingly, the organizer, Brian Elliott, became in-famous after the Eco-Challenge in 1997, when the Discovery Channel de-picted him with a cheese board in his enormous pack. The event provides a great taste of the Emerald Isle, and you can always warm up in a pub along the way if (when?) the usual inclement weather strikes. The Adrenalin Rush covers about 300 miles over 5 to 7 days. Teams of four (with at least one female member) trek, mountain bike, kayak, as-cend and descend fixed ropes, and even horseback ride to the finish. For more information, check out www.asportsone.com.

PARTTWO

Team Eco-Internet treks toward Mount Cotopaxi in the 1998 Raid Gauloises in Ecuador.

"All human beings should try to learn before they die what they are running from, and to, and why."

—James Thurber

FANCY FOOTWORK

HOW TO COVER GROUND QUICKLY WHEN ON FOOT

The 2000 Outdoor Quest in LiJiang, China, included a partial ascent of Snow Dragon Jade Mountain, a 17,000-foot glaciated peak in the foothills of the Himalayas. Day 4 of the event culminated in a final "run" up the mountain to one of its lesser peaks, followed by a run back down to the finish line.

As luck would have it, a heavy, wet snowfall enveloped the mountain on the first day of the race. By day 4, one of the competitors, an Ironman Triathlon world champion, found the going so difficult that she sobbed as she crawled the final 300 feet to the peak. Another world-class endurance athlete was caught on camera saying, "I've done 11 Ironmans, and I would rather do 11 more than do this again."

Indeed, as those athletes learned that day, your foot-travel skills may be the most important in your arsenal of talents. Television shows inevitably depict adventure races as grueling suffer fests, with teams of bickering athletes hobbling slowly forward on bloody and blistered feet. This image is not too far from the reality for a large number of teams;

however, it needn't be this way. In this chapter, you'll find out how to ameliorate the effects of prolonged punishment of your feet. If you build the specific skills for each type of foot travel—whether by snow, ice, trail, or road—with plenty of practice, you'll be able to navigate your way from start to finish without the bloody and blistered feet.

Conditioning

People often ask how some competitors' feet can look so good at the end of a long race when most racers' resemble hamburger. The answer is very simple: conditioning. The human body is incredibly good at adapting, be it to heat, cold, altitude, endurance, or physical load.

Most people are well aware that regularly lifting heavy weights will produce bigger muscles, and that eating too much food creates bigger fat cells. If you ever get a chance to study the feet of someone who lives in a culture that doesn't value shoes, you'll notice very large and incredibly tough feet. Nepalese porters carry astoundingly large loads at altitude wearing only flip-flops. Fijian islanders happily run around on coral reefs with no shoes at all. If you gradually increase distance while carrying your pack, you'll eventually be able to breeze through a race and avoid "hamburger foot" and other nasty afflictions.

There's a delicate balance to conditioning your feet. You need not train the full race distance with the full amount of weight on your back. The resulting damage and necessary recovery from such long "training" sessions far outweigh the benefits. Most exercise physiologists readily agree that you must learn to balance your intensity with your distance in order to strengthen your feet—or any other part of your body— without injuring yourself in the process. To do this, you substitute intensity for distance (up to a point), stimulating your body to adapt to the stress. For example, marathon runners never train by running 26 miles at race pace in training. Instead, they usually complete a long, slow run of about 20 miles once a week and then a series of shorter, faster runs at race pace at other times during the week.

To build time on your feet, schedule low-intensity sessions into your training program. For example, try a long day hike once a week in the mountains at a social (conversational) pace. Since long races can include

INSIDE FACTS

John Howard has enormous feet. His 165-pound, 6-foot frame is supported by size-14 shoes. John attributes his phenomenally large dogs not to genetics, but to the fact that he rarely wears shoes. This is also his recipe for toughening his feet, something that carried him to 10 major international adventure-race victories over 10 years. Ironically, the 2000 Eco-Challenge in Sabah, Borneo, ended prematurely for John because he wore shoes for the entire event. One of his teammates had suffered a puncture wound from a sea urchin and the team decided to protect their feet from further injury by keeping their shoes on at all times. After 5 days of his wading through the ocean and struggling through saturated jungle, John's feet had become so soft and tender from the relentless moisture, he was forced to retire.

Since I started competing frequently in long-distances races, my feet have also grown, from a size 8½ to an 11. The robustness of my feet has improved significantly as a result. In my first long race with John Howard (the 1995 Eco-Challenge in Utah), my feet suffered terribly. After a week of my running around in the deserts of Utah, my feet had blisters on blisters, sacs of fluid on top of each other between successive layers of skin. For a month after the race, I tottered around like an invalid from the pain and tore huge sheets of skin from my feet on a daily basis. Two years later I not only could complete a weeklong race with minimal damage but could compete in successive events with very little recovery time in between.

foot sections that last over 20 hours, aim to hike comfortably over a weekend for this length of time. Hike or ski to your location one day. Set up camp, spend the night, and then hike or ski back the next day.

The second part of the conditioning puzzle involves load. Inevitably, you will end up carrying much more in the race than you anticipated. As a rough guide, the best teams with the lightest equipment in a long multiday race will have packs as heavy as 30 pounds. Loads are lighter for shorter races, with the lightest packs weighing around 10 pounds for 24-hour races. Sprint and stage races still require you to carry some sort of small pack, so it's a good idea to become comfortable wearing your

French teams try to make up ground during the 2000 Raid Gauloises in Nepal.

pack for all races, long or short. You should train with a pack at least as heavy as the one you will wear during the race.

The third piece of the conditioning puzzle involves terrain. If you train on rough, uneven surfaces, you can make up serious ground on these same surfaces during a race as poorly prepared teams tear their feet apart. In the 2002 Eco-Challenge in Fiji, the vast majority of athletes suffered debilitating foot problems, a result of rough terrain and the ever-present water on the course. We waded through rivers hundreds of times in the first few days of the race, with slippery, uneven rocks and steep, muddy jungle as footing. After a week of this, even the best-prepared feet were feeling tender, and the vast majority of athletes were reduced to stumbling around on shredded stumps. The lesson we all learned: Train in all conditions on all types of terrain to ready your feet for any conceivable situation during the race.

Tips and Tricks

Maintenance of your feet during a race is critical to prolonging their well-being. Apart from putting in time on your feet, there are a few other tricks that will prolong the endurance of your feet in a race. The top four most important things you can do for your feet while racing are keep debris out of your shoes, keep your feet lubricated, keep your feet dry, and elevate your feet when resting. To maintain foot health during a race, you need the right shoes, socks, and other types of apparel. Below, you'll find some of my tips for properly outfitting your feet.

SHOES

Your footwear is critical as you want a shoe that is not too heavy, not too flimsy, and not at all waterproof. You want the fastest-draining shoe you can find that still provides you with your desired support. The reasons you want a fast-drying shoe are twofold. First, water is heavy, weighs down your feet, and makes moving forward more difficult. Second, moisture softens your skin, making your feet less resistant to abrasion and blistering. Look for a shoe that is lightweight, has an aggressive outsole (good traction), a solid foot plate (to prevent stone bruising), a generous midsole for cushioning, and plenty of mesh in the upper for drainage and breathability.

You also need the proper size. In general, you will want to race in a shoe that is a half to a full size bigger than your street shoe, as your feet swell and spread during training and the race. For multiday races, buy a "bailout" pair of shoes that are an additional size larger than your racing shoes, in the not unlikely event that you suffer from a foot injury or an infection that swells your feet even more. (For more tips on purchasing the right shoes, see chapter 13.)

SOCKS

Your socks provide a layer of fabric between your foot and the shoe, allowing your foot to slide without catching your skin. This reduces

HOW *NOT* TO . . .
Hike through a Desert

The 1995 Eco-Challenge in Utah was sponsored by HiTec, which provided each athlete with three pairs of footwear: a light hiking boot, heavy waterproof boots, and sandals. We made the mistake of wearing our waterproof boots for the second leg, a 90-mile canyoneering and desert hike across the San Rafael Swell. Temperatures ranged from below freezing at night to over 90 degrees during the day. After 2 days with our feet saturated from sloshing around in canyons, our skin was soft and heavily blistered. Upon reaching the rafts at Mineral Bottom on the Green River, I felt hugely relieved to take off my boots and put on my sandals. When we left the rafts, we couldn't face putting our boots back on and found the airy sandals perfect for hiking and canyoneering the final on-foot legs.

the risk for blisters. There are three schools of thought regarding which types of socks work best for adventure racing. One school favors light, meshy acrylic sports socks that breathe well and dry fast. Another school advocates heavier, cushioned socks, the type used by backpackers, with the idea that they provide more protection for your feet. The last and least of the sock think tanks uses two thin socks or a sock liner, which creates a second boundary layer between you and your shoe. It all boils down to personal preference, so you should train with different combinations to discover the right sock style or strategy for you.

In very sandy, muddy, or cold conditions, you'll need waterproof/breathable socks such as SealSkinz. Sand and mud are like sandpaper against skin, and can quickly rub your feet raw, effectively producing an open wound that's prone to infection, especially in tropical regions. If you encounter extremely low temperatures in high-alpine and high-latitude races, wear a large, waterproof sock as an outer layer with a warm inner sock for insulation, and then slip on an oversize, lightweight running shoe. The resulting setup keeps your feet warm and dry without your having to wear a heavy (and slow) winter boot.

LUBRICANTS

In addition to socks, a lubricant will help prevent friction and abrasions. You want an emollient that lubricates without sealing the moisture into your foot, a condition that leads to saturated and overly softened skin. There are several products available that do the trick; Hydropel, Sportslick, and Bodyglide meet the above requirements and are available from outdoor and athletic stores. You can also make your own concoction by blending a mixture of 94 percent by weight silicone grease

HOW NOT TO . . .
Race in the Mud

The Elf Authentic Adventure was a short-lived race dreamed up by Gerard Fusil after he left the Raid Gauloises organization. Gerard wanted to create an "authentic" adventure, one that was a true journey expedition through remote and untrammeled country. The first edition of the race in 1999 traversed the remote east coasts of Samar and Layte in the central Philippines. Unfortunately, a nearby typhoon bombarded the islands with torrential rain for a week, turning the normally dry trails into knee-deep mud.

We struggled through these miserable conditions for more than a week, and suffered severely traumatized feet as a result. The mud in the region proved to be highly abrasive, and we all ended up with diabolical deep-tissue infections that caused some astonishing swelling (and just as astonishing pain). My feet were so big by day 9 that I had to remove the inner boots from my inline skates so we could complete the 60-mile off-road skating section. Needless to say, the experience was not pleasant.

Cathy Sassin of Team Spie Battignol was the only top athlete not to suffer this malady, as she wisely wore SealSkinz for the entire event, effectively preventing any of the mud and bacteria-riddled bat guano (we had to wade through several caves full of the stuff) from coming into contact with her skin. Spie won the race after 11 days, about 2 hours ahead of my team of relative rookies. Cathy and her team repeated their win the next year, using the same trick in similarly saturated conditions in Brazil.

and 2 percent antifungal, 2 percent antibacterial, and 2 percent antibiotic ointments. Avoid petroleum-based grease, such as Vaseline. This lubricates well, but tends to seal moisture into your skin.

Pushing, Pulling, and Carrying

Adventure athletes are often heard saying, "You are only as fast as your slowest teammate," but this only applies to teams that lack synergy. True teams pool their resources and average their available power. Stronger people carry more weight, and faster people push or pull slower people. The net result is that the team goes considerably faster than its slowest teammate would alone.

Use the following simple 3-step process when assisting on foot.

1. If a team member starts fading, shift some weight from the weakening person to stronger teammates. Small, heavy items are the easiest to move around, such as water bottles and food bags.

2. If there is room on the trail, place a couple of fingers along the small of the teammate's back and gently push your teammate forward. Make sure the person being pushed does not increase his or her effort, as this could exacerbate fatigue. Likewise, the person pushing should not be too aggressive.

3. Attach a simple towline from one teammate to another to move hands-free and on very narrow trails. Use 6 feet of $\frac{1}{8}$-inch-diameter high-strength cord with a small key-chain carabiner at each end. Clip one carabiner to the hang loop of the tower's pack and the other to the waist belt of the towee. Tie an 8- to 12-inch section of $\frac{1}{8}$- to $\frac{1}{6}$-inch-diameter bungee cord into the system to take up shock.

If you race for long enough, you will eventually have to accept a tow, even though admitting this can bruise your ego. I am fortunate to race with people who are physically fitter and faster than I am on foot, so I am often the lucky one hanging on to the towline. Even a small difference in speed makes it practical to hitch up.

In 1999 I was racing the Outdoor Quest in China with Robert Nagle, Keith Murray, and Danelle Ballangee. As we approached the end of the final day of the race, we were trailing the leaders, team Nokia, by only a

TIPS FROM THE TOP

Below, you'll find three running tips from Michael Tobin, a former professional runner and an X-Terra world champion and winner of the Eco-Challenge, Primal Quest, and the Balance Bar 24-hour series.

1. Running and hiking downhill are tough on the legs. When coming down a mountainside, take short, quick steps to reduce the impact to your thighs and lower the risk of spraining your ankle. Stay loose, relax your shoulders, and breathe naturally.

2. To run uphill, try a technique I call ski hiking. Bending forward a bit, use your quadriceps muscles to swing your extended leg forward, landing on your heel. This will increase your stride length, reduce wear and tear on your calves, and increase your traction.

3. Look around and take in where you are only when you're either on smooth terrain or not moving. I roll my ankle most often when I'm coming to a stop, so take care when braking, especially on downhills or on rough ground.

few minutes. Unfortunately, I had run full tilt into a tree branch. A torrent of blood gushed down my face and clouded the vision in one eye. As we sprinted down the hill to the final paddle, officials informed us that the run had been lengthened with an additional out-and-back loop around the lakeshore. As we approached the turnaround, I started feeling weak and woozy, and began lagging behind. Keith was already towing Robert, who was ill, so Danelle threw me a towline. She pulled so hard I felt I needed to only periodically spring into the air to move forward. We didn't catch Nokia, but we did stay ahead of the third-place team, a testament to Danelle's incredible running ability and the efficacy of towing.

Former professional mountain biker and Eco-Challenge winner Isaac Wilson demonstrates proper climbing technique.

"The business of life is to go forward."

—Samuel Johnson

 # TWO WHEELS

HOW TO IMPROVE YOUR ROAD, MOUNTAIN, AND CYCLOCROSS SKILLS

Residents of developing countries have watched with bemused curiosity as athletes (literally) cycle through their backyards. In the 2000 Raid Gauloises that crossed Tibet and Nepal, the local inhabitants couldn't quite fathom why such desperate-looking and emaciated foreigners, dressed in filthy rags and wearing strange headgear, were in such a hurry. We were forever making excuses as to why we couldn't stop in for a nice cup of chai tea or a social suck on the hashish hookah. I'm sure they figured we were refugees, riding for our lives from the communist menace up north!

Adventure racing encompasses every known style of cycling, and, consequently, to be a successful adventure athlete, you must be competent in all aspects of riding, including pushing, pulling, and carrying. To ride long distances with the least discomfort, start with the basics: setting your bike to fit your physiology.

Bike Setup

How you set up your bike—generally called bike fit—can dramatically effect your comfort and bike handling. The most comfortable position is not the most efficient, and the fastest position is not the most ergonomically appropriate, so you must make a compromise between the two. Spend some time playing with different bike fits to see what works for you. The three main adjustments you can make are seat height, handlebar height, and back-to-front positioning.

SEAT HEIGHT, TILT, AND FORE/AFT POSITIONING

Position your seat so that your legs are nearly straight, but not locked out, when either pedal reaches the bottom of the downstroke (in line with the leg). Your foot should remain horizontal to the ground. If your hips rock from side to side as you pedal, your seat is too high. If your heel drops below horizontal at the bottom of the downstroke, your seat is too low.

You'll also want to tilt the seat for comfort. In general, males feel most comfortable riding with a slightly high front (seat tilted up) and females with a slightly low front (seat tilted down). Start with a horizontal seat and adjust as needed.

Finally, adjust the seat fore and aft by sliding it along its rails. Pedal, and then stop with the cranks in the 3 and 9 o'clock positions. Ask a friend to drop a plumb line (a couple of washers tied to a string will do) off the front of the bony bump just below your kneecap. The line should align with the pedal axle. Generally, if you favor spinning, move the seat so that the plumb line falls slightly forward of the axle. If you favor pushing harder gears, move it so that the line falls slightly behind it.

HANDLEBAR HEIGHT

Ideally, you'll position your handlebars an inch or two lower than your seat. The low position allows you to sit in an efficient aerodynamic position when you reach speeds faster than 18 miles per hour, making this position most useful if you are on smooth roads or fast trails. Keep in mind that while lower is faster, it also puts more strain on the back, neck, and shoulders. Raise the bar for increased comfort.

HANDLEBAR REACH

You can change the distance from the seat to the handlebars by changing the stem that joins the handlebars to the steering post. A long stem length results in a low, stretched-out riding position with a very acute angle between your thigh and torso at the top of your pedal stroke. This provides speed and stability, but can also be debilitatingly uncomfortable. A short stem length allows you to sit upright, increasing your leg angle and reducing pressure on your hands. Generally, you should set the bars so that in your normal riding position, the handlebar obscures your view of the hub of the front wheel. If you are riding primarily on the road, you might want to consider using clip-on time-trial (aero) bars. These bars give you additional hand positions and allow you to rest on your elbows when you're riding on smooth surfaces.

For adventure racing you will want a bike fit that errs on the side of comfort rather than speed, as your comfort will ultimately dictate your endurance in the saddle. Try various positions on a long ride, making incremental adjustments as you go. Incorporate various kinds of terrain to see how your bike fit works for each condition.

Skills for the Trail

Good bike-handling skills allow you to ride fast through a variety of terrain, including technically demanding trails. The most important skill of all is dynamic positioning, the ability to move the bike around under your body in order to maintain balance and negotiate the terrain. With a dynamic stance, your body moves forward relatively smoothly while your bike moves around under you to absorb and avoid bumps, dips, and obstacles on the trail. If you watch good technical riders, their bodies appear as if they are riding a smooth surface, while their bikes jump all over the place. The trick here is to keep your elbows and knees bent and relaxed when standing on the bike, allowing those joints to quickly respond to changes in terrain. With good body position and a dynamic stance, you can negotiate some impressive terrain, including precipitous drops and large obstacles such as logs and boulders.

BRAKING

Without proper braking skills, you will skid and lose lateral traction, increasing your risk of falling. Braking is a subtle art, one that takes some finesse, a lot of practice, and possibly a bit of dirt hugging, to master. To hone your braking skills, walk forward next to your bike with

HOW TO . . .

Brake on Foreign Soil

If you travel internationally to races and rent or borrow a local bike, check which hand operates which brake. In general, U.S. mountain bikes route the right-hand brake to the back wheel and the left to the front wheel, whereas in Australia and New Zealand, they do the opposite. If you forget to check, and the routing is the opposite from your personal bike, you may be in for a nasty surprise when you jam on your "back" brake and suddenly find yourself contemplating the sky rather than the trail in front of you.

your hands on the handlebars. As you walk, feather (lightly squeeze) the front brake to keep the bike's rear wheel off the ground, without letting the bike flip over. Experiment with your braking pressure. Once you can brake smoothly on a variety of slopes, try it while walking backward and grasping the rear brake to bring the front wheel off the ground.

Once you can do that smoothly, try to find the braking limits for each wheel on a variety of slopes and surfaces. Find a flat, open surface and ride at a moderate speed. Increase brake pressure on your back wheel until it starts to skid. Try to maintain a straight line as the tire slides. If the rear end starts to drift sideways, release the brake so that the wheel rotates and the tire regains traction. When you feel comfortable skidding in a straight line, practice letting the wheel slide sideways. Compensate by steering the front wheel in your direction of travel as the back of your bike starts to slide around. Keep your shoes out of the clips so you can put a foot down when needed, and don't ride too fast. Bear in mind that 70 to 80 percent of your braking power comes from the front brake, making it easy to flip yourself over the handlebars if you get too enthusiastic with your front-brake hand.

GEARING AND SHIFTING

Choosing the right gear for riding will help you stay in the saddle and allow you to supply consistent power to the wheels. Anticipate the gear you need rather than let your effort determine it. Because you can spin your legs through a wide range of speeds, you should change into a slightly lower gear than you need as you start to climb a hill, and keep changing down as your speed decreases. If you let your cadence drop too much, you won't be able to change gears. The slower you spin, the more force you need to apply to the pedals, and the harder it is to change gears. If you find it difficult to pedal once you reach your lowest gear, you may be better off walking.

Avoid setting the gears in the smallest and largest cogs at the same time. Doing so causes the chain to bend aggressively where it leaves the cogs, which can break the chain. Avoid setting the gears with the big chain ring with the two or three biggest rear cogs, and the small chain ring with the two or three smallest rear cogs. Because there is a lot of overlap in gear ratios between cog combinations, you can always find a gear you need without going to the extremes at either end.

BODY POSITION

To maintain control of your bike in rough terrain, you need five points of contact between you and your bike. This means each hand, each foot, and something against the saddle, either your rear end on it or your thighs gripping its sides. There are some exceptions to this rule: Stand in your pedals when you hit technical or rough surfaces to allow your arms and legs to negotiate the shock. When you stand, ride with your arms flexed at the elbows and your legs flexed at the knee and hip. When you ride over an obstacle, allow (or assist) the bike to rise over it while your body stays on the same horizontal line.

JUMPING AND RIDING OVER OBSTACLES

Sometimes you will encounter logs and rocks that take a bit of finesse to cross. To clear these obstacles, you can either jump them or ride over them. Jump obstacles by standing high on your pedals, compressing your weight onto the bike, and then aggressively pulling the bike up off the ground, all in one smooth, controlled motion. If you encounter an obstacle or hole and can't simply jump over it, you can cross it one wheel at a time. Crouch over the bike, compress the front end, and then aggressively pull up on the front wheel. Once the front wheel clears the top of the obstacle, rotate your weight forward and pull up on the rear of the bike so it can roll over the obstacle. Jumping logs and rocks is a great skill, and one well worth practicing. If you can't jump logs (and they are quite common on wilderness trails), you will be forced to get on and off your bike, a slow and energy-consuming task.

WATER CROSSINGS

Water crossings are quite common. These vary from water-filled vehicle tire tracks to open-water swims. Ride through water no deeper than your pedals at the bottom of a pedal stroke. For deeper water, get off your bike and carry it.

Anticipate the slowing effect of the water as you enter it. As you approach the water, crouch, placing your weight over the rear tire, and thrust the bike forward to absorb the impact. Start pedaling as you sit and get a feel for the nature of the bottom. If the surface below the water is rough or uneven, it may take exceptional bike-handling skills to negotiate. In this case it is much smarter to dismount and wade than risk a catastrophic crash.

If you encounter a deep river or lake, you can get your team and bikes across safely and swiftly—if you know what you are doing. First, seal any holes in your frame with waterproof tape, remembering that there are hidden holes in the bottom bracket and head tube. Mountain bikes are surprisingly buoyant, in part due to the volume of air in their large-diameter tires, but only if you keep the water out of the frame. If you must wade, hold the bike out of the water. This will reduce drag, keep water out of the bike components, and overcome the buoyancy effect of your body.

If the water is really deep, you may have to swim. Swimming is very cumbersome with a bike, as the bike has a large surface area, which creates significant drag. If you have the opportunity, time, or forethought, it is better to float the bike on a raft. If you know the course will include a long deep-water swim, pack a child's inflatable pool toy to serve as the

BETWEEN YOU & ME

Our team Salomon/Eco-Internet nearly met disaster in the 2001 Eco-Challenge in New Zealand. We were partway into the final mountain bike section at night during a ferocious blizzard when Sara Ballantyne tumbled on a stream crossing. We were both surprised (she is a three-time mountain bike world champion) and dismayed to see her completely submerged in the frigid water. Under normal circumstances, Sara would have sailed through the crossing with barely a second thought, but on day 3 of the race, with little sleep and profound fatigue, this was not the case. Only her quick actions and iron will staved off hypothermia as she dragged herself out of the creek and proceeded to devote all her energy to climbing the next hill. Fortunately, we came across a hut an hour later, and napped and warmed up. Unlike the Kiwis, who had pushed on through the night, our conservative tactics gave us an edge that led to our eventual win—by only 20 minutes—2 days later.

bike's personal flotation device. Make sure you test the toy first, or you may end up dragging around a useless, if colorful, piece of plastic. Tow the raft on a line that allows you to use both arms, as one-arm swimming is as effective as, well, swimming with one arm.

Swift water is the most dangerous and difficult to cross. You can easily lose your footing, lose gear (including your bike), or lose your mind when you lose the former. Riverbeds and streambeds are extremely uneven and slippery. As a rule of thumb, if the water is fast flowing (you can see rapids) and more than knee-deep, don't cross it! Find a more benign section of the river rather than risk losing everything.

Once you decide to cross the stream, hold your bike with one arm through the frame and hold on to a teammate for stability. Don't try to use your bike as a crutch, as it will most likely be swept away in the current. If your team makes a line of pairs, with the heaviest, strongest person on the upstream side to break the current, you should be able to cross in one pass.

SAND, SNOW, AND MUD

Any soft, low-traction surface tests the skills of all riders, especially when they are fatigued, sleep-deprived, and loaded down with gear. If you are faced with a short soft section in an otherwise hard-packed trail, maintain your speed, shift down to a lower gear, and stand low crouch as you hit it. Keep your body weight slightly back to maintain traction and allow some float in the front so you can steer. This will allow you to absorb the added resistance and set you up to ride through as the bike slows. As you feel the nature of the surface, settle into your saddle and start spinning to maintain power. Concentrate on riding a straight line because the instant you lose it, your rear wheel will spin out or your front wheel will dig in.

UPHILL RIDING

Technical uphill riding demands a whole new level of skill. You must keep sufficient weight over the back wheel so that you maintain traction, but not so much that you lift the front wheel. In general it is easier to ride uphill in the saddle. Keep the bike in a low gear, which will make it easier to deliver power to your wheel when you hit a tough section.

To negotiate steps and large rocks while riding uphill, you must transfer your weight. Stand up and move forward over the frame. Lift the front wheel over the step, and then thrust the bike forward and under your body. As you negotiate rocks, ruts, and roots, you need to maintain balance as the bike moves over or around the obstacles. Here, dynamic positioning is important, so you should develop the ability to get into and out of your saddle and move the bike around aggressively while maintaining your momentum and keeping your wheels in contact with the ground. To keep a good line, look far enough ahead that you can place yourself and your bike where you can comfortably ride. This sort of anticipatory viewing takes practice. Just remember to look where you

Ian's Adventure-Racing Wisdom

Look where you want to ride, not at what you want to avoid.

want to ride, not at what you want to avoid. Your head follows your eyes, your body follows your head, and your bike follows your body.

STARTING ON A HILL

If you miss a gear, lose balance, or lose traction, you may have to start riding again from a stalled position during a climb. This can be quite difficult, but not impossible, on steep hills. Stand with your bike at an angle to the fall line, the line that an object will naturally follow if left to its own devices under the force of gravity. This may or may not be facing the direction you want to head, depending on the angle and camber of the trail. Next, stand with one foot planted on the ground on the uphill side of your bike and one foot in the opposite pedal at the top of the pedal stroke. Start in a very low gear and push off from the ground to get some forward momentum. Start pedaling quickly as you steer the bike back on course. Once you are moving, clip your shoe into the cleat. It may take a few attempts to get moving on rough, slippery, or loose surfaces, and if you can't do it quickly, then it is usually faster to push or carry your bike.

DOWNHILL RIDING

When riding downhill, keep your weight well back on the bike so you don't topple forward. Also, feather your brakes so that you maintain tire traction. Locking your brakes will skid your wheels, which will inevitably result in a crash. Under certain circumstances you can use a controlled rear-wheel skid to assist in negotiating tight corners, but in general you will want to avoid skidding. It is quite possible to ride fast over rough downhills, but you need to be aware of possible dramatic consequences. If you have the nerve to do it, stand in your pedals and move really fast, letting the bike move under you, to avoid the worst obstacles. As your wheels spin faster, they become stabler due to gyroscopic forces, giving you stability when obstacles knock you sideways. Your wheels also spend more time in the air; this, of course, is much smoother than bumping over every rock and rut, which you would do if you were riding more slowly. The downside is that coming off your bike could be disastrous, so you need to weigh the risk against your skill level.

Roman Dial demonstrates his hike-a-bike prowess during the 1996 Eco-Challenge in British Columbia.

HIKE-A-BIKE

Unfortunately, many races include significant sections of hike-a-bike, which is anywhere you cannot, or choose not to, ride. If the hill is too steep (up or down) or the terrain too technical, you may choose to carry your bike.

Most adventure-race bikes weigh in at well over 22 pounds. The first line of defense in hike-a-bike is to push, rather than carry, allowing the bike to support its own weight. If the slope is too steep or the surface too rough, you may have to carry. In this case you have several options, depending on your frame type.

Bike on pack: To support the weight of the bike on your pack, hold it by the seat tube and down tube and hoist it behind your head onto your pack. You will have to juggle it around until it is balanced.

Bike on shoulder: Grasp the top tube and lift it to your shoulder. Carry it either front wheel or back wheel forward, depending on preference.

Bike in hand: If you are crossing a small obstacle you can't ride, you may simply want to grab the bike by the frame or handlebars and haul it over rather than lift it completely. Some riding surfaces may not require a full-on carry, and you can half push, half lift the bike as necessary.

Head through frame: If the main triangle of the frame is large enough and not adorned with bike bottles and other accoutrements, you can place the bike over your head so that a tube rests on each shoulder.

TIGHT CORNERS

Riding through tight corners takes exceptional balance, precise handling, and braking finesse. Steer your front wheel around the outside of the curve, allowing your back wheel to follow a tighter curve. Lean slightly into the turn, as your momentum will throw you to the outside, and brake the front wheel just enough to prevent it from losing traction. A good rider can turn through an arc the length of a bike, and really good riders will do a series of standing jumps (or hops) to get around the corner.

DRAFTING

Depending on conditions, a group of cyclists can ride faster than even their strongest cyclist, provided they work together and draft one another. To draft, team members ride extremely close together in a single-file "pace line." A pace line allows a team to move faster because only the person at the front of the line has to overcome the full effects of wind resistance. Everyone behind benefits by sitting in the "draft" as they are sucked along in the wake of the front rider. When the front rider tires, he or she drops to the back of the pace line and takes a rest. Thus, in a team of four riders, you can work very hard for 1 minute and recover for 3 minutes as you rotate through the pace line and maintain a high average speed.

There are a few important caveats for safe drafting. Never brake unless it is absolutely necessary, as this is the fastest way to cause a pileup. You need to be confident that you can ride within half a wheel's distance behind the rider in front of you, or the drafting advantage is not fully effective. With a line of four riders this close together, even the slightest change in speed can have a dramatic (or disastrous) effect. If the front rider sees an obstacle, such as a hole in the road, gravel, rocks, or sticks, he or she should signal by pointing down at it as it appears. If braking will occur, the front rider should sit up and spread his or her hands wide, palms back. Indicate sudden or sharp turns by holding the turn-side arm out to the side. Yelling is useful, especially when visibility is poor or the team is getting woozy.

PUSHING

On steep uphills or more technical trails, some of your teammates may need a push. If the road is wide enough, you can form a reverse pace line, with the weakest rider in the front and the stronger riders behind. The easiest way to push is with your left hand on the other rider's behind. This allows you to steer, brake, and change gears with your right hand.

TOWING

The majority of conditions in adventure races favor towing rather than pushing. Towing is usually done in pairs, but under really good conditions you can hook up several riders in a line. In any event, all people involved should ride smoothly, much as you would in a pace line. Sudden changes in direction or speed by either the tower or the towee will most likely result in at least one of the parties crashing. The person being towed should follow the line of the tower as closely as possible because riding to one side will pull the front rider off balance and make the pulling harder (a "heavy" tow).

There are many effective towing systems. I recommend you use one that is as simple and foolproof as possible. Mountain bike and three-time Eco-Challenge world champion Mike Kloser uses a tow system made from a steel car-radio aerial and a $1/8$-inch-diameter bungee. He secures the aerial to a seat rail (one of the two metal bars under the bike saddle, used to attach it to the seat post) with a small metal hose clamp, available from any hardware store, and ties the bungee to the top end of the aerial, which is suspended over the back wheel of the bike. The aerial prevents the towline from getting tangled in the back wheel and posi-

Mike Kloser (left) and Michael Tobin (second from left) tow their teammates during the 2001 Discovery Channel Adventure Race in Switzerland.

tions it so that it is easy for the towee to grab. Choose a bungee that is long enough to stretch and accommodate the small speed differences between the two riders, but not so long that it can snag in a wheel.

For towing to work, you must communicate. As the towee, do not simply grab or release a towline without alerting the tower, as this could result in a crash. When the tower is ready, position yourself with about a foot between the front and rear wheels of each bike, and slightly to one side. Grasp the towline with either hand by hooking one or two fingers through the loop and holding your handlebars normally. Ride so that the towline pulls straight back, not off at an angle, so that you don't pull your tower off balance or off track. The closer your hands are to the center of the bike, the easier it will be to steer, since the force of the towline pulling on one side of the handlebars pulls and steers you to one side.

In any towing situation, neither person should increase his or her effort, as the idea is to average the power of the two riders. The net effect is to slightly speed up the slower person and slow down the speedster so that the team moves at the same (increased) speed.

Getting the Right Equipment

The most commonly asked question about mountain biking in adventure races is "Should I use a full-suspension mountain bike, or not?" The answer depends on your skill level, the length of time you will be on your bike, how much weight you need to carry, and how much weight you can stand to lose from your hip pocket.

If you have the financial resources to own three styles of mountain bikes—a hard tail, soft tail, and fully suspended—you are among the blessed few. A hard tail is relatively light and stiff, perfect for short, fast races where you can maintain focus on all the technical sections. A soft tail is almost as light as a hard tail, but has 2 inches of front-and-rear travel (suspension); it's a good choice for races around 12 to 24 hours, where a combination of darkness, fatigue, and weight carrying put you in the saddle most of the time. A full-suspension bike is an opulent comfort machine and may have adjustable rebound, a fair amount of suspension travel, and the ability to lock out the suspension. Rebound is the speed at which the suspension responds to a bump, and is similar to damping in the shock absorbers of a car; travel is the range of movement of the suspension; and lockout allows you to make the suspension rigid, so that you are essentially riding an unsuspended frame. Lockout is quite useful for climbing smooth hills, since it eliminates energy-wasting bounce in the suspension. The extended travel on a full-suspension bike allows you to sit through technical terrain, both up and downhill, giving enormous control and forgiving errors and sloppy technique that can infiltrate your riding during multiday races.

For short races, such as HiTec or Salomon X-Adventure, most people need only a lightweight front-suspension bike. Front suspension gives you much better control and greater riding comfort than a fully rigid frame, and now comes as standard equipment even on entry-level mountain bikes.

Soft-tail mountain bikes' small amount of rear suspension is not enough to truly absorb large shocks, but is enough to soften the ride through technical terrain. Typically, a soft tail will have about 1 inch of rear travel and will be as lightweight as a hard-tail bike. Soft tails work well for people who race long distances but who do not want to carry the weight of a full-suspension bike. These days, soft tails are disappearing as full-suspension rigs approach the lightness of hard tails. However, soft tails bridge the expense gap between hard tail and full suspension, so if you want to move up from a hard tail but don't have the money for a full-suspension bike, consider a soft tail.

High-end, expensive, fully suspended bikes typically weigh more than hard-tail bikes, at a price that exponentially increases as weight decreases. For longer, multiday races, however, full-suspension bikes can keep you safer and faster, as they are much more forgiving and comfortable than their more rigid brethren. Another advantage: Longer races generally require a significant amount of mandatory safety gear, and the vast distances require a moderate amount of food and water. As a result, you may end up carrying a load weighing 20 pounds or more over a significant distance. Bikes such as the Cannondale Jeckel, Giant NRS Air, and Trek Fuel have a significant amount of travel front and rear, up to 4 inches in most cases. This gives you more control on technical trails and more comfort with a load on your back. With full suspension, you can also load up a seat-post rack with about 15 pounds quite safely, as the rear suspension will attenuate any damaging shock load from the extra weight. This is something hard-tail bikes do not accommodate well.

What if you can buy only one bike? In this case, I recommend a good-quality hard tail. Invest in a suspension seat post for longer races. It will absorb some of those nasty bumps that can throw you off the trail or break your back wheel.

WHAT GOES AROUND . . .

When choosing a tire for racing, you have options in diameter, width, tread pattern, weight, maximum and minimum pressures, tubeless or inner tubes, folding or rigid bead, and several other, minor characteristics.

In general you want the lightest tire you can find that meets your core requirements. When selecting the core features of a tire, consider the terrain and conditions you will be riding through. If you will be racing largely on smooth roads, you will want minimum width (1.25 inches or less), high pressure (100 psi or more), and minimum tread rubber. At the other extreme, you may be preparing for a race that takes you primarily

BETWEEN YOU & ME

New Zealander and family doctor Keith Murray is one of the most gifted athletes in adventure racing, and as a result he often carries a heavy load. In the 2002 Primal Quest, we were on the third and final mountain bike leg when his new tubeless tire punctured. It sounded like a rifle shot. The failure caused a large section of the treaded surface of the tire to be torn free, leaving a flap of rubber the size of a silver dollar. We figured that his extra weight and great physical strength had combined to shred the tire on one of the many sharp rocks forming the trail. The likelihood of this happening was so low that we had chosen not to bring a spare. Instead, we used a little trailside ingenuity. We repaired the tire with several potato chip wrappers and a dollar bill folded around a regular inner tube. The wrappers and paper money are fairly rigid, so they didn't bulge out of the hole under pressure.

through technical steeps, so you'll want a wide (2.2 inches or more), minimum pressure (35 psi), and aggressive knobby (tread) tire.

Tubeless tires have become very reliable, and many professional mountain bikers are making the transition from standard tube/tire combinations. Since a tubeless tire does not contain a soft rubber inner tube, it is significantly less susceptible to pinch flats, where the inner tube gets caught between the rigid metal rim of the wheel and a hard obstacle, like a rock, and is punctured.

Tubeless tires can also resist needle punctures, small holes caused by glass fragments, nails, thorns, cactus spines, and so on. Because of the rigidity of tubeless tires, they are an ideal receptacle for self-sealing "slime," or liquid latex. Pour a small quantity of slime into the tire as it is being mounted on the rim. Inflate it and spin it a few times to allow the latex to coat the inside of the tire. In the event of a puncture, the slime will get forced into the hole and solidify under the pressure, sealing the tire. Riders in Arizona report riding whole seasons on a single pair of tubeless, latex-filled tires without having to fix a flat, despite their having accumulated large numbers of cactus spines on a daily basis.

Pedals and Shoes

Your leg transfers power through your pedal, crank, chain ring, chain, gears, and wheel, and then to each tire. Each link in this system creates a little friction and a small loss of energy, but by far the biggest loss is between your foot and the pedal. Clipless pedals reduce this loss by providing a rigid attachment between your shoe and the pedal. Wearing a stiff-soled shoe eliminates any other losses.

One possible equipment option for races with endless hike-a-bike is to use "flip" pedals, which have a clipless mechanism on one side and a platform on the other side. This would require that you carry a pair of bike shoes plus a pair of running shoes, switching out the shoes depending on whether you are riding or running. Alternatively, you can choose bike shoes that are reasonable to hike in. Either way, it's a compromise you will have to figure out based on your riding skill and ability to suffer.

Most of the top athletes in adventure racing use ultralight shoes, such as the Sidi Dominator 4 mesh, with clips pedals like the Shimano PD-M959 Pro, which both are featherweight and shed mud and other debris with alacrity.

Give Me a Brake

Motorcycle components have been finding their way onto mountain bikes over the years, first with frame construction, then front suspension, rear suspension, and tubeless tires, and more recently in the form of disc brakes. Early adaptations of this equipment were problematic, but today's lightweight designs are reliable and effective. The advantages of disc brakes include superior braking force, minimal loss of braking power in the wet and cold, slow wear rates of the brake pads and braking surface, low rotating mass, and increased tire-to-frame clearance (important when you're riding in mud).

Disc brakes are available in either mechanical (cable) or hydraulic versions. Both work well, but hydraulic brakes can be difficult to adjust (although they rarely need adjusting) and mechanical brakes need

TIPS FROM THE TOP

Below you'll find three tips from Mike Kloser, former mountain bike world champion, three-time Eco-Challenge champion, and winner of Primal Quest and the Balance Bar 24-hour series.

1. Choose comfort over weight when choosing a bike. Although weight is extremely important when choosing a bicycle for adventure racing, comfort and control are even more important. It is well worth sacrificing a pound or two in weight if it means you can ride your bike in comfort for a few hours longer.

2. Pace yourself. Adventure races can include extremely long bike sections. Curb your urge to race the bike leg, and remember you have more weight, more distance, and more sports to cover than in a single-sport event.

3. Maintain your investment. Bikes are expensive and require frequent and obsessive care. Maintenance begins before the start line, but continues throughout the race, so take care of small problems before they become big problems.

more maintenance. The sealed nature of a hydraulic system is a blessing and a curse. Cable "sticktion," which results from friction between the cable and cable housing (the single biggest headache for any cable system), is not an issue, but hydraulic leakage, although rare, leads to degrading braking power and eventually failure. That said, I have been racing on hydraulic discs for more than 3 years without a single breakdown.

V-brakes are highly reliable, easy to adjust, easy to replace, and swappable between bikes. The three main disadvantages are high wear of the rubber pads in abrasive mud, a propensity to gum up in sticky mud, and a tendency to seize up in extreme cold. Some people opt for a front disc and rear V-brake, since 70 to 80 percent of your braking power is in the front and in the event of a disc failure, you can always ride with a rear brake only.

Maintaining Your Investment

If you're going to race bikes, you need to be familiar with basic bike repair and maintenance. Buy *Bicycling Magazine's Complete Guide to Bicycle Maintenance and Repair* and study it. Bicycles are like cars. They will last a very long time if you regularly tune them up. Conversely, if you don't maintain them, they will deteriorate rapidly and, via Murphy's Law, will fail catastrophically during a race.

To keep your bike in top shape, do the following on every ride:

- Fill the tires to the correct pressure for your ride.

- Check and adjust brakes and brake pads.

- Run through the gears and adjust as necessary.

- Clean and lubricate the chain. You should wipe all excess oil and dirt from the chain and apply a light film of oil to all links, then wipe off any excess with a clean rag. The chain should look clean and dry on the outside.

- Check the rebound on your shocks and adjust and fill them with air as needed.

- Remove any accumulated dirt, especially around moving parts.

- Check wheel-true (the symmetry of the rim) by spinning each wheel and adjusting as needed.

Every 300 miles, or whenever you ride through really muddy, dusty, or sandy conditions, you should:

- Clean your bike thoroughly with a high-pressure hose at a car wash. This is an extremely effective and quick way to get rid of caked grease and dirt in

Mike Kloser

hidden crevices. Be extremely careful not to blow hot, soapy water into bearings (around the headset, crankset, and wheel hubs).

- Clean the cables and cable housings. Dirt in these areas is the main culprit in stiff brakes and skipping gears. Remove the cables and housings, and clean them with a citrus solvent, dry them, and lightly oil them with a wet lube. If necessary, replace the cables and housings.

- Check, clean, and replace brake pads if needed. Embedded grit in rubber pads can cause a nasty grinding or screeching noise and will wear away your rims.

- Clean your chain with a citrus solvent and chain-cleaning tool (or remove the chain and clean it by shaking it in a sealed jar half-full of solvent). You will be amazed at how much abrasive grit can accumulate in the links.

- Check for tire wear, cuts, and foreign objects.

- Clean and lubricate clipless-pedal mechanisms.

- Clean and lubricate your derailleur.

Each year you should:

- Replace your chain. Stretched and worn chains will quickly wear the teeth on your chain rings and cluster. Replacing a $20 chain is much less expensive than replacing $200 to $300 worth of cogs.

HOW TO . . .
Lubricate Your Components

Spray lubricants are a great way to lubricate components that are difficult to access, such as derailleurs and gears. If you use a spray lubricant, be extremely careful not to get any on your brake pads, discs, or rims if you have V-brakes. You can safely spray around these components if you shield them with a clean rag. Make sure you wipe off excess lubricant; otherwise, it will collect dirt and other abrasive grit.

- Check and replace tires if necessary.

- Lubricate all moving parts—headset, hubs, bottom bracket, brakes, cables, derailleurs, and so forth.

- Service your shocks.

- Check for play in all moving parts, and adjust as necessary. If bearings are grinding, you may need to replace them, most commonly in your hubs and bottom bracket.

Emergency First Aid for Your Bike

You don't need to be a bike mechanic or have a fully stocked workshop to perform effective trail maintenance on your bike, but you do need familiarity with your ride, and hands-on experience tinkering with it. The following is a short list of the breakdowns you are most likely to suffer and how to fix them.

Flat tire. A flat or softening tire (puncture or slow leak) is the most common repair you will ever make. With some practice you can change a tire in less than 2 minutes. Mike Kloser, Danelle Ballangee, and Michael Tobin changed one in 1 minute, 40 seconds, at the Chicago Wild Onion in 2002. At the other end of the spectrum, rookie teams can struggle for over half an hour.

Despite their wide proliferation, you don't need tire irons. Just disengage the "bead" of the tire from the rim and maneuver it into the middle of the rim once the tire is completely flat. Most regular tires have a "hook bead" that jams into a recess on the inside of the rim when the tire is inflated and prevents it from coming off. Since the middle of the rim is a smaller diameter than the outside, you can then "roll" the tire off the rim quite easily. Make sure you leave one side of the tire on the rim, since you need to remove just the old tube. Check the inside of the tire for the cause of the flat and remove the object if it is still embedded in the tire.

Partially inflate the new tube (by mouth or pump) and install it on the rim, inserting the valve through the hole in the rim first. Partial inflation of the inner tube helps keep it from folding over itself when it is fully inflated, another cause of punctures. Reseat the tire on the rim, and check that the inner tube is not caught between the tire and rim, yet another cause of flats. Then reinflate the tire.

Torn tire. Sidewall tears are quite common, from sharp rocks, sticks, or badly adjusted brake pads. The easiest way to patch up a torn sidewall is to insert a large patch between the tire and inner tube. Use a material that doesn't stretch or tear. You can buy sidewall patches, but paper money is cheaper and more convenient. It's also very robust, especially if you have access to $1 bills. For really large tears, several bills, a section of inner tube cut from a spare, and some strong duct tape can do the trick.

Broken chain. A chain breaker will have you back in business in no time, less a pair of links. Make sure you practice breaking and reattaching your chain, and don't push the pin out completely when making the new connection. Newer chains use a very simple master link to connect the chain together. These links are much easier to master than trying to press pins back into the chain.

Broken cable or lost brake pad. You can't fix a broken cable or lost pad (unless you carry spares), but you can swap back cables and pads to the front if you lose a front brake, the one you need the most.

Skipping gears or stiff brakes. If you ride through dust, mud, or sand, the soil can quickly find its way into your brake and gear cables. This first manifests itself as skipped or sticky gears and stiff brakes. Cables are quick and easy to clean: Just undo the nut that clamps the cable at the business end of things, pull it out, and wipe it clean. If the cable is dry, you can sometimes blow debris out of the cable housing, using your breath. Otherwise, you may have to slide the cable backward and forward through the housing and clean as you go.

Better still, if you have a solvent, you can pour some into the housing(s) and then work the cable through and clean it. When you are ready to reassemble everything, lightly lubricate the housing and cable and put it all back together. The most likely culprit to interfere with gear changing is the rear derailleur housing next to the back wheel, since this section of cabling tends to accumulate a lot of dirt. If you have trouble changing between chain rings, the housing adjacent to the bottom bracket is usually guilty.

Broken rear derailleur. A broken rear derailleur is a major inconvenience, but not catastrophic. Ride your bike as if it only had single speed, choosing a gear that can get you up most hills. Use the middle chain ring at the front and a low (big) cog in the back, and then shorten the chain appropriately, using your chain breaker.

Broken spoke. If you don't have a spare, or you don't want to spend the time replacing it, wrap the broken spoke around an adjacent one, and tighten the two adjacent spokes to correct rim alignment. Wrapping the broken spoke around adjacent ones prevents it from flailing loose and causing secondary damage.

Broken frame or fork. Depending on how bad and where the break is, you can shore up a broken frame by reinforcing it, using a stick, frame pump, or other object as a splint. Use a bandage from your team's first-aid kit, duct tape, or a cord to secure the splint.

Packing Tricks for Transport and Racing

If you travel with your bike on airplanes, you will quickly learn that baggage gorillas take a particular dislike to bike boxes. I used to own a beautifully constructed BikePro bike bag (used by the U.S. Cycling Team) with an internal steel frame, caster wheels, and semirigid sides. Unfortunately, the bag alone weighed more than 20 pounds, about as much as my bike. I was forever struggling to get it under the 66-pound maximum weight for flying. As a result of its size and excessive weight, it managed to attract an inordinate amount of abuse. After one international flight, I retrieved it from the oversize baggage claim to find that someone had dropped the bag from a great height, breaking the bike loose from the frame, to which it had been bolted, and bending and denting the frame. Fortunately, a bike shop was able to bend it back to a form where I could mount the wheels, and we were able to show up at the race gear check with a functional bike in tow.

Bikes are often transported by the race organization during an event, and you have to pack and unpack your bike as part of the competition. The following tips can save you a lot of headaches when racing or traveling.

Choose the right box. I have used almost a dozen different bike boxes over the years, from discarded cardboard shipping boxes to the high-tech but unlucky BikePro. To date, the best container I have found is a corrugated plastic box from CrateWorks (in the United States, 800-934-5214, www.crateworks.com). For about $100 (about one-third the price of similar boxes) you get a really lightweight (11-pound) box that meets UPS shipping dimensions. This model comes with optional removable wheels (very useful for carting the thing around in airports), external straps, a wheel separator, and Velcro straps for holding everything in place. Its almost 50 percent more usable volume and considerably lighter weight mean you can cram in a bunch more gear than in a regular box. I can fit either two bikes or a bike and several breakdown kayak paddles along with the helmet, shoes, and other required biking equipment. The shape and size mean you can ship it cheaply ($20 to $30 via UPS within the States, as opposed to $60 to $80 each way when you fly).

Don't overpack. Putting too much weight (or volume) in a bike box results in overweight charges from airlines and can lead to broken parts. I prefer to pack the bike, wheels, helmet, shoes, and accessories with a few lightweight soft items (spare tires, PFD, fleece jacket, sleeping mat) between them. If keep your bike clean, you won't get dirty chain grease everywhere. If you are concerned, just wrap an old T-shirt around the chain and rear derailleur (you will want one to clean the bike anyway!). Under no circumstances should the box be so overpacked that you can barely jam the lid on—you can easily bend or break something in the process.

Protect delicate components. The bike parts most commonly damaged in transport are the wheels, rear derailleur, and cables. I prefer to separate the wheels from the rest of the bike, using a rigid plastic dividing sheet, although a thick foam pad also works. This prevents other hard objects from poking through the spokes and warping the rims. The rear derailleur must be unbolted from the frame, since it is unprotected when the rear wheel is removed. I secure it to the frame with a plastic zip tie so it won't come loose or twist the chain. If you leave the chain unsecured, it can bang around inside the box and cause a really confusing puzzle. To avoid cable kinking, make sure the cable housings are fully seated in their cups (so that the cable ends are not hanging free from the end of each cable assembly), and make sure there are no free cables loose in your box. Reattaching the brakes (which you had to undo to remove the wheels) helps keep the cables under tension and seated correctly.

Secure all parts. Damage often results from loose parts careening around inside your bike box as ham-handed baggage handlers throw it around. You can't do anything about baggage handlers, but you can secure your box's contents. There are three basic methods for holding things in place in a bike box: a rigid frame such as that from TriAll3Sports (www.triall3sports.com), straps such as those made by CrateWorks, and foam pads, such as those by Trico Sports (www.tricosports.com). The most damaging offenders—and those most likely to migrate inside your box—are those with heft, such as tools, shoes, wheels, and the bike frame itself. To secure your tools and shoes, put them in a small bag and tie the bag onto the rear triangle or main triangle of the bike.

Teams take off at the start
of the 1995 Raid Gauloises
in Patagonia, Argentina.

"I believe in getting into hot water; it keeps you clean."

—G. K. Chesterton

PADDLE CRAFT

HOW TO IMPROVE YOUR CANOEING, KAYAKING, AND RAFTING SKILLS

Paddle sports can be very simple or very complicated, depending on where and how you decide to dip a blade. At the most basic level, paddling involves jumping on a sit-on-top kayak in a T-shirt and shorts and going for a spin around the reservoir. At the other extreme, you may tour in arctic whitewater in a canoe loaded to the gunwales (atop the sides) with equipment and apparel.

No matter where or how you do it, paddling usually requires more than simply dipping your blade in and gliding across the water. With the explosion in extreme sports, kayaking is now on the cutting edge of the wild and exciting, and adventure racing has taken full advantage of this. Most adventure races include some sort of paddle sport, such as canoeing, kayaking, or rafting on still water, moving water, whitewater, or open water. Longer races often include all three types of paddling, and conditions may vary from the sublime to the seriously scary.

INSIDE FACTS

In 1957 German physician Hannes Lindermann spent 72 days kayaking across the Atlantic in a 17-foot-long folding boat. He was rewarded for his efforts by being placed on the cover of *Life* magazine, an honor garnered by very few endurance athletes. In 1931, Richard Grant and Ernest Lassy circumnavigated the eastern United States (6,102 miles) in 11 months, setting the record for the longest continuous canoe trip. In 1997 I was fortunate to have favorable conditions on the Colorado River to paddle 203.3 miles in 24 hours in a Prijon K1 downriver racing kayak, breaking the old *Guinness Book of World Records* distance by 46.2 miles.

Types of Boats

The most commonly used type of boat in adventure racing is the Sevylor Tahiti K, an inexpensive two-person inflatable kayak. The HiTec adventure-race series and Action Asia Challenge series both use this craft exclusively because it is lightweight, easy to store, easy to transport, easy to paddle, and cheap to buy. The ubiquitous Sevylors are not bad boats for adventure races, as they can carry one or two people, allowing for teams with an odd or even number of people. Also, they are safe in most conditions. On the downside, they are at the very bottom end in terms of performance.

In North America, two-person, open canoes (Canadian style) are very popular simply because they are the most common rental boat. Open canoes are generally stable, high volume, robust, and relatively quick, which allows them to be used in a variety of conditions.

Another boat style that has become popular internationally is the sit-on-top kayak. This style of boat has been used major races, including the Outdoor Quest, BalanceBAR 24-hour series, and Expedition BVI. Sit-on-tops are virtually impossible to sink, and easy to reboard if you fall off. They work well in a huge range of conditions, and they are incredibly robust. By contrast, conventional, decked kayaks (the ones you sit inside) can fill with water and require a spray skirt (also known as a spray deck) to keep water out of the cockpit. If you fall out of the boat, they are difficult to reenter and generally fill with water when you do so. The whole reentry and emptying process can be dangerous in rough, cold, or windy conditions.

Expedition-length races, such as Eco-Challenge, Raid Gauloises, and Southern Traverse, tend to use hard-shell tandem sea kayaks, open canoes, four- to six-person whitewater rafts, and inflatables—often all four in one race. Raid and the Salomon X-Adventure Raid Series use a French boat called a Jumbo, which is a large three-person inflatable canoe made from an extremely tough rubberized cloth called Hyperlon, used in whitewater rafts. This boat can easily handle class IV whitewater, even if the people paddling it cannot. The Raid group also uses plastic sea kayaks, both tandem and solo, when long open-water paddling is involved.

Unlike Raid, the Eco-Challenge does not own its watercraft, preferring to use sponsored boats or to rent them. Over the years the Eco-Challenge has used four- and six-person whitewater rafts, open canoes, composite and plastic sea kayaks, tandem and solo inflatable kayaks, and a variety of "native boats," such as *perau* outrigger sailing canoes, wooden canoes, and bamboo rafts.

Southern Traverse is unique among the major races in requiring teams to supply their own tandem kayaks to a minimum set of specifications. Consequently, an industry has grown up in New Zealand around building high-end carbon/Kevlar racing kayaks for the local athletes. Visiting internationals can sometimes get lucky and can rent one of the local boats, but generally they have to settle for standard touring sea kayaks, creating a significant disadvantage in the race.

Paddles

A race organization usually supplies the paddles as well, but they are inevitably heavy, low performance, and made from plastic and aluminum. Race rules usually allow you to supply your own paddle(s), which is definitely advantageous, especially if the paddling legs of the race will last more than a couple of hours. To paddle a narrow boat most efficiently, use a double-bladed (kayak) paddle. Kayak paddles allow you to have the free blade (the one in the air) well on its way to the start of the paddle stroke while the other blade is still delivering power in the water. A canoe blade, on the other hand, spends a much greater proportion of its time in the air. Anytime the canoe blade is not in the water, it is moving forward through the air and not providing forward propulsion to the boat.

KAYAK PADDLES

For stroke efficiency, use a wing-bladed kayak paddle. This was developed in Sweden in the early 1980s for Olympic sprint paddlers and is now used almost universally for competitive sprint, marathon, and ultradistance paddling. A wing blade looks somewhat like a spoon and works as a hydrofoil or underwater wing: When you move the blade through the water, water flows over its surfaces in one direction, just as air does over an airplane wing. The lift created as it slices through the water pulls the blade forward. With a flat blade, the paddle blocks the water, forcing it to flow around both edges and creating turbulence behind the blade. This dissipates the energy of your stroke.

Adventure racing is extremely demanding on equipment, so several manufacturers have developed sport-specific wing-blade models. The best have metal tips (to prevent end damage in shallow or rocky conditions), adjustable lengths (to accommodate water and boat-size variables), and adjustable feather (the angle between the left and right blade). They can also be pulled apart for transporting. There are only a few paddles that meet these criteria, including the Descent Flite series from New Zealand (available from Futura Surf Skis in California at www.surfskis.com), Quickblade (www.quickbladepaddles.com), and Prijon, based in Germany and Boulder, Colorado (www.wildnet.com).

The traditional, teardrop-shaped "flat blade" paddle offers an alternative to the wing blade. Epic Paddles (www.epicpaddles.com) in the United States makes an exceptionally lightweight flat blade for racing that is significantly lighter than the best wing paddles and is worth considering.

Whatever your choice of kayak paddle, it should be light, strong (fiberglass or exotic fiber, depending on your budget), and stiff (it should not easily flex when you apply force to it in the water). To choose the

HOW *NOT* TO . . .
Paddle Whitewater

One day a good friend of mine, Cameron Jenks, and I were setting the course for the 2000 Mild Seven Outdoor Quest adventure race and wanted to scout a section of the Xue Shan river in southeast China as a potential paddling leg. This is a nice, big whitewater river, although most regular people find *nice* and *big* incongruous when associated with rivers of this type.

There is no land access to the river because of the desperately rugged canyon walls, so our only option was to paddle in. As we entered the rapids, it became apparent that we had misjudged the scale of the water. We found ourselves flying over 8-foot pressure waves and wound up doing a rear endo. We were ejected into a huge eddy and whipped around in several tight circles by the power of the water.

After that, we decided to portage anything that looked exciting.

Several hours and about a dozen long, difficult portages later, we reached a dead end at a tiny beach. The only way to progress was on the water. We made a plan to paddle like crazy into the flow, using our momentum to push past the nasty-looking turbulence and holes along the precipice.

We pushed off and hurtled toward the foam and spray. The next thing I knew, the boat was pointing skyward and my world became a dark, seething mass of cold gray water. I eventually found myself circulating in a huge whirlpool against the cliff, bumping around with flotsam and jetsam. I spotted Cameron clinging to the cliff, but no boat. Moments later, a large yellow boatlike object appeared. The bow was bent over at 90 degrees, and the rear third of the hull was folded over on itself.

Cameron muttered something about never setting foot in a *&%!@ kayak again, but I pointed out it was our only way out. We spent the next 30 minutes bashing the boat into a usable shape. Finally, we had a craft that we could at least sit in, and we made attempt number two at surviving to the end of the rapid. Luck was with us this time, and we made a serviceable if not elegant turn into the flow. The boat no longer handled like a kayak, but it stayed afloat and we were able to nurse it down to the takeout.

right length, stand barefoot and hold the paddle vertically against your body. You should just be able to curl the tips of your fingers around the top of the blade. Rough or technical conditions and low seats will require shorter paddle lengths. Wide, slow, or high-seat boats will require longer paddles. In theory, the most efficient feather angle is 90 degrees, since the free (returning) paddle blade is cutting through the wind with the least frontal area (the reason a paddle is feathered). Unfortunately, many people end up with tendinitis problems at 90 degrees, and find 70 to 80 degrees much more forgiving.

CANOE PADDLES

Certain races and conditions will require you to use canoe paddles. Conditions where you will definitely want to use a single-blade paddle include whitewater rafting (the boats are too wide to use a kayak paddle), outrigger-canoe sailing (the rigging prohibits the use of a kayak blade), and paddling very large or very heavy boats, such as large dugout canoes or rowboats/dories (these are too slow for a kayak blade's cadence advantage). Also, a lot of overhanging vegetation will interfere with efficient kayak technique.

Canoe paddles come in a huge variety of shapes, sizes, and materials. By far the best for adventure racing is a carbon-fiber "marathon" blade. These are available from a few specialty manufacturers, including Zaveral (www.zre.com) in the United States, and are startlingly lightweight—as light as 7 ounces, although a blade that light is not strong enough to withstand the abuse of an adventure race. My choice for most conditions is a medium-weight marathon-racing blade, still very light at 11 ounces.

If you have the resources to buy racing blades (such as those available from Zaveral Racing Equipment, www.zre.com/gearshop/paddlesport/paddles/770013.html), you should make sure that you get the strongest construction available. Even the heaviest composite (synthetic fiber/resin) raft paddles will be less than half the weight of a standard plastic/aluminum rental paddle, and that advantage can save you a huge amount of energy over the length of a typical raft leg in a long race.

Wash Riding and Towing

Paddlers could stand to learn a couple of important lessons from fluid mechanics. First of all, as you move through the water, your boat creates a wave, which in turn creates resistance, and this resistance is increased if the wave is disrupted in some way. Most of the time this happens when you paddle in water that is shallower than the boat is long, or if you paddle too close to a bank. Second, the wave itself is a small hill. Because of this, you can use the wave behind a boat to provide assistance to a following boat. Measurements in test tanks show that a 15 percent advantage can be gained if a boat is placed on the displacement wave of another boat, similar to the effects of drafting in a pace line on a bike, only it is called wash riding.

The trick to wash riding is positioning. The best place to ride is on the front of the first wave being created by the front boat. The bow of the wash-riding boat should be immediately astern of the front boat. If this is not possible—due to adverse conditions where steering or positioning are too difficult—there is a useful wave off the side of a boat called a bow wave. To ride a bow wave, the bow of the wave-riding boat should be positioned approximately three-quarters of the way along the hull of the front boat and as close to the side as practically possible. Sitting on a bow wave is tricky because the wave tends to pull the boats together, and their proximity makes for some interesting language as paddles clash and fight for real estate between the two hulls.

TOWING

If individuals on a team are not evenly matched, or it is impractical to wash ride, towing may be the answer. Successful towing requires good boat-handling skills by the steerers of both boats. And if towing is not well-implemented, the potential outcomes vary from slowing down the team to sinking the boats. But done properly, it can have huge rewards.

Towing in a boat is similar to towing on a bike in that both parties need to keep good lines and an even speed. If the back boat wanders too far to one side, it will pull the front boat off line, and this inevitably sets up a slomlike set of maneuvers as each boat tries to get back on course.

It is not uncommon to see novice paddlers who are attempting to tow wind up with their boats gunwale to gunwale (side to side) because their slaloming exceeds their ability to steer.

To minimize the steering effect of the back boat on the front boat, clip the towline as close to the center of the front boat as possible. You can clip the line either behind the stern paddler or onto the stern paddler's body. I like to wear a small waist pack the way tourists do, pockets in front, the buckle in the small of my back, and clip the towline into the belt behind me. This allows me to put food and other items within reach in the pockets. You can also purchase a PFD (personal flotation device) with a ready-made towing strap with metal D ring in place. Some of these have a built-in bungee cord, so all you have to do is clip the D ring and you're ready to tow. Another solution is to use the chest or waist strap on your PFD, which will be somewhat more comfortable than a waist pack.

Clip the towline as far forward on the back boat as possible, as this assists in keeping it in line with the front boat. Most kayaks and canoes have carrying handles at either end; otherwise, you can use deck lines, hatch straps, or cross beams.

Andrea Spitzer and Ian Adamson give John Howard a lift on the way to winning the 1997 ESPN X-venture race in Baja, Mexico.

HOW TO . . .

Make a Towline

If you are boating in rough conditions, you'll need to strengthen your towline. You can do this with ¼-inch-diameter climbing cord and ¼- to ⅓-inch-diameter shock cord. Tie the boats together no more than 3 feet apart, as any greater distance will cause the aft boat to push uphill on the back of the front boat's wave. Clip two small nonlocking carabiners to each boat and tie them to each end of your towline. Tie 3 feet of the shock cord to the body of the climbing cord in a loop with an overhand knot in each end of the shock cord (to stop it from pulling through the towline). Then tie this to the main body of the towline with another overhand knot at each end. The shock cord will absorb the dynamic loads of the two boats surging back and forward in the waves.

If you are towing using a boat with a stern hug rudder (most sea kayaks use these), you need to be aware that the towline can get caught in the rudder or steering lines. To avoid this, secure the towline to the boats or people as high off the water as possible, and keep the line taut.

Sailing

If you have a strong wind from behind or even off to the side, you can use sails to add speed to a canoe or kayak. The force of the wind is considerable if harnessed effectively, and the power produced by sails can easily exceed that delivered by the paddlers. In really strong winds it is quite possible to get a kayak hydroplaning. Kiwi adventure athlete Steve Gurney and I have hit at least 20 knots in a tandem racing kayak. At those kinds of speeds, it takes exceptional skill to keep a boat upright, so do not attempt to sail a kayak or canoe in strong winds unless you have a background in kayaking *and* sailing, and plenty of experience with the specific rigs.

If you decide to set up to sail, you have several choices. The fastest and most portable system is a high-performance kite used for kite-boarding.

Kite-board sails are expensive (upwards of $500) and take a lot of practice and skill to master. Another option is to buy or make a fixed sail. Though not as powerful as a kite, it is much easier to use, and can be set up to be hands-free, unlike a kite, which must be tended continually.

If you decide on a kite, you need a model that can be self-launched from the water (even experienced kite sailors ditch their rigs occasionally). There are two basic types of kite: those you steer and those you don't. Only the steerable kind work in the range of conditions that make them useful, as you have the ability to "park" them in a neutral position where they don't pull you around, or to place them at an angle that pulls you in your desired direction even if the wind is not ideal. Steerable kites come with either two or four lines, and most can be set up either way. My preference is to use four lines because it allows you to steer the kite backward as well as forward, park it easily, and lower it to the ground at will.

Fixed, or "V," sails have two rigid poles attached to a flexible joint on the deck of the boat, and fit inside sleeves in a V-shaped sail. Two or more lines support the sail and poles, and tie to the boat deck in a way that allows you to paddle and adjust them to steer your course. Wildwasser Sport, the U.S. representative for German kayak manufacturer Prijon, based in Boulder, Colorado, carries by far the best V-sail I have found (www.wildnet.com). The Wildwasser sail is lightweight, compact, and fast to set up and adjusts to sail hands-free in most wind conditions. In heavy winds you can stow it in seconds or reset it automatically by simply releasing a hold-down bungee.

Portaging

When conditions are too rough for your skills, you may need carry your boat overland, called portaging in paddling parlance. This is mostly a painful exercise, since loaded boats are heavy and awkward to handle. In general two people must carry a two-person boat, which creates communication and coordination challenges. A typical tandem kayak or canoe used in a multiday race is about 80 pounds and 16 feet long. If you add in equipment, apparel, and food, you are up to around 120 pounds, a significant weight to carry over long distances.

A team portages its kayak during the 2000 Southern Traverse in New Zealand.

Most races prohibit dragging boats, so you can either carry them or tow them on a set of portage wheels (available from boating and larger outdoor stores). Wheels are a great asset if the portage surface is smooth, but their bulk, weight, and expense usually make them impractical. If you carry a boat over a short distance, it is often most convenient to simply grab the ends and go. For longer distances, however, your shoulder, arm, and grip muscles will give way. In this case it is easiest to put your pack on your back and hoist the boat to your shoulder or head.

(continued on page 82)

BEAUFORT WIND SCALE

Use this chart to judge wind speed while paddling.

Beaufort Force	Wind Speed (Knots*)	Description	Sea Condition
0	0	Calm	Sea like a mirror
1	1–3	Light Air	Ripples but without foam crests
2	4–6	Light Breeze	Small wavelets. Crests do not break
3	7–10	Gentle Breeze	Large wavelets. Perhaps scattered white horses
4	11–16	Moderate Breeze	Small waves. Fairly frequent white horses
5	17–21	Fresh Breeze	Moderate waves, many white horses
6	22–27	Strong Breeze	Large waves begin to form; white foam crests, probably spray
7	28–33	Near Gale	Sea heaps up and white foam blown in streaks along the direction of the wind
8	34–40	Gale	Moderately high waves; crests begin to break into spindrift

Beaufort Force	Wind Speed (Knots*)	Description	Sea Condition
9	41–47	Strong Gale	High waves. Dense foam along the direction of the wind. Crests of waves begin to roll over. Spray may affect visibility
10	48–55	Storm	Very high waves with long, overhanging crests. The surface of the sea takes on a white appearance. The tumbling of the sea becomes heavy and shocklike. Visibility affected
11	56–63	Violent Storm	Exceptionally high waves. The sea is completely covered with long white patches of foam lying in the direction of the wind. Visibility affected
12	64+	Hurricane	The air is filled with foam and spray. Sea completely white with driving spray. Visibility very seriously affected

* 1 knot = 1.15 mph

Kayaks are usually carried on the shoulder, since they are relatively narrow in the ends; canoes are easier to carry over your head (upside down), since you can rest the crossbars on your shoulders. If you carry this way, your head will tend to be inside the hull. A major consideration: limited vision. Pay attention to your footing, and if you are in front, tell your teammate behind you what is coming up.

Loading and Packing

A slightly bow-heavy boat travels more quickly, but is difficult to steer. A stern-loaded boat travels slowly, but steers more easily. To compromise, stow most of your gear in the middle. This keeps the ends light and buoyant, making the boat easier and faster to turn. It also reduces the likelihood of swamping (flipping).

Adventure races will often require you to take a large amount of gear with you in your boat. At a minimum, you'll need safety gear, food, and water. It is not uncommon to carry other equipment, which in past events has included bicycles, mountaineering equipment, and climbing and trekking gear. All this paraphernalia has to be safely and securely stowed in waterproof bags somewhere so it doesn't impede a paddle stroke or cause grievous pain to lower body parts.

The most commonly used method for sealing and securing gear is with "dry bags." These are available in a variety of sizes, from something barely big enough for your cell phone to cavernous expedition packs that could comfortably house half your team. Less common due to their weight and rigidity (difficult to fit into odd-shaped holes) are "rocket-style" boxes and hard-side "Pelican" cases. The Raid Gauloises specifies a small waterproof drum as mandatory paddling equipment, but otherwise you are free to choose your weapon.

I usually use lightweight roll-top nylon dry bags. If we are in an open boat, such as a raft or canoe, I prefer to have a single big bag for the bulk of my gear, and then a small transparent bag for items I want ready access to. Portage packs allow you to carry all your gear on your back, leaving your hands free to carry your boat and paddles.

Load the center of the boat with your heavy gear, and always strap it in securely in case of capsize and to prevent it shifting position as you paddle. Use 9- to 12-foot-long roof-rack straps, the kind with ½- to ¾-inch nylon webbing and a spring-loaded metal buckle, since they are immensely strong and very fast to use.

Kayaks have considerably less room than open boats and usually have fore and aft hatches that force you to put your gear into each end. Some kayaks have elastic cords and/or netting to accommodate limited deck storage, and this should be reserved for essential items like food, maps, and safety gear. Wildwasser makes a really useful dry bag that clips to the deck of a sea kayak and has a map sleeve and external mesh pocket built into the top flap.

All Water Is Not Created Equal

Wind, waves, and current all dramatically affect the speed of a boat over the ground, the only speed that counts in racing.

WIND

A really strong headwind will slow down your speed to the point where it may be better to stop or portage. Anything over 20 miles per hour (Beaufort Scale Force 5; see table on page 80) will be difficult even for good paddlers, so you need to consider possible alternatives if you get in these conditions. It may be possible to choose a course that avoids the worst wind, something that may be an option if you see a sheltered shore or have other large objects to shelter behind. The side of a river or lake from which the wind is blowing (the "windward" shore) is always more sheltered than the other ("lee" shore) side. Even if the wind is blowing straight down the lake, or up the river, bends, bays, and headlands along the bank can provide small areas of shelter. Conversely, if you are traveling in the direction of the wind, you will want to paddle where it is strongest and most consistent.

WAVES

Wind creates waves, and the longer the wind blows, the bigger and faster the waves. Windward shores, islands, and enclosed waterways generally provide the smoothest water, but sometimes it's better to

BETWEEN YOU & ME

The final leg of Eco-Challenge, Sabah (Borneo), came down to the wire. We had to navigate our way through a maze of small islands and over 60 miles of open sea to the finish. We were sharing the lead with team Spie from France and team Aussie, the strongest kayakers in the race.

As we paddled out of the final transition, we saw Spie running in, and we had seen Aussie hot on their heels only a few hours before. A strong headwind was rising as we turned our bow toward the open ocean, and we could see whitecaps building in the distance. I pored over our nautical charts as we pounded our way into an increasing gale, looking for an alternative route that would save us some effort. I saw one possibility that involved something of a detour, but could potentially save us a useful amount of time. The next checkpoint lay in a group of islands to the northeast, but the charts indicated a sheltered route behind the islands directly to the east. If we paddled around the islands and then north to the checkpoint, we would avoid the worst of the wind and waves, and hopefully make up some time in the smoother water.

Several long hours later, we nervously approached the checkpoint, not knowing if we were first, second, or third to check in. Pandemonium broke loose as we announced our team number. It transpired that the race organization had completely lost track of us when we made our little detour, and we were indeed first by almost an hour. Our choice to travel faster but further in better conditions paid off handsomely, and we were able to hold on to our lead for the overall win.

travel on foot a little further to find sheltered conditions than to expend a lot of effort paddling in difficult ones. If the wind forces you to paddle at an angle into waves, you should steer a slalom course so that the bow of your boat points directly into the wave as you crest it, and then steer the bow in the direction you are heading as you head off down the back. This will prevent waves from broadsiding and rolling your boat.

If the waves are behind you, they provide an excellent opportunity to surf, a practice that can dramatically increase your speed. Surfing allows you to use gravity to pull you along, since the front of a wave is a small downhill slope that can help propel you forward. On really short, steep waves, it is possible to get a kayak hull planing—that is, the boat moves so fast it sits on top of the water rather than pushes it aside. If you have a quartering swell (one that approaches your boat at an angle from behind), steer a slalom course to avoid getting pushed sideways down the wave and having your boat roll, landing you in the river. To steer through a quartering swell, point your bow directly down the wave as it starts to lift the stern of the boat, and then resume course as the wave passes under you. Compensate for steering down the waves by steering toward the waves in a zigzag motion, or you will end up off course and have to paddle across the waves to get to your destination.

CURRENTS

Good things always come in threes, and water conditions are no exception. Where there is wind there are waves, and where there are waves, there is current.

The biggest wind waves we typically see are ocean swells which are formed over thousands of miles of open sea. All this water being moved around by the wind also results in a net movement of the water in the direction of the wind, effectively a wind current. Significant wind currents can occur on relatively small bodies of water, such as lakes and reservoirs, and although you may not be able to see it, you can assume it is there anytime there are wind and waves. Paddlers often overlook wind current because it is difficult to differentiate from the effects of the wind.

Tidal currents are much more obvious. Any body of water open to the sea will be at the mercy of tidal current, and the bigger the tidal range, the bigger the body of water, and the smaller the opening to the ocean, the stronger the current. The most extreme effect of tidal current is called a tidal bore, where the current is so strong and the change so rapid that a large, extremely fast wave (the bore) that looks like an ocean wave can rush up an inlet.

Tidal currents can be so fast that they become impossible to paddle against. I have been in several races where we were faced with tidal currents in excess of our paddling speed of about 7 knots. In these situations you should refer to tide charts that list tide and current information for a calendar date and the time of day, and try to time your paddling to match the best conditions. It is sometimes possible to make your way against a strong current if you stay close to shore (where the current is weakest) and use eddies, the pools where the cur-

TIPS FROM THE TOP

John Jacoby, winner of the Eco-Challenge and the Raid Gauloises, and four-time World Marathon kayak champion, offers these paddling tips.

1. Train regularly in the fastest boat you can handle, such as an Olympic class K1. If you can't balance in this boat, practice over the summer months (when the water is warmer!). Being confident and stable in a K1 will extend your paddling skills so that you can handle just about any type of paddling that an adventure racecourse might throw at you.

There is no good substitute for training by paddling, but if you can't get on the water, some basic upper-body exercises will help you maintain paddling strength. Chinups, pushups, dips, and situps all are great exercises for paddling muscles. And you can do them anywhere, with or without a gym.

2. Use a fully adjustable wing paddle. They are easy to travel with, and the adjustable length and blade offset mean you can adjust the length depending on the type of boat and conditions you are racing in. Using a paddle that is too long will create an excessive workload on each paddle stroke and cause premature fatigue. Make sure you reinforce the "locking" system on the paddle shaft with tape. Besides helping to prevent breakage, taping the lock will also assist in maintaining the paddle angle and length and help keep water out of the paddle shaft.

3. Train in tough conditions to prepare for poor conditions on race day. Rough water in the ocean, windy lakes, and flooded rivers are great places to boost your competence and confidence in paddling. Being confident in difficult conditions is a key component to successfully and efficiently negotiating them when the going gets tough in a race.

John Jacoby

rent reverses behind a large stationary object such as an island or a headland.

It is quite common to have a current moving across your direction of travel, and in this case you will have to adjust your course to accommodate the resulting drift. To do this, angle your boat into the current, and, using two fixed objects on shore for reference, increase the angle until they remain lined up. Note that you will not be pointing in the direction you are moving with relation to the land, but instead will be pointing up current of your destination.

SURF

Negotiating surf—launching into it, landing on a beach through it, or surviving in extreme open-water conditions with breaking waves—is one of the most challenging (and exciting) aspects of open-water paddling. It is quite possible to get caught in rough conditions at any time on a large body of water, and it pays to be able to handle it. In fact, in *most* long races that have featured open-water crossings, the race organization has had to rescue teams due to their inability to handle the conditions.

Extremely high or even moderately strong but prolonged wind can cause waves in open water to collapse (Beaufort Scale Forces 6–8) so that surf appears in water too deep for a bottom effect. If you ever encounter these conditions, you need one of two things to survive: world-class kayaking skills or lots of luck.

If you must launch into surf off a beach, pick a lull in the surf to start out in, since breaking waves always come in sets of bigger and smaller waves. If you spend a few minutes watching the surf, you will notice patterns in the way the waves break. On a sand beach, the moving water shifts the sand around on the bottom, creating sandbars and channels. Avoid sandbars because they are more prone to large waves. Channels are usually favorable routes out, since they are deeper and flow away from the beach (that's how they form).

However you tackle the surf, once you're there, point your boat directly into or directly away from the waves, depending on whether you are entering or exiting the water. If the conditions are extreme, you should run with the wind and waves, as this will reduce the effects on you and your boat. It is entirely possible you will get thrown sideways against surf because it can move considerably faster than you can paddle. Speeding surf makes steering extremely difficult or impossible. If you get caught sideways, lean aggressively into the wave and brace against the whitewater with your paddle. It is quite possible to brace down some quite large ocean waves, and Eskimo roll to right yourself if you lose it.

As the wave dissipates its energy and decreases in size, you can often break free by doing a wide, powerful sweep stroke to face your boat into the wave, or a deep rudder stroke to face back down the breaking edge of the wave. In any event, all this takes practice, so it pays to find some safe surf you can handle (something on a surfing beach or lakeshore) and practice going into and out of the waves. As your skill improves, look for increasingly difficult conditions until you are comfortable you can handle those expected in the race.

With enough practice you may be able to use surf to your advantage and play like a surfboard rider. The trick to surfing a kayak is to keep it pointed directly down the wave and to lean back. Even the big rudders on sea kayaks are insufficient to keep you on line in big conditions, so you will have to use your paddle as a rudder to steer. If you don't lean back far enough, or if the wave is too steep, you will end up pearling— that is, the bow of the boat buries into the trough of the wave in front of you, and you lose control as the boat slows and the stern lifts out of the water. If this happens, you will lose the wave, get thrown sideways (most common), or perform a somersault.

An athlete rappels (abseils) above Lake Wanaka during the 2000 Southern Traverse in New Zealand.

"Accomplishment, like life, will prove to be a journey, not a destination."

—Anonymous

VERTIGO

HOW TO IMPROVE YOUR CLIMBING AND ROPES-COURSE SKILLS

Most ropes courses in adventure racing have very little in common with technical rock climbing. Both use ropes, anchors, and dramatic relief in the natural landscape, but that is where the similarities end. Although it is very helpful on a ropes course to have technical rock-climbing experience, it is by no means necessary.

Most races with climbing sections (I call them "ropes" sections, which is more accurate) include at least rappelling (abseiling). Highly technical races, such as Raid Gauloises or Eco-Challenge, may also include fixed-rope ascending and traversing. Races rarely include free climbing. If you don't know what rappelling, ascending, and other types of ropes sports are, no worries. I'll explain them all now, one at a time.

Rappelling (Abseiling)

Rappelling is the art of making a controlled descent, usually off a cliff, with the aid of a rope. You can also rappel off buildings, bridges, and other tall structures. Although there are many tools you can use to rappel, the two most common aid devices are a figure eight and an ATC (air traffic controller)/tuber-style device (descender). Occasionally, a race will allow you to use other mechanical systems, such as a Petzl GriGri, a stitch plate, or a rack, but I don't recommend them for adventure racing due to their bulk and weight. Although ATCs and figure eights thread differently, they use the same principle: Each increases the friction of the rope through the system by forcing it through a series of tight bends. The person rappelling controls his or her rate of descent by increasing or decreasing the rope's angle and hence the surface area of the rope in contact with the device.

Both the figure eight and ATC are relatively inexpensive, so it is worth buying one of each and practicing with both. The ATC system is lighter and smaller than a figure eight, but it is much harder to thread the rope through and can be considerably slower, especially if you are tired and the rope is old and stiff. Apart from size and weight, a figure eight's main disadvantage is that it twists the rope, and this can lead to some really messy tangles if you rig several ropes too close together.

In addition to the main equipment, race organizations usually require you to use an automatic backup system to prevent a free fall in the event of hardware failure or human error. Eco-Challenge specifies the Canadian Mountain Guide system, with a prusik above or below the descender, clipped with a carabiner to the harness. Raid Gauloises X-Adventure specifies the French system, with a figure eight on a 24-inch lanyard above a Petzl Shunt (which clamps and grabs the rope as it passes through) that is clipped by carabiner to the climbing harness. Some races use a fireman's belay, where a person pulls on the bottom of the rappelling rope if he or she thinks the person descending is out of control.

In addition to the rope equipment, you'll need leather-palmed gloves. These will protect your hands from the friction generated when you brake. This friction is so intense that it will melt synthetic gloves and burn flesh. One of the cheapest and most effective kinds are leather gardening gloves (about $7 at a hardware store). Of course, if you are so inclined, you can also shell out four times as much for climbing-specific gloves from an outdoor outfitter.

Ascending

The ability to climb up a rope is without question the most challenging ropes skill for most adventure racers. Few people know how to do it, and few training organizations know the best equipment or techniques. Luckily, ascending is not difficult; it just takes some practice and a little conditioning to master the technique.

EQUIPMENT

To ascend, the key piece of equipment you'll need is, not surprisingly, an ascender. You'll need at least one, and you may need two because you can ascend by using either two hands on one ascender (one-handled ascender) and a single foot loop or one ascender per hand (two-handled ascenders) and one or two foot loops. Ascenders are variously called jugs or jumars and come in a large variety of shapes and sizes. The one most commonly used in adventure racing is the Petzl Ascension (6.9 ounces), as it is relatively light and easy to use. The lightest ascender available is the Petzl Tibloc (1.4 ounces), but it's difficult to use and impractical for long or technical ascents. An intermediate device is the Petzl Croll (4.6 ounces), which is basically an Ascension without a handle. The Petzl Pantin (4.3 ounces) is a useful device for long ascents, but it doesn't qualify as a safety piece, since it straps to your foot, not your harness. Other mechanical ascenders worth looking at are the Gibbs #2 (7.0 ounces), the Jumar (9.2 ounces), and the Wild Country Ropeman II (3.0 ounces), although the Jumar is the only one of these with a handle. Petzl's Web site, at www.petzl.com, has a good page explaining equipment and techniques for adventure racing.

In addition to two ascenders, you need a climbing harness, one or two full-strength leashes (sewn slings, via ferrata lanyards, and climbing rope tethers all work), one or two foot loops, and two to four carabiners, depending on the race requirements. Consult the charts on pages 94 and 95 to see what brands I recommend.

Ascending with two-handled ascenders. Use the two-handed method as long as there are no significant overhangs on the ascent route. Significant overhangs force the rope out away from the rock face below

RECOMMENDED EQUIPMENT

The following equipment is recommended for two-handled ascenders.

Quantity	Item	Use	Recommended Brand
1	Climbing harness	Secure gear	Petzl Pandion
2	Mechanical ascenders	Clamp to rope	Left- and right-hand Petzl Ascensions
2	Full-strength slings	Secure ascenders to harness	60- to 100-cm × 10-mm Spectra slings
1 or 2	Foot loop(s)	Step for each foot	Petzl Footcord
4	Small hair ties	Secure foot loops and slings	1–2-mm diameter elastic
2	Locking carabiners	Connect equipment	Lightweight screw gate

and make it difficult to climb under racing conditions (that is, you're tired and have a weighted pack).

Efficient two-handled ascending starts with setting up your equipment correctly. Follow this sequential process to find and set the lengths of your slings and foot loops.

1. Secure a length of climbing rope against a wall so that you can safely put your full weight on it and climb up a few feet.

The following equipment is recommended for one-handled ascenders.

Quantity	Item	Use	Recommended Brand
1	Climbing harness	Secure gear	Petzl Pandion
1	Chest harness	Secure Croll	Petzl Serpentine
1	Mechanical ascender	Clamp to rope	Right-hand Petzl Ascension
1	Mechanical ascender	Clamp to rope	Petzl Croll (or Ascension, if mandatory)
1	Full-strength sling	Secure ascenders to harness	60- to 100-cm × 10-mm Spectra sling
1	Foot loop	Step for both feet	Petzl Footcord
2	Small hair ties	Secure foot loops and slings	1–2-mm diameter elastic
3	Locking carabiners	Connect equipment	Lightweight screw gate

2. With your harness on, girth hitch both slings through your belay loop or harness loops.

3. Attach the left and right ascenders to the slings, using a locking carabiner on each, with the gate facing down and toward you. This will allow you to put on the foot loops later.

4. Hold your right ascender in your right hand with your upper arm at right angles to your body in front of you (horizontal) and your

An athlete uses a two-handed ascender to climb Herbert Falls during the 1997 Eco-Challenge in Queensland, Australia.

forearm at right angles to your upper arm (vertical). The sling should be taut and pulling on your harness. The length of the sling will depend on how tall you are, and may require adjusting. If you can't find a sling of the right length, buy one that is the next size longer, and tie one or more figure-eight knots in it until it is the right length. Make sure the sewn overlap on the sling is not bent around the carabiner, in the knot, or in the girth hitch.

5. Repeat step 4 with the left ascender, carabiner, and sling, but make sure the top of the left ascender just clears the bottom of the right ascender's cam housing. The left sling should be about 6 inches shorter than the right sling. This allows both ascenders to slide freely on the rope without jamming against each other.

6. Clip the foot loop(s) to the carabiner(s). It is quite possible to ascend using only one foot loop, but you need to be comfortable with this procedure. I suggest using two to start with and then experimenting with using only one on a variety of surfaces and angled slopes.

7. Adjust the length of the foot-loop tethers so that each ascender is at chest height when you are standing erect with your feet in the loops.

8. Use the hair ties to secure each foot loop to your feet and each sling to the carabiners. To do this, wrap the ties (as you would a ponytail) several times around the sling and foot loop and slide them against the carabiners and feet so that they won't slip. This will prevent you from losing the carabiners if you drop them while taking gear on and off, and will stop your feet from falling out of the foot loops when you start to move up the rope.

9. Clip the ascenders, right above left, on the rope you set in step 1.

10. Make sure all carabiners are locked and that your harness is doubled back if it is not a Petzl Pandion, which doesn't need doubling back.

Two-handled ascender technique requires an unusual gait, in which your right hand and right foot move together and your left hand and left foot move together. This is counterintuitive, since walking and running require you to move opposite hands and feet to maintain balance. To ascend smoothly and effortlessly, get your weight over your feet and move as if you were climbing a ladder. In this case, the ladder steps are the foot loops. Transfer your weight between left and right in a waddling motion. Try to lift your leg and foot loop with very little assistance from your arms; otherwise, you will fatigue your arms quickly. The arms should only lift the mass of the ascender, carabiner, sling, and foot loop, letting the larger muscles of your legs to do the rest of the work.

When you start moving up the rope, especially on a long ascent, it will take a while to completely stretch out the rope. Don't sit down in your harness when you first clip to the rope, or you will end up in a heap on the ground when the rope stretches. Instead, start by sliding the right ascender up the rope as high as you can while standing on your left foot. Don't forget to flex your right leg as you do this so you don't have to lift its weight with your arm. Now stand in your right foot loop; the rope will stretch and your foot will hit the ground. Slide your left ascender up the rope so that the left sling is taut and the left ascender is just below the right ascender. It helps to have someone hold the bottom of the rope, since the friction of the ascenders will tend to lift the rope, preventing the ascenders from sliding upward. You may have to take several steps before the rope fully takes your weight and you start moving up the wall.

Once you start moving upward, you'll begin to get a feel for the side-to-side climbing motion as you move right foot and right hand together and then left foot and left hand together. Keep your weight over your feet, with your chest close to the rope and your head close to the cliff (or wall). If you get tired, you can sit in your harness and shake out your arms and legs.

Ascending with one-handled ascender. The technique for using one-handled ascender requires a completely different motion because you hold only one ascender in both hands and have both feet in one foot loop. This technique is virtually essential if you have long, overhanging sections of rope or if you're carrying very heavy packs on vertical walls. Follow these steps.

1. With your harness on, girth hitch the sling through your belay loop or harness loops.

2. Attach the right ascender to the sling, using a locking carabiner, gate facing down and toward you. The gate pivot should be on top, close to the ascender.

3. Hold the ascender in front of you in your right hand, with your upper arm at right angles to your body and your forearm at right angles to your upper arm. The sling should be taut and pulling on your harness. The length of the sling will depend on how tall you are, and may require adjusting. If you can't find a sling of the right length, buy one that is the next size longer, and tie one or more figure-eight knots in it until it is the right length. Make sure the sewn overlap on the sling is not bent around the carabiner, in the knot, or in the girth hitch.

4. Clip the foot loop to the carabiner.

5. Adjust the length of the foot-loop tether so that it is at chest height when you are standing erect with your feet in the loop. You will have both feet the one loop.

6. Use the hair ties to secure the foot loop to your feet and each sling to the carabiners. To do this, wrap the ties (as you would a pony-tail) several times around the sling and foot loop and slide them

against the carabiner or feet so that neither will slip. This will prevent you from losing the carabiner if you drop it while taking gear on and off, and will stop your feet from falling out of the foot loop when you start to move up the rope.

7. Put your chest harness on according to the instructions on the packaging, and secure it with the second carabiner with the gate facing away from you.

8. You'll most likely be clipping in to a mechanical ascender designed specifically for use with a chest harness, such as a Croll. Clip the third locking carabiner through your harness, *not* the belay loop, since you want your Croll to be as low as possible in the system, with the gate facing out and up.

9. Attach the Croll to the carabiners on both harnesses so that the Croll gate faces away from you. Adjust the chest harness until it is uncomfortably tight, forcing you to hunch over. When you sit on the rope with weight in your harness, you will sink into the system and it will be much more comfortable. If it is too loose, you won't be able to move up the rope effectively.

10. Clip the ascenders to the rope, right hand above the Croll, and put one or both feet in the foot loop.

11. Secure the foot loop and carabiner with the hair ties.

Ascending using one-handled ascender looks something like a frog hopping, since you stand on both feet together as you pull up with both hands together. As you stand, the Croll slides up the rope, and then you sit in your harness and slide your handled ascender up the rope as you lift your legs. This "stand and slide" motion gives you a lot of power because you are using the power of both legs and both arms simultaneously to push and pull up the rope. As with two-handled-ascender technique, you need to keep your weight over your feet as you move, or your arms take too much of the load.

Traversing

You traverse anytime you use ropes or other equipment to cross otherwise impassable obstacles, such as a canyon. Race organizers usually include traverses for the spectacle and the thrill, and design their courses specifically to include them. Various types of traverses are used in races, including fixed ladders, Tyrolean (rope) traverses, zip lines, and commando lines.

LADDERS

Ladders (the kind you might use around the house) can bridge small chasms, such as crevasses on a glacier. It is quite possible to walk across a ladder even with crampons on over your boots, but it takes a lot of confidence. Most people crawl across really deep voids, and this is quite acceptable, if somewhat undignified. If you know you will be crossing ladders in a race and want to impress your mates, practice with one on the ground at home. Crossing a ladder is a lot like crossing a tightrope. It's easy when the ladder or rope is only a few inches off the ground, but extremely difficult if it is 100 feet high. To cross without losing your balance, keep your head up. This will stabilize the balance centers in your brain. Look down with your eyes without lowering your head. Step on each rung with the instep of your shoe, and keep your arms out wide for balance. If you have walking poles, it helps to hold these out to the sides as well; it will give you more inertia to correct a misstep.

TYROLEAN TRAVERSE

Tyrolean traverses are the type most commonly seen in races, since they are relatively easy to set up and can be configured to fit a variety of locations. Tyroleans are generally made with $7/16$- to $1/2$-inch static climbing rope, but may be made with wire rope if the traverse is particularly long. The maximum distance of a rope Tyrolean is about 1,000 feet. Anything over that gets extremely difficult to rig.

Although single-rope traverses are quite safe, most Tyroleans use two parallel ropes for each person, so you are required to clip your backup to the second line. Usually, you will set up a pulley on the main rope to take most of your weight, and hitch a sling girth to your harness with a locking carabiner clipped to the backup line. Some races require a short tether between you and the Tyrolean so that you can't get caught between the rope and the pulley; if not, make sure you stay clear of the rope. It is not uncommon for clothing, hair, or loose equipment to jam in the pulley, so ask your teammates to check you—and each other—for loose odds and ends before traversing.

Most Tyrolean traverses include a gradual downhill portion at the start and a short, steep uphill at the finish. Negotiating such a traverse takes a surprising amount of technique. You must push off strongly at the start, maintain an aerodynamic body position on the downhill, and then, at the end, use a swimmer's butterfly kick with your legs.

Your push-off will depend on the topography of the start. Get as much speed as you can to launch across the rope. In some cases it may be possible to run. Other times you may have to spring off a wall like a backstroke swimmer. In general, it is best to go headfirst and hold your body in a horizontal position, with your feet and legs acting like a weather vane. This should minimize wind resistance and keep you pointed in the right direction. You can maintain your orientation to a small extent by holding the tether or primary carabiner and twisting it if you start to turn to the side.

Once you slow down to a manageable speed, pull yourself hand over hand until it becomes too steep to do so. It's at this point that you will have to employ the butterfly kick. Draw your legs into a crouching position and grasp the rope ahead of you with both hands, arms extended. Vigorously extend your legs as you pull hard on the rope, and you should shoot forward. Repeat this motion until you reach the ground at the other side or you can get a helping hand from a teammate. The first person across a Tyrolean should be the most proficient traverser on the team, as he or she won't have a helping hand at the other side.

Zip Lines

A zip line is similar to a Tyrolean traverse, only the rope or cable is angled downhill so that gravity pulls the person across to the far side. The techniques for negotiating a zip line are the same as for a Tyrolean, except you don't have to pull up at the end. Speeds can be quite high on a zip line, so you need to make sure you don't get anything caught in the pulley.

Races sometimes set zip lines and Tyroleans to end in water, which means you will make a splash landing and have to pull or swim your way out. If this is the case, make absolutely sure you have a clean landing, or you face the possibility of lost gear or even injury. As you approach the water, keep your arms and legs clear so that your rear end hits the water first. If you are going really fast, you may bounce and skim across the water. Try to maintain that momentum for as long as possible, to travel the maximum distance before you have to swim.

COMMANDO LINES

Commando lines allow you to cross a chasm using two parallel ropes or cables that are kept taut and horizontal. You walk on one line like a tightrope. You use the other line—often placed at chest or head height— as a hand line. If more than one person is allowed on the line at a time, be careful not to bounce or you'll knock the other person off. Use a sliding motion, as if you were using Nordic skis, rather than a stepping motion, as if you were walking or running.

TIPS FROM THE TOP

Team Montrail captain Rebecca Rusch, professional climbing guide and winner of Raid Gauloises, Extreme Adventure Hidalgo, and Raid the North Extreme, shares these three key climbing tips.

1. Don't take your preparation for ropes courses lightly. Ropes courses pose serious safety concerns. Also, proper preparation can greatly improve your race times and reduce your energy expenditure.

2. Make sure your entire team is comfortable on ropes. I have seen many racers with the tags still on their harnesses at race check-in. I have also seen the same racers waste hours and precious emotional and physical energy struggling on a ropes section. Your race is not the time to practice your rope work. Put the time in before the race, just as you do with biking and hiking.

3. Become intimate with your gear. Spend the time to get your ascenders and footloops custom fit to you, find carabiners that you can quickly operate with one hand, and choose a harness that is light and comfortable.

Other Fun Stuff

Ropes provide endless creative possibilities for devious riggers to confound adventure athletes. Here are a few of the most common.

RAPPELLIAN TRAVERSE

A rappellian traverse, or zipolean abseil, is a hybrid exercise combining a zip line or Tyrolean traverse with a rappel. The athlete clips into a rappelling rope that is tied to a pulley on a traverse line, so that he or she can simultaneously descend and traverse. It is up to the athlete to control the descent and try to land in the most desirable spot. This may involve avoiding water, trees, or other obstacles.

Rebecca Rusch

CARGO NETS

Cargo nets are very common in events such as HiTec, Action Asia, and the Outdoor Quest. In general, these entail simply climbing the net like a ladder, using it for a traverse, or setting it up as an obstacle. Nets are quite difficult to climb, since they are not rigid and they move about a great deal. Having more than one person on a net tends to exacerbate the motion and can easily cause someone to fall. To climb a net, ask your teammates to stabilize the net by hanging, standing, or lying in it, depending on its orientation.

HAND LINES

Hand lines are often used in areas of moderate exposure to heights, such as a cliff edge, where climbing ropes are not warranted. Large-diameter (1 inch or greater) knotted ascent lines may also be used to ascend small cliffs or walls (typically 10 to 12 feet) that are too high to

NEAR-DEATH EXPERIENCES

Gravity and altitude can be a lethal combination, and as a consequence, ropes courses have a high potential for disaster. Not surprisingly, there have been a few incidents, including at least one fatality, in adventure races. In a major event in the United States in 2002, several athletes had extremely close calls on the ropes sections.

The worst incident involved two athletes and a separation of the sheath (the protective outer layer) of a rappelling rope. This was due to extremely sharp but unprotected rock ledges on the top of the cliff sawing through the sheath as the athletes bounced the rope while lifting it through their rappel device. The rappel was about 280 feet, with several small steps in the rock. The combination of the weight and the friction of the rope over the steps made bouncing unavoidable. Contrary to the claims of the race director, who said that it was the fault of the athletes and that the rope was quite safe after losing its sheath, consecutive cuts on different ropes in the same location (the original rope was replaced) indicated it to be a rigging error. The first of the two athletes managed to grab the last few inches of intact rope as it slid through his descender, but the second athlete was not so fortunate and took a 30-foot plunge as the sheath started sliding down the core. By some miracle he didn't fall to the bottom, and was rescued by the rigging staff.

Another scary episode occurred on a 270-foot rappel down Herbert Falls in the 1997 Eco-Challenge in Australia. One of the athletes had started down the rope when he lost concentration and let his prusik go. It jammed, and rather than step up on a sling to release the knot as you are supposed to, the athlete decided to use his emergency knife to cut it free. Not only was the prusik above his descender, but he decided to cut the coils that were wrapped around the main rope. In the process, he managed to cut into the sheath before he realized what might happen. The horrified race staff quickly jumped into action and removed him from the course before he could write himself into race history.

scramble up but too small for climbing ropes. Climbing knotted ropes requires a strong handgrip and reasonable upper-body strength. If a teammate is incapable of doing a hand-line ascent under his or her own power, teammates can help by lifting, pushing, and pulling.

Staying Safe While Moving Fast

Several factors affect the safety of a ropes course: the condition of the equipment, the competence of the rigging crew, and your own ability and state of mind. Ultimately, it comes down to you. If you feel physically or mentally unfit to go on the ropes, don't tackle them. No one is forcing you, and the worst that can happen is that you will take a time penalty. Competent race organizations make it easy and painless to bow out of ropes sections. They often allow you to walk around the area, if possible, or provide rigging staff help you through. The consequences of attempting ropes without the proper equipment or ability can be disastrous.

If you know a bit about rigging and rope safety, you can evaluate the ropes set up at a race to make sure they're safe to use. Look for large steel carabiners (as opposed to small aluminum ones); $7/16$-inch static, clean, and unfrayed climbing rope; neat double or triple knots as backup on all anchors; 1-inch-wide slings; oversized climbing hardware, such as pulleys, bolts, and rope jams. In general, ropes should be anchored to really solid-looking trees or bolted into immense, solid rocks with no cracks, crumbling, or flakes.

In addition to keeping you safe, familiarity with your equipment will let you move fast. Absolutely the best thing you can do to move quickly on the ropes is practice doing the basic skills over and over. Eco-Challenge has traditionally had impressive and very long ropes sections. The 22,000 feet of set ropes through the Cathedral Spires in Argentina in 1999 was probably the biggest, and it took even the fastest teams the better part of 6 hours to negotiate.

Team Montrail discusses their navigational options during the 2001 Primal Quest in Colorado.

> *"The principal mark of genius is not perfection but originality, the opening of new frontiers."*
>
> —*Arthur Koestler*

 # STAYING FOUND
HOW TO IMPROVE
YOUR NAVIGATION SKILLS

Anyone can hike with a pack, sit in a boat and paddle, or roll around on a mountain bike. Navigation, on the other hand, is a discipline that you simply can't fake. Many teams train like crazy in the physical skills, but neglect their orienteering. On race day, they end up going very fast, but in the wrong direction. For every one step you take in the wrong direction, you must take three steps to get to where you want to be!

I was racing with a very fit, very fast team in the 2002 Wild Onion Urban Adventure Race in Chicago. We stayed with the teams at the front of the race until we had to "navigate" through the city on one of the last legs. Despite running literally twice as fast as one of the local teams, we were unable to match their net speed through this section and lagged more than 30 minutes behind them. All of us being mountain people, we spent too much time scratching our heads and asking strangers for directions as we tried to orient ourselves within the cityscape. The "urban jungle" defeated us, giving me a taste of how city dwellers experience the natural wilderness.

As you can see, one navigation mistake can negate all the physical training you have done over the previous 6 months. The rest of this chapter provides you with a good basic understanding of navigation and orienteering—but as with any other sport, you must spend time doing it to improve your skills.

Topographic Maps

Unlike a standard road atlas or trail guide, a topographic map includes contour lines to portray the shape and elevation of the land. These wave-like lines appear at regular intervals, rendering the three-dimensional shape of the terrain on a two-dimensional surface. Mountains, valleys, plains, lakes, rivers, and vegetation are depicted or indicated. Manmade features, such as roads, boundaries, transmission lines, and major build-ings, are portrayed using a set of symbols that are either printed on the map (internationally) or in a separate booklet (in the United States). Im-portant information on a map includes age (year created or updated), scale (including contour interval), and map symbols.

The most commonly used map scale in the United States is 1:24,000, which means 1 inch on the map equals 24,000 inches (2,000 feet) in dis-tance in the real world. The most detailed maps printed by the United States Geologic Survey (USGS), 1:24,000 scale maps are known as "7.5-minute series," with 7.5 minutes describing the surface area covered by the map (7.5 minutes of latitude by 7.5 minutes of longitude). (Infor-mation on USGS maps is available at http://mapping.usgs.gov.)

Most other countries use metric maps (and metric marine charts), generally done on a 1:50,000 scale, in races. Metric scales are very easy to use, since Universal Transverse Mercator (UTM) coordinates (more about these later) are in meters and correspond to millimeters on a ruler. Elevation and depth are shown in meters on metric maps and charts.

U.S. and British Admiralty Charts still use fathoms for depth, and feet for height, or a combination of measures. Distances can be shown in fathoms, cables, chains, nautical miles (1,852 meters), statute miles (1,609 meters), kilometers (1,000 meters), or, often, a combination of all of them. Coordinates can be given in latitude and longitude (although this system is rapidly disappearing, thank goodness!), UTM, or a local grid system.

This can all be very confusing, but primarily you need to know what scale map you are using and become familiar with how it relates to the real, three-dimensional world around you. The single most useful skill in wilderness navigation is feature recognition, the ability to recognize terrain features in the landscape and place them on the map, and vice versa. To learn how to do this, get a map of an area you are familiar with and study it intently. I also recommend you read Cliff Jacobson's *Basic Essentials of Map and Compass* and then, for more advanced navigating, Bjorn Hjellstrom's *Be an Expert with Map and Compass*.

The Compass

A compass typically shows direction with a magnetic needle that swings freely on a pivot and points to magnetic north. Although electronic compasses are now quite common and can help pinpoint a *general* direction (+/- 15 degrees), they are difficult to use with accuracy. For adventure racing, I suggest you use an orienteering compass with a liquid damped needle and a rotating bezel (circular ring around the outside of the needle) with numbered bearings from 0 to 360 degrees. My favorite is the Suunto MCB Amphibian (www.suuntousa.com), which is lightweight (1.3 ounces), comes in easy-to-see bright yellow, has a sighting mirror with a 45-degree index, and has a microscopically small whistle—and it floats! (Having lost dozens of compasses in races, I need all the help I can get to keep track of them.)

If you travel to international races, you'll need a global compass (or a compass calibrated for your destination). The Earth's magnetic field is angled, and varies considerably in different locations, so a compass needle that is well-balanced in North America will drag or stick anywhere south of Mexico. As a result of these magnetic variances, the compass industry has divided the earth into five zones. When you travel to a zone where the field is at a different angle, the needle of the compass that works in your home zone gets pulled against the inside surface of the compass housing (a condition known as compass inclination) and can become stuck. Global compasses overcome this problem with the use of bearings, which allow free movement regardless of the angle of the magnetic field.

One of the most confusing things about compasses and maps is the distinction between magnetic north and true north (also called grid

INSIDE FACTS

If a metallic object is close enough and large enough to create a magnetic field, it can affect the compass needle and create a faulty reading. For this reason, compasses do not work well when you are in or on a vehicle, at a table with metal bolts or supports, or close to high-voltage sources such as power lines or transmission boxes. The difference between magnetic north and the direction a compass points in due to another external force is called the magnetic deviation.

north). True and magnetic north may vary by up to 40 degrees in the mid latitudes closer to the Earth's poles. Maps are always drawn to true (grid) north, whereas compasses always point to magnetic north. The resulting difference is called magnetic declination. The declination for a given topographic map is shown in the map's data or symbol area.

To deal with declination, I draw a few lines of magnetic north on my map, effectively making my own magnetic grid for use with the compass. This avoids my having to perform arithmetic to convert between map and compass orientation, true and magnetic north, east and west declination, of which there are eight possible permutations. When it is wet, dark, and windy, and you are hungry, sleep-deprived, and exhausted, arithmetic becomes an impossible task. That's why I do it ahead of time and prepare my map accordingly. It's entirely possible to accidentally subtract a west (or add an east) declination instead of add it (or subtract, if east). Of course, this depends on whether you are taking a bearing off the map or writing one on it, in which case you should add it, not subtract it. The same thing happens if you confuse true and magnetic north, either on the compass or on the map. So you can see that addition and subtraction are something less than elementary when you are working with maps. To keep things simple, use these steps when preparing a map for use in a race.

1. Determine the declination for your maps from the map key or declination symbol. If you have more than one map, declination can vary for each, so make sure you do this for each map separately.

2. Use a protractor or your compass to measure the declination angle in the center of the map (this is generally where the declination is specified).

3. Place a straightedge such as a long ruler (36 inches is ideal) against the protractor or compass and draw a line across the entire map. Use a color, such as fluorescent pink, that stands out against the other colors on the map.

4. Repeat step 3 twice more, so that your map has three evenly spaced magnetic lines crossing it.

5. Draw a large arrowhead at the north end of each line so you can find north when you are really loopy. You will be surprised how easy it is to get the wrong north when your mind goes south!

UTM Grid Coordinates

Universal Transverse Mercator (UTM) grid coordinates are rapidly becoming standard in the United States and the rest of the world. This metric grid system drawn over the globe specifies units in meters east and meters north of the southernmost and westernmost borders of each zone (north of the equator). UTM coordinates can specify a location with extreme accuracy, down to a square meter. As an example, the flagpole in front of the courthouse in Boulder, Colorado, is in NAD (North America Datum) Zone 13T, at 476286 meters east and 4429834 meters north, as shown on the accompanying map on page 112. UTMs are most commonly used in races to specify the location of the start and finish, checkpoints, waypoints, and transition areas.

In most races that involve any sort of navigation, you will be given a "race book," "road book," "rule book," "course description," or other, similar pile of information describing how to get to the start, the finish, and everything in between. At checkpoints, you get your passport stamped and/or time taken to verify that you followed an intended route and that you didn't end up in the wrong country. Don't laugh too hard. Adventure racing teams have wandered into the wrong river valley (quite a common occurrence), the wrong mountain range (not quite so common, but a surprisingly frequent occurrence), and even the wrong

FINDING THE FLAG POLE

Consult the map below to practice your UTM skills and find the Boulder courthouse flagpole.

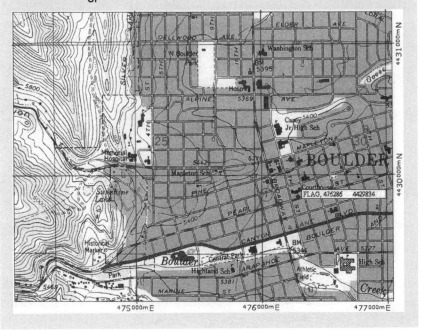

country (in at least two races that I know of), searching endlessly for their checkpoints.

Whatever grid system you use, make sure your maps have the appropriate grid marks along all four sides. Ideally, the map will already have the grids drawn onto the map. If not, you will have to do this yourself. You only need grid lines where you plot coordinates, so if the maps don't have the grid predrawn, just draw in the segments of the lines you need.

Plotting grid coordinates is really straightforward, but there are a few shortcuts you can use to make life easy (and fast), which is necessary if you have to plot more than a few during a race. You'll need a brightly colored fine-tip permanent marker, a long straightedge, and a UTM grid card. Global Positioning System (GPS) compasses often have a handful of common UTM scales along their edges, but it is easier to use a UTM card, which has multiple UTM grid scales (in 1,000-meter scaled squares) printed on transparent plastic that you can lay over the map.

To plot using a UTM card, do the following:

1. Read the easting and northing for the coordinate and find the grid lines (or tick marks) on the map for the first few digits. This will be three or four numbers, depending where you are in a zone. Using the Boulder courthouse as an example, this would be an easting of 476282 and a northing of 442841. You will always have three digits on the right of your grid line number, as UTM grid lines are at 1,000-meter intervals. In our courthouse example, there are grid marks at 476 east and 442 north. There are also UTM grid marks on both sides and the top and bottom of the map that will help you draw a complete grid on the map.

2. Draw a vertical line on your map between the two 476 easting marks (on the top and bottom edges of the map) and a horizontal line between the two 442 northing marks (along the sides of the map).

3. Place the appropriate UTM grid scale (in this case 1:24,000) at the intersection of the grid lines in the top right quadrant. This

TOOLS OF THE TRADE

Several basic tools will help you in wilderness navigation. Below, you'll find my list of the minimum needed to keep you out of trouble in any condition.

- Your senses (sight, hearing, smell, touch)
- Map, preferably topographic and recent
- Compass, ideally a high-quality orienteering compass
- Altimeter, and the knowledge to use it effectively
- A small, reliable writing implement such as a soft pencil

TOOLS OF THE TRADE

To prepare a map either before the race or at a transition area, you'll need the following additional tools.

- Brightly colored fine-tip permanent markers and a pencil with an eraser, for writing on maps
- Set of highlighters for marking routes and locations
- Long straightedge, preferably transparent and long enough to cover the entire length of a map. The side of a map will do in a pinch
- Protractor or compass for marking angles in degrees
- UTM grid reference cards in various scales. A grid can be made using a piece of paper and some guesswork
- Scissors for cutting maps
- Waterproof map sleeves
- Circle gauge for marking checkpoints and transition areas (optional)
- Distance measuring wheel (optional)

places the 0,0 coordinate on the grid at the intersection of the two lines.

4. Count two grid squares and estimate an additional eight-tenths of a grid square to the right (east), and then eight- and four-tenths grid squares up (north), corresponding to the last three digits on the UTM coordinates (282 and 841). You can drop the last number on each coordinate, since it's beyond our visual resolution and outside the map error range.

5. Place your uniquely colored marker (fluorescent pink works well) on the point you found on your UTM card, and remove the card while holding the pen in place over the map. You should have a dot on the map at the exact location 476286 4429834.

6. Draw a small circle around the dot and label it with a useful description, such as "CP12 Boulder courthouse flagpole." The circle

should be no smaller than $\frac{1}{2}$ inch in diameter, so you can easily locate it, but not so large that you obstruct any useful navigational information. It sometimes helps to mark your circle and label with a brightly colored highlighter.

Global Positioning Systems

Global Positioning Systems (GPS) are seldom permitted in adventure races, though they can be quite useful when allowed. Although GPSs accurately discern location in most conditions (+/- 50 feet) and are quite reliable, they do have their limitations. Knowing where you are and where you need to go is all very well, but finding the best route for getting there is another matter—something no GPS to date can provide.

If you do have the luxury of using a GPS, you should understand some of its basic operating parameters. This includes knowing how to initialize the unit, entering the relevant map datum (there are dozens to choose from), specifying your desired coordinate system (another large number of choices), and setting up the appropriate units (metric, nautical, or imperial/statute/American). For example, a GPS in North America will generally require NAD 27 (North American Datum 1927) or NAD 83 map datum, and you will probably be plotting in UTM coordinates with units in miles.

GPS use is quite simple once you understand how to navigate the menus. You can enter checkpoint, waypoint, and transition-area coordinates; read off your location, altitude, speed, distance traveled, and distance to destination (in a straight line); and determine your estimated time of arrival (ETA) at your destination. If you use a GPS in a race, make sure you have plenty of spare batteries, and keep them in a waterproof bag. To work properly, a GPS needs a direct line of sight to satellites; so carry it as high as possible on your body, ideally on the top of your head.

Map Preparation

Once you receive your race maps and instructions, you can begin marking your route, using these steps.

1. Review the basic information on the map, including date of last revision, units of measurement, scales, map symbols (if unfamiliar), coordinates, and declination.

2. Draw in magnetic north lines, using a unique color such as bright red.

3. Plot the start location, noting any useful instructions from the course notes on the map. This will save you from having to refer to the notes later.

4. Continue plotting each checkpoint in order on your maps, writing in useful information from the course notes.

5. Highlight any mandatory routes between checkpoints, and note any forbidden or dangerous areas.

6. Once you have plotted all course information, review the course from the start. Using a highlighter, mark in the most likely routes between checkpoints. You may have several options, which will require evaluation once you see the terrain.

7. Plot any bearings you may need later.

8. Measure distances for each leg of the course, so you plan how much food, water, and equipment you'll need between transition areas.

9. Cut off and put aside any unnecessary sections of the maps, and number each of the remaining maps in the order you expect to use them. Make sure you place the cut-off pieces in a safe place, in case you need them, too, later.

10. Fold the maps and fit them in your map sleeves or map case in a way that you can see all necessary information.

11. Get going!

Feature Recognition

People who have spent their entire lives in the outdoors generally have a good sense for terrain, whereas those who have spent most of their time in urban environments often struggle. If you are good at math, a natural musician, a chess wizard, or adept at visualizing complex shapes, you will probably be able to understand the land features a topographic map describes. If you are really good, you will be able to do this practically blindfolded—a huge advantage, since at least a third of most long races are completed in the dark.

Basic features you'll need to understand include:

Mountain. A mountain is generally defined as more than 1,000 feet above the surrounding land, with at least 500 vertical feet between it and another high point. If two high points are closer than 500 feet, they are generally regarded to be peaks (see below) of the same mountain. Mountainous regions are easily identified on a topographic map by the large number of closely spaced contour lines and the map labels identifying various peaks.

Peak. These high points on a mountain are where the contour lines of concentric rings (usually uneven in shape) diminish to a point. Peaks give great vantage points, affording you a view of the surrounding terrain. The only reason to climb a peak in a race, however, is to see the view or visit a checkpoint. Maps often represent peaks with a small triangle (a trigonometric point—there is actually a round brass plaque with "USGS" and a bunch of numbers stamped into it at these locations in the United States).

Hill. A hill is a small peak, typically less than 1,000 feet high. On maps, these look like small mountains; in fact, most mountainous regions are a mixture of hills and larger peaks.

Knoll. Even smaller than a "hill," knolls are generally shorter in height than a tall tree. On maps, these look like small hills.

Ridge. Any feature of high ground where the land drops away on either side is considered a ridge. Ridges generally slope from a high point, such as a peak, down to the base of the feature, but can also maintain height or undulate. Like peaks, ridges often provide a vantage point for observing the land around you and frequently are easy to traverse, since they are typically free of thick vegetation. On a map, a ridge has contour lines descending from either side, starting as parallel lines with the highest lines of elevation.

Spur. These small features are similar to ridges, but they cut off at the end with a steep or vertical terminus. Spurs often divide watercourses or small depressions. Spurs are often obstacles if you are trying to descend a ridge, but can provide a good vantage point. On a map, the contour lines of a spur create a series of V-shaped lines pointing down the hill.

Plateau. This large, flat area is elevated above the surrounding land. Mesas and buttes are types of plateaus, generally surrounded by cliffs. Mesas are wider than they are high, and buttes are higher than they are wide. Since plateaus are relatively flat on top, the contour lines are widely spaced, with the outline of the plateau defined by lines close together around the perimeter where the land drops away steeply.

Saddle. A saddle is a low point on a ridge, or the land connecting two high points, such as two peaks. It is very common to plot a course through a saddle, since it is generally the most efficient route over a ridge or between valleys (across a mountain range). A saddle can be identified on a topographic map by the convergence of the concentrically larger contour lines circling two peaks.

Gully. A small depression caused by water eroding the land, leaving a dry watercourse that is only a few feet deep. On a map, gullies can be identified as small discontinuities (small wiggles) in contour lines on a slope. Successive lines lower down the slope show the discontinuity increasing in size, while successive lines up the slope show it diminishing in size.

Valley. These large depressions between ridges and peaks vary from large, open, and mostly flat depressions several miles wide to tight, steep, cliff-ridden, impassable barriers. In general, valleys are more sheltered from the wind and sun than high points, so they tend to accumulate thicker vegetation, making them more difficult to negotiate without trails. A valley almost always has a watercourse in the bottom. You can identify one on a map if you see the markings for a river or stream surrounded by high ground on either side.

Canyon. Canyons are very steep or vertical-sided valleys that are formed by water cutting through an obstacle. Canyons are often impossible to cross without the aid of ropes, and range from slot canyons only

UNDERSTANDING MAP FEATURES

Below you'll find common symbols used on maps to indicate specific land features.

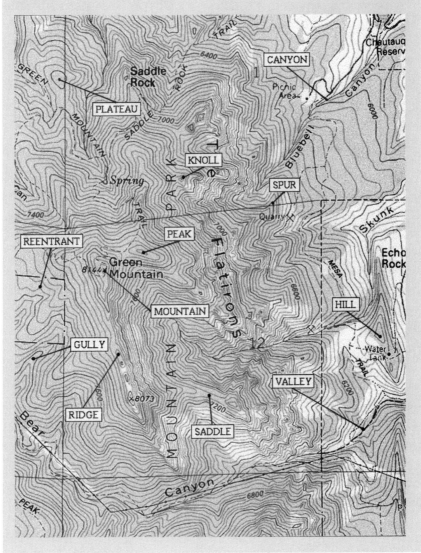

a few yards wide and hundreds of feet deep, to the Grand Canyon. On a map, canyons are identified by the two opposing cliff faces or extremely steep slopes (close or intersecting contour lines).

Reentrant. This is a small depression in the land, often the top end of a watercourse where it originates on a hillside. Reentrants are quite small map features, but are obvious once you know what you are looking for. Orienteering races use them to "hide" the orienteering controls (marker flags), and once you get used to identifying them, they provide a very useful way to track your location and progress on a map.

Staying Oriented

Once an hour as you move through a course, use your compass to check your general direction, as it is easy to get turned around when it is dark or you are not thinking straight, which is most of the time during a long race. In addition to your compass, you can also use a large terrain feature, such as a mountain, or a celestial body, such as the sun, moon, or a bright star, to orient yourself in the right direction. Other than following obvious features, such as trails, rivers, shorelines, or ridge tops, you can also use your senses of hearing and smell, and the altitude, to stay on track.

USING YOUR EARS

If you have acute hearing, you can estimate your location from features that generate sound, such as rivers, waterfalls, vehicles, transition areas, or population centers. There is a running joke among top teams that they practice NBH, which means "navigation by helicopter." Quite a few of the larger race organizations use helicopters to shuttle film crews and race staff around, and by watching or listening to where they land, you can often locate checkpoints and transition areas.

You can also listen for radio chatter. People talking over a radio tend to talk very loudly, with an unnatural frequency and cadence. If you hear "Crackle, hiss, CP23, come in, please . . . BEEP . . . crackle, hiss . . ." somewhere in the wilderness, it is unlikely to be a large, ferocious animal.

WINNING BY A NOSE

How many times have you driven by a skunk, rotting roadkill, a garbage dump, or a refinery and had to roll up your window? Although our sense of smell is only one-thousandth as sensitive as that of a dog (which makes one wonder why dogs like to sniff garbage and their own feces), it is more than adequate to detect some quite useful odors when racing. If you pay attention, you may be able to pick up quite a few that indicate the location of a valuable feature. In particular, keep your nose out for the smell of:

- Freshly cut grass

- Oceans, lakes, or rivers

- Automobile exhaust

- Aviation fuel

- Cooked food

ALTITUDE

Knowing your altitude can be a lifesaver if visibility is low, as it can keep you from approaching too close to a cliff edge or from dropping too low beyond a feature you are looking for.

To find out your altitude at any given time, you'll need an altimeter, a device that uses a pressure sensor to determine altitude in exactly the same way an aircraft does. The only difference between a mountaineering wrist altimeter and an aircraft altimeter is the way they are calibrated. Aircraft use ambient pressure, and mountaineers (generally) use a known altitude from a map.

Most altimeters are equipped with altitude alarms so that you know when you reach your preset elevation. Once you reach this height, you know from your map that you are somewhere on the corresponding contour line. You then need only one other indicator that intersects this altitude to know your position, such as a geographic feature (a watercourse or ridge, for example), manmade feature (road, trail, power line, railroad, pipeline, and so forth), or compass course.

TIPS FROM THE TOP

Below you'll find three navigation tips from Novak Thompson, winner of the Eco-Challenge, Raid Gauloises, and Raid the North Extreme, and a former world champion in rogaining (see glossary on page 240) and triathlon.

1. As soon you receive your race map, study it. Take note of the scale of the map (1:50,000, 1:100,000, etc.) and the contour interval. Then calculate the magnetic variation or declination.

2. Once you are familiar with the map, plot your control points and work out the best possible route, remembering that the shortest route is not always the quickest route. Identify some features on the map to give yourself a feel for the type of terrain and vegetation you will encounter. Use colored highlighters to mark the route and points of interest on the map. Remember to keep your map safe and dry.

3. Now the real fun begins. Orient the map, using the compass and remembering to add or subtract the magnetic variation for that map. Now the map should represent what you see around you. When traveling long distances between known points, keep track of your position on the map as you go. Sometimes you have to slow down to go faster. As night falls and shapes start to take on a different appearance, it is always easier if you know where you were before the sun was gone.

Many people falsely believe their altimeters are inaccurate or faulty, when in fact they don't calibrate them often enough—or ever. Atmospheric pressure can change rapidly and dramatically, and since pressure and altitude are directly related, this affects the reading on a pressure-sensing altimeter. Airplane pilots know this, so they calibrate their altimeters every time they take off and land; otherwise, they could erroneously try to put their wheels down up to 300 feet above the ground, or try to dive 300 feet underground.

Pressure changes so rapidly that a weather front moving over you can change your apparent height above sea level up to 300 feet in either direction within a matter of minutes. We were fooled by our altimeters in

Novak Thompson

the 2002 Eco-Challenge in Fiji and spent over an hour looking for a trail because we thought we were 200 feet lower than we actually were. Ultimately, we realized our error, but not until we were caught by our archrivals from New Zealand.

To accommodate the natural fluctuations in atmospheric pressure, check your altimeter at least once an hour against a known elevation on your map. If the weather is stable and you are making large gains in elevation (which can fool your altimeter into thinking the change is atmospheric), you should not see any significant variations. It is sensible to have at least two people with working altimeters on your team. Although altimeters are highly reliable, they are sophisticated electronic instruments and can easily fail.

Using Your Tools to Orient Yourself

Now that you understand how to use the basic tools of navigation, let's put it all together so you can see how to use them in any situation. You'll start by orienting your map to the real world. This procedure should take no more than 5 seconds.

Step 1

a) Place the compass on the map so that the long edge connects the starting point with the desired destination.

b) Make sure that the direction arrows point from the starting point to the place of destination (and not the opposite way).

Step 2

a) Hold the compass firmly on the map in order to keep the base plate steady.

b) Turn the rotating capsule until the north-south lines on the bottom of the capsule are parallel with the north-south lines on the map.

c) Be sure that the north-south arrow on the bottom of the capsule points in the same direction as north on the map.

Step 3

a) Hold the compass in your hand in front of you. Make sure that the base plate is horizontal, and that the direction arrows are pointing straight ahead.

b) Rotate your body until the north-south arrow on the bottom of the capsule lines up with the magnetic needle, and the red end of the needle points in the same direction as the arrow.

c) The directional arrows on the base plate now show your desired travel direction.

Drawings courtesy of Suunto USA, www.suuntousa.com

FOLLOWING A BEARING

If you are on open water, grassland, desert, or other open terrain, or if you have no visual or topographic clues (such as a slope or an angle), you may have to follow a compass bearing. To set a bearing on your map, do the following:

1. Using a straightedge, draw a line on the map from your origin to your destination. If this is a kayak leg through islands or along a convoluted coastline, you may have several straight lines, each of which will require a bearing.

2. Place the side of your compass along the line you have drawn, with the center of the rotating bezel located over a magnetic north line. Make sure the *direction of travel arrow* points in the direction you want to go. Most compasses have a direction of travel arrow drawn at one end, indicating which way to hold it.

3. Rotate the bezel so that the north lines drawn on its base are parallel with the magnetic north line. Your desired compass heading

(bearing in degrees) is indicated by the index mark on the compass housing. The orientation of the needle is not important at this point.

4. Write the bearing along the line, something line "056M," where the M stands for magnetic.

Later in the race, when you get to a section where you have preset some bearings and you want to pursue them, do the following:

1. Read off the relevant bearing and rotate the compass bezel until it lines up with the index mark.

2. Holding the compass in front of you with the direction of travel arrow facing away from you, move around until the needle lines up with the north mark on the compass bezel. Do not move the bezel, as this will change your compass bearing. Make sure it is you that move, not just the compass. You may have to turn around completely, if you are facing the wrong way.

BETWEEN YOU & ME

The 1999 Raid the North Extreme at Elliot Lake, northwest of Toronto, was held during full spring growth, resulting in vegetation that reduced visibility to about 3 feet. One particularly difficult foot section pitted teams against a wall of vegetation 30 miles deep, over a mountain, and around numerous lakes and streams. The only way to move effectively through the section was by shooting bearings between obvious features, such as lakeshores, small hills, and watercourses. Navigating in this fashion meant shooting a bearing every few hundred yards, resulting in hundreds of course adjustments. Any mistake resulted in complete confusion, since it was impossible to see more than a few yards at a time. Our navigation was error-free, and we made it through the section in under 8 hours, but most teams took more than twice as long, with several taking more than 2 days! Navigating in these conditions is similar to navigating at night, and it pays huge dividends to know exactly where you are at all times.

3. If you are on foot, hold the compass level (this keeps the needle swinging freely) and at about waist height, so that you are looking directly down at the compass. Make sure the compass is square with your body and everything is lined up. Now look up and you should be facing in the right direction.

As you move, you need to continually look back and forth between your compass, your distant surroundings, and your footing. This takes some practice, but really good navigators can keep an accurate course at a full run.

Following an accurate compass bearing in thick forest is difficult, but not impossible. Use teammates as a single-file human compass needle. One person on the team takes "point" and leads the team through the terrain. The point person micronavigates to avoid obstacles, keeping an efficient route, while the person with the compass guides from behind. Ideally, a third teammate keeps track of the team's course with the map, noting any changes in elevation, slope, vegetation, and so on.

SHOOTING A BEARING

Shooting a bearing allows you to confirm your position on a map. If you shoot one bearing and transfer the line to the map from the feature you are shooting, you know you are somewhere on that line. If you shoot two bearings to features roughly at right angles (for example, one to the north and one to the west) the intersection of these two features gives you a reasonably accurate location. Here are the basic steps to shooting a bearing.

1. Orient the map to magnetic north.

2. Locate the desired feature on the map and in the surrounding countryside.

3. Point the compass and direction of travel arrow toward the feature with as much accuracy as you can. A sighting mirror helps enormously if you have one.

4. Rotate the compass bezel so that the north end of the needle is between the index marks on the bezel. If you use a sighting mirror, angle the mirror facing the compass at 45 degrees, then sight along the notch on the top of the lid. You should be able to see the compass needle and bezel in the mirror at the same time you see the distant feature. Compasses with sighting mirrors come with instructions and diagrams on how to do this.

5. Place the end of one side of the compass on the feature on the map. Make sure that the compass needle is still between the index marks and that the map is oriented to magnetic north.

6. Draw a line along the side of the compass toward your location on the map. You are somewhere on this line.

DETERMINING YOUR LOCATION FROM KNOWN FEATURES

A single bearing line can be very useful in determining your location on a map, and if you have another known feature, such as a road, watercourse, fence line, power line, or elevation, you can simply intersect the two and have your position. In the event that you have no other positive location features, you can shoot a second or third bearing to confirm your location. Here's how to do this.

1. Shoot a bearing to a known feature and draw in the bearing line.

2. Shoot a second bearing to a known feature roughly perpendicular to the first, and draw in the line. The intersection of these two lines is your approximate location.

3. For more accuracy, shoot a third bearing. Your location is in the small triangle formed by the three lines. If you have drawn a big triangle, then one or more of your features or bearings are incorrect and you will have to reshoot them. Shooting three bearings is called triangulation, and is the most accurate way to determine location given three distant features.

4. Quite often, you don't need to shoot bearings at all. You simply have to look around you and, with a quick glance at your compass

SPEED ESTIMATES

The following table can help you estimate speed on flat ground. Uphill or downhill slopes will affect your estimates.

mph	On flat ground with a 10-pound pack	On a steep uphill grade (8%+ slope)
1	Casual stroll—easy	Walk—comfortable
2	Pedestrian walk—comfortable	Moderate walk—some effort
3	Fast walk or very slow jog—some effort	Hard walk—moderate effort
4	Very fast walk or slow jog—moderate effort	Jog—hard effort
5	Jog or slow run—moderate/hard effort	Run—very hard effort
6	Hard run—hard effort	Hard run—extreme over distance
7	Fast, hard run—hard/very hard effort	Possible for extremely fit athletes only
8	Very fast run—very hard effort	Only possible for short distances
9	Sprint—extreme	Only possible for very short distances
10	Short sprint—superelite athletes only	You're dreaming

for the general direction, you have a good idea of your location. This, of course, relies on proficient terrain recognition, something you can master with training.

DISTANCE, SPEED, AND TIME

Without any features to go by—for example, if you're paddling across a lake in the dark or hiking through a desert or forest with little variation in the topography—you need another method for estimating distance. You should know your direction based on your compass heading, so if you know how far you have moved, you can plot your position. Distance can be calculated from time (you should always carry a working timepiece) and speed. The speed part you have to estimate, something you can do as you train. If you get in the habit of checking the time at the start and finish of each training session, and knowing the distance you traveled, you can easily work out your speed through various terrain types. The table on page 129 gives a good starting point for speed estimates on flat ground. Uphill or downhill slopes will affect speed accordingly.

USING COMMON SENSE

If you are unsure of your navigation skills, you can generally tell whether you've led the team in the wrong direction by tapping into the mindset of the race director. For example, no sane race director will put a transition area in a location that has no access to get equipment like boats, bikes, and gear containers in and out. If you plot a transition to kayaks on a mountaintop, recheck to see whether you've made a mistake. Similarly, most race directors are smart enough to design courses that minimize logistics. If you are launching into the wilderness and start heading through an area of complete inaccessibility toward a transition area, consider how the race staff or support crews will get there. If you genuinely can't see how vehicles could possibly get to where you are going, stop blaming the course and start blaming your navigation skills.

Making Decisions

Once you have been set free to roam around the countryside, you'll *always* first orient the map with the surroundings. Your next step, however, will vary depending on the terrain. To figure out how best to navigate, ask yourself:

1. Where am I? Look to features, terrain, bearings, and triangulation for the answers.

2. Where do I want to go? Use grid coordinates, features, and description.

3. How will I get there? Consider your compass course, terrain, and obstacles.

Then launch off into the unknown and stay found. Oh, and remember these words of wisdom: Great navigators always know where they are, even when they're lost.

Teams inline skate during the 2001 Salomon X-Adventure World Cup in Utah.

"Getting ahead in a difficult profession requires avid faith in yourself. That is why some people with mediocre talent, but with great inner drive, go much further than people with vastly superior talent."

—Sophia Loren

 # SPORTS UNLIMITED

HOW TO IMPROVE YOUR SKILLS IN THE EVENTS YOU'VE NEVER HEARD OF

Adventure races consist of any nonmotorized means of forward propulsion a race director can dream up—everything from paragliding to camel riding to outrigger canoe sailing. Event organizers will generally give competitors a heads-up on any unusual skills that are required for a particular race. New disciplines have, however, been sprung on teams unexpectedly. If you end up getting truly addicted to adventure racing, you will eventually come up against some really obscure and interesting activities, so pay close attention and be prepared for the worst (or the best) a race can throw at you. It is time to give you an idea of some of the more obscure sports that can make an appearance in adventure races.

BILIBILI, ANYONE?

If a large man in a skirt walked up to you and asked, "Where is your *bili-bili?*" you might at first think he was mistaking you for a guy named William who owns a pet named Bill. Either that, or the strange individual had a stutter and only a rudimentary understanding of the English language. Regardless, you probably wouldn't think, "Aha, this fine gentleman wants to know if we know where to find our bamboo rafts."

In the 2002 Eco-Challenge, this was precisely our situation. Five hours after the race's start, we arrived at the first checkpoint to find a large pile of bamboo logs and instructions on building a raft. My teammates Mike Kloser and Michael Tobin unpacked 300 feet of cord, along with other assorted objects, and began binding the logs together into a large, flat, and extremely heavy raft. As they worked, Danelle Ballangee and I pored over a large pile of maps and instructions, looking for a way to avoid small, watery explosions.

After 35 minutes of furious activity, the boys had completed their masterpiece and we launched into the sluggish water of the Navuniyasi River, promptly dislodging some carefully placed bamboo, and careening out of control as the current caught our ungainly craft. Steering and propulsion proved very challenging with the two thin poles provided for the task. The few teams that had anticipated the bilibilis had carried canoe paddles through the jungle. Other teams improvised by creating paddles that were crudely fashioned from an odd assortment of driftwood, string, climbing helmets, and chewing gum. Ultimately, the teams that were smart or flexible did well in the bilibili section, whereas those who weren't did not fare so well.

Mountaineering

When asked why he wanted to climb Mount Everest in 1924, British mountaineer George Leigh Mallory replied, "Because it's there!" This exasperated answer from the famous climber beautifully sums up the numerous reasons people embark on any adventure. High alpine regions can be both magnetic and intimidating, and clambering around high peaks is not without its dangers.

The high altitude, severe weather, and extreme exposure frequently create a lethal combination. As altitude increases, so does the fatality rate from mountain-related accidents, from essentially zero at sea level to as high as one in four for technical peaks higher than 25,000 feet.

You'll need technical mountaineering skills for about 40 percent of major expedition-level events. You must take the training very seriously because your life and the lives of your teammates can depend on your expertise. To become proficient in mountain environments, you need knowledge, skills, appropriate physical and mental preparation, judgment, and experience. This all takes time (and money). You can't simply buy a bunch of gear, hike up into the hills, and expect to stay safe.

To get started, first read the seminal text *Mountaineering: The Freedom of the Hills* by "the Mountaineers." Then sign up for training with any number of outfitters in any number of mountain states. Safely traveling through high mountains requires skills for climbing and traversing rock, ice, and snow, as well as an understanding of the inherent dangers of the weather, crevasses, and avalanches. Each event will require different skills, depending on the geography, climate, and course, so you need to exercise your discretion.

To stay safe in the mountains, you should seek training in the following:

- Proper clothing and equipment

- Mountain weather

- Rope skills, rappelling, traversing, and ascending

- Avalanche awareness and rescue

- Snow travel and climbing

- Glacier travel and crevasse rescue

- Alpine survival skills

Danelle Ballangee

Winter Sports

Winter adventure races are becoming more popular, making the "off-season" less and less sedentary. Numerous 1- and 2-day winter races have sprung up that include Nordic and alpine skiing, mountain biking, snowshoeing, ice-skating, ice climbing, and running. The biggest and toughest team race is Raid Ukatak, which is a nonstop multiday race for coed teams of four, held in midwinter in Quebec (www.ukatak.com). On the extreme end of things is the Iditasport Impossible, a 1,100-mile non-stop solo race in Alaska's frigid north in the depths of winter.

TIPS FROM THE TOP

The following are Danelle Ballangee's tips for winter racing. Ballangee is a winner of the HiTec Sprint and Balance Bar 24-hour adventure-race series, Primal Quest and Outdoor Quest adventure races, and a former world champion in trail running, snowshoeing, and Ironman Triathlon (age group).

1. Winter sports provide a fun and exciting way to stay in shape during the off-season, as well as a mental break from the typical run, bike, and kayak format. Adding snowshoeing, Nordic or downhill skiing, and snow biking to your fitness routine will keep you fit and ready for year-round competition. When training for these sports, gradually increase your training time and intensity. Because you will be using new muscle groups, you may fatigue earlier than usual.

2. Dress in layers. Start off with two or three layers, and take layers off as you warm up. The high-tech water-wicking fabrics work great in winter conditions. To stay dry, take layers off if you start to sweat, and put on a waterproof shell if it starts to snow or sleet.

3. Take precautions when going into the backcountry. Take an avalanche safety course before you head out. Carry the appropriate safety gear with you, which may include a beacon, a probe, a shovel, and additional insulating clothing. Always tell someone where you are going and what time you expect to be back. Bring a friend along whenever possible.

The Winter Classic (www.canoevic.org.au) in Australia's southeast alps is one of the original winter adventure races (held every year since 1983). The original format started with a Nordic ski followed by orienteering, biking, and whitewater kayaking on the first day, and whitewater kayaking, orienteering, and biking on the second.

Winter sports revolve around snow skills and the ability to cope with a vast range of conditions. Unlike summer sports, snow sports are held in an inhospitable climate, with the possibility of severe weather at any time. Seemingly benign conditions can turn lethal in a matter of minutes, and freezing, windy conditions are not conducive to taking a quick nap under a likely-looking bush. Moving from summer to winter conditions in the higher latitudes or altitudes requires a whole new world of apparel and equipment, and the knowledge to use them.

Inline Skating

Adventure racing first embraced inline skating in a big way when the Salomon X-Adventure World Cup (www.raidseries.com) introduced it to their world cup races in 1998. Today, races across the globe include inline in various forms. One of the most innovative products to reach commercial reality is a true off-road inline skate called Crosskate (www.crosskate.com). This product is the first to allow athletes to move off smooth surfaces and into the wilderness. Inflatable tires, disc brakes, articulated wheels, and a one-way clutch on the front wheel allow skaters to go anywhere a mountain bike can, including steep up- and downhills, singletrack, and snow.

Aquatic Endeavors

Beyond paddle sports, dozens of other interesting water-based activities make an appearance in adventure races. The century-old Australian sporting beach culture has included water-based competitions since 1907 in its Surf Life Saving Championships (http://slsa.asn.au/doc_display. asp?document_id=1) programs. Australians developed a sport decades ahead of triathlon called Surf-IronMan, a high-profile professional sport that combines ocean swimming, surf skiing, knee boarding, and beach running. In the 1970s and 1980s, various surf clubs introduced early ver-

BETWEEN YOU & ME

The day before the 2000 Eco-Challenge event in Sabah, Borneo, athletes were presented with a pile of assorted sizes of wood and a primitive canoe hull. The mandatory equipment list included various lengths of rope, cord, and fishing line with which to construct a native-style *perau* outrigger sailing canoe. The organizers let us scrutinize a completed boat and then gave us several hours to build our own and sail it to a remote island, where the start would take place the following day. Many teams experienced difficulties with their rigging during the prologue and spent a good part of the night adapting their craft for the ocean conditions.

sions of adventure racing with odd sports and activities such as solving a chess problem, rappelling off a cliff with a bicycle, and running or swimming around rocky headlands between beaches (now called coastaleering or coasteering).

In recent years aquatic endeavors have gone mainstream with events such as ocean swimming, scuba diving, snorkeling, underwater navigation, Boogie boarding, hydro speed (whitewater sledding), canyoneering, and coastaleering.

Creatures Great and Small

Large, irritable animals always add an element of luck to keep things interesting. Many athletes believe the random allocation of a beast of burden can be unfair, but most feel it adds a level of complexity and enhances the adventure. Horses, mules, donkeys, camels, and elephants have all been used in various races, each time making for some comical and sometimes heart-stopping action.

Despite the lotterylike distribution of animals in an adventure race, you can mitigate the possibility of landing a nag with a little training. Inevitably, the horse's owners or experienced wranglers will decide which teams get which animals. They can also tell within seconds if you are comfortable and familiar with riding. If you are, you will almost certainly be given a lively mount, one that will move quickly and stay on track. If you are a raw beginner, you'll end up with the slowpoke of the bunch. Of course, if you overstate your experience, you could well end up with even more trouble than having a nag. Many people who try to ride at a level over their heads end up *on* their heads, or at least out of their saddles. Visit the HorseWeb (www.horseweb.com) home page for more information on training and all things related to horses, or Endurance Net (www.endurance.net) for specific information on the sport of endurance horseback racing.

Air Travel

Hang gliding, parasailing, parapenting, base jumping, and parachuting all fall into the category of "quite likely to suffer injury or death." In the past, race directors have made para-sports optional in their events, simply because the potential for mishap is relatively high. Soaring through the air at up to 20 miles per hour is by far the fastest way to get to your destination, especially when the alternative may involve navigating on foot through the wilderness, a mode of locomotion that typically has a top speed of 3 miles per hour. In the 1990 and 1993 Raid Gauloises in Costa Rica and Madagascar, for example, teams had the option of parachuting out of a light plane or hiking for 20 miles to the drop zone, with the gravity-assisted alternative proving by far the faster.

The Alaskan Mountain Wilderness Classic allows any mode of non-motorized transport, provided you take all your equipment with you. This led one adventurous soul to carry his parasail with the intention of climbing one of the high mountains on the course and then gliding over the swamps and forest to an easy first place. Things didn't go according to plan, however, and he dragged his starving and beaten body into town just as authorities were about to launch a search-and-rescue attempt.

Not surprisingly, many teams opt for the slower route—choosing to hike rather than fly—simply based on their evaluation of the risks. If you choose to leave solid ground, you had better have a lot of training under your belt, or a good life insurance policy. Investigate the United States Hang Gliding Association Web site (www.ushga.org) and the Paragliding.net home page (www.paragliding.net) for more information.

PART THREE

An athlete trains under tough conditions, carrying a heavy load.

> *"Our plans miscarry because they have no aim. When you don't know what harbor you're aiming for, no wind is the right wind."*
>
> —*Seneca*

 # BODY BALANCE
EVERYTHING YOU NEED TO KNOW TO GET IN SHAPE

Because of the vast distances they travel, the lack of sleep, and the frequent lulls in their forward motion as they make decisions, eat, and resupply or fix equipment, most adventure athletes do not perform anywhere near their top speeds during a race. The longer a race—any type of race—the slower the top speed from start to finish.

To illustrate, John Howard, Steve Gurney, and three local Malaysians completed the fastest ever expedition-length adventure race when they covered 350 miles in 4½ days, at an average speed of 3.24 miles per hour, during the 1994 Raid Gauloises in Borneo. Their speed approximated that of a brisk walk, seemingly pedestrian until you consider everything else involved: To get from start to finish, they had to navigate through thick jungle, spelunk, canoe, climb, mountain bike, and carry all of their food and survival equipment.

So you can see, to succeed in adventure racing, it's just as important to train for *endurance*—the ability to sustain your effort over a long period of time—as it is to train for *speed*. It's equally important to hone your strength, creating well-rounded overall fitness that will help you get from point A to point B with the least wasted effort. In this chapter you'll discover the ingredients to a successful adventure-training program. In "Sample Training Programs," page 249, you can see how to apply those ingredients.

The Four Basic Elements

To be a successful adventure athlete and to become a well-rounded competitor, you need to develop and maintain each of the four basic elements of fitness: speed, strength, endurance, and skills. Lacking any one of these elements in any sport drags down your overall performance. Let's take a closer look at each of these fitness elements.

Speed. To develop the ability to move quickly, you must train by running, biking, or paddling at a fast clip. The technique most widely used to develop speed is called interval training. In this system you perform several very fast but relatively short bursts of effort, interspersed with intervals of rest. This allows you to train for a useful length of time at high speed without exhausting yourself. Speed intervals for endurance generally last from 1 to 5 minutes, with enough rest to fully recover in between (30 seconds to 1 minute, or enough time for your heart rate to drop to a comfortable level, say, 140 beats per minute or less). The lengths of each interval and rest period, as well as the total number of repetitions, will very depending on your fitness level. As a rough guide, you should spend 10 to 20 percent of your total training time on speed sessions.

In addition to speed intervals, do "threshold" sessions once a week for each sport. Threshold sessions increase your anaerobic threshold, the upper limit of your muscles' ability to utilize oxygen. Perform your threshold sessions with relatively long intervals at high intensity, such as your 5-K running race pace for 1-mile intervals, or your 10-K race pace for 3-mile intervals.

Strength. For endurance racing, you need a balance of absolute strength (the total weight that can be moved) and relative strength (the strength per unit of body weight). If you have too much absolute strength, your heavy muscle mass will weigh down your body, making it harder to cover long distances. On the other hand, having too little absolute strength means you won't be able to carry the heavy pack and other adventure-racing essentials.

To build an appropriate amount of strength for adventure racing, you don't need to spend lots of time in the weight room. Resistance training using weights and machines can be useful, but you get better results if you simply increase resistance while doing your target sport. For example, hike while carrying a heavy pack or dragging a car tire, cycle or run up hills with a load on your back, and kayak while towing a plastic shopping bag.

Endurance. Your endurance is the total time you can maintain a specific level of muscular power output. Endurance training is only effective, however, if you allow for adequate recovery between sessions. The longer and harder the session, the longer you need to recover. There is also a point of diminishing returns for endurance training. If you go too far, the damage and repair cost will exceed any gains.

You need to build endurance gradually. Start with your comfortable distance limit; then you can increase your distance (or the intensity, if you have reached your target distance) by no more than 10 percent each time you train. Back off every fourth or fifth session to allow for long-term recovery. For adventure-race training, you can do only one long session per sport per week, taking 1 or 2 days to recover between endurance sessions. You can reduce your total number of endurance-training sessions per week (great for busy lifestyles) with "Bricks" (two back-to-back sports), "Tricks" (three back-to-back), and "Quicks" (four back-to-back-sports) in a session. For example, you might do a Brick by running 1 hour, then mountain biking another 2 hours.

HOW TO . . .
Find Your Maximum Heart Rate

You can estimate your maximum heart rate by halving your age and subtracting that number from 205. This will only give you a rough estimate, as everyone's maximum heart rate varies. To get a more accurate number, hire an exercise physiologist, who will put you through a battery of tests to figure it out more precisely.

Endurance sessions are often also called long, slow distance, which adequately describes the way you should approach your distance sessions. You want to maintain a heart rate that is high enough to stimulate a training effect, but not so high that you can't recover. To do this, shoot for between 70 percent and 90 percent of your maximum heart rate.

Skill. Fine-tuning your technique—for example, your kayaking paddle stroke or your running foot strike—helps you move more efficiently, allowing you to go longer, faster, and harder with less effort. Consider a mountain biker who has expert technical skills over rough terrain. While he or she is smoothly riding around the obstacles on the trail, the beginners are expending more energy by running into them, bouncing around, and getting on and off their bikes.

A keen observer once said that practice makes permanent, which is why it is important to train *with* good technique *for* good technique. Training *with* good technique means that you should consciously critique your form at all times. Training *for* good technique means you should specifically gear some of your training to improving your efficiency. Skills and technique are not mutually exclusive, but they are not quite the same, either. Skill is the ability to perform a task proficiently, while technique is the method used to perform that task. It is quite possible to have the skill to kayak a class III river but also have such poor technique that doing so takes an inordinate amount of time and energy. Conversely, you could have beautiful paddling technique, with a smooth, powerful stroke, but lack the skill to paddle on anything other than flat water.

By training under difficult conditions, such as running or riding on rough trails, you will eventually learn the skills to perform efficiently under those circumstances.

Recovery. Recovery is not training per se, but it is a very important part of any training program. Recovery allows your body time to rebuild damaged tissue and recharge its energy systems. Plan rest and recovery into your training program and listen to your body, taking more rest if you feel like you are overtraining. Symptoms of overtraining include elevated heart rate at rest, unusual feeling of fatigue while training, and difficulty maintaining times and speeds in training sessions.

Recovery can include anything from shorter or lower-intensity training sessions to complete rest. Quite often, busy people with work and family pressures skimp on their sleep, a sure way to negate some of those hard-fought gains from pounding the pavement.

The Four Training Principles

To build your speed, strength, endurance, and skills for any given sport, follow these training principles.

Consistency. You must train consistently to improve your fitness. There is no point in doing a stop-start program to achieve your desired goal, just as you wouldn't stop and start during a race. Inconsistency leads to injuries, since you are subjecting your body to high stress without allowing it to build a base of strength.

Effort. You must put effort into any training to stimulate a *training response*. Human physiology responds to a physical stimulus by adapting to the stimulus. If you lift increasingly heavy weights over time, you provide a stimulus (the weight lifting) to elicit a response (stronger muscles). Similarly, if you run very fast for as long as you can at regular intervals, you will be able to run increasingly faster, up to the limit of your specific physiology. This also applies to endurance and skills (efficiency), provided you give your body sufficient time to recover, and the nutrients needed to repair and build tissues and systems.

Specificity. You must train for the specific sport you wish to improve. That means cycling to improve your fitness on the bike and kayaking to improve your fitness on the water.

INSIDE FACTS

According to Greek mythology, Hercules gained his immense strength by carrying a calf every day. Over time, the calf grew in size and weight, eventually growing into a full-size bull. Hercules became so fit because he *consistently* carried the animal (every day), he put in *effort* to lift the beast, performed the *specific* task in which he wished to improve, and put in the *time* needed to see results.

Time. There's a fine line between undertraining your body and over-training your body—and both can be equally disastrous to your fitness. Put too little time into your training and you won't improve. Put too much time into your training and your body and muscles will not recover or grow stronger. You must find the happy medium that allows you to put enough time into your training to improve your strength, speed, and endurance, but not so much time that you lower your immunity, feel fatigued all the time, or injure your joints, tendons, or muscles.

Interestingly, the above principles are a good basis for success in almost anything, be it learning to fly an airplane, climbing the corporate ladder, obtaining a degree in sports medicine, or training for a long adventure race (all of which I can attest to, since at one point I was doing all four at once).

The Four Basic Disciplines

Though adventure races will throw many sports your way, the four main disciplines are running and trekking, cycling, paddling, and climbing. Let's take a closer look at how to apply the training principles and elements to these core sports.

RUNNING AND TREKKING

You will not run much in expedition-length adventure races, since generally you'll carry quite large loads—up to 40 pounds in extreme circumstances. Having the strength to run with a load is quite advantageous, however, as it increases your ability to move quickly in most conditions.

Speed. Without question, the best way to increase speed is by running faster in training than you will during your race. You can do this easily by joining a track club and running intervals. For those with an aversion to the track, fartlek (speed play) can be effective. Find a gently undulating, smooth trail and run a moderate distance with 3- to 5-minute bursts of speed separated by 3 to 5 minutes of slower running.

Strength. You can increase your strength either by running while wearing a weighted backpack or by doing hill repeats. Find a nice, long hill that takes 3 to 5 minutes to run up. Run repeated intervals up and down, resting between each climb and descent. Training by running downhill is just as important as running uphill. Just ask anyone who has run the Pikes Peak Ascent and later tried the marathon. Most of the effort is expended going up the mountain, but most of the muscle damage and soreness are from running down.

Endurance. Developing endurance for running and trekking is only useful up to a certain point. Beyond about 30 miles most people suffer too much collateral damage (and thus spend too much time injured) to make regular runs of this length effective in training. Increase your long run by about 10 percent (time or distance) every 2 weeks until you have reached a point where you find you are not recovering adequately. Then back off for a week to recover before building distance again.

Skills. Put yourself in the roughest conditions you can safely tackle. This will vary widely depending on your background. Someone with a road-racing background may find that trails are tough enough, whereas orienteers may be able to run across talus slopes with no problem. Ultimately, you need to be able to cover rough ground (talus, undergrowth, marsh, and so on) quickly while carrying a load.

BIKING

Without question, the most important single factor for cycling in adventure racing is the ability to endlessly grind out the miles, making endurance the most important training element to master.

Speed. Training for speed on the bike is similar to that for running. You can join a bike group or design your own interval training program.

Strength. There are two ways to develop strength on the bike, by either riding hills or riding with a weighted pack as you would in a race. Ideally, you should do both at the same time. If you don't have ready access to natural hills, you can make do with freeway on-ramps and headwinds. You can also lower your tire pressure or tighten up your brakes so you are peddling against extra resistance. Or you can create a hill-like effect by pushing big gears—that is, riding in a higher (harder) gear than normal, forcing yourself to use more force on the pedals.

Endurance. To develop endurance on a bike, you must spend at least 60 percent of your time riding with a consistently elevated heart rate. This is best done on the road (or stationary bike trainer, if you can't get outside). Biking, whether on a road or a mountain, uses the same muscles, but road biking uses them more the consistently, providing better cardiovascular fitness in the process.

Bike endurance is more than simply fitness; it is also your ability to put up with endless hours on a hard, skinny seat, with a pack on your back, and over rough terrain. To develop this type of endurance, you need lots of miles on your wheels, and most of these miles should be on the road, where you can maintain your target heart rate (about 80 percent of your maximum for most long, slow distance training).

Skills. Ride hills and rough ground and make sure you are comfortable in all conditions. Proficiency in riding through sand, mud, water, grass, and steep terrain, and at night, are all skills necessary to keep you safe and fast in a race. Find a piece of trail that is a little above your comfort level and try to ride it repeatedly until you can ride it smoothly and with confidence. Once you can do this, try adding a race-weight pack and repeat the process until you feel confident. Then set up your lights and tackle it again in the dark.

PADDLING

Canoeing, kayaking, rafting, and rowing are all commonly included in adventure races, and each of these sports has been used on the ocean, rivers, and lakes. If you had to choose one craft and one body of water to train on, a fast, unstable kayak (like a surf ski or a downriver racing kayak) on a whitewater river would be the best choice. Each combination of craft and conditions creates a unique environment, so you should train for the worst you can find.

Paddling over long distances puts more emphasis on certain muscles than short-distance or technical paddling. Over time, the muscles supporting the paddle will fatigue, forcing the paddle lower and resulting in poor technique and a slower boat speed. The remedy is to develop strength and endurance in your deltoids (the support muscles) with a combination of strength and endurance training.

Paddle skills are much maligned by many athletes, since just about anyone with no previous experience can sit in a boat and propel himself or herself over the water. But is that really true? Eight teams had to be rescued from the ocean in Australia in the 1997 Eco-Challenge when conditions got a little lively. Eight-foot swells and 40-mile-an-hour wind gusts bombarded the fleet, creating some anxious moments for most teams. The better paddlers from Australia and New Zealand loved the conditions and sailed home extremely quickly (in 7 to 8 hours for 50 miles), taking the top 5 places, while the tail-enders wallowed and sank.

Endurance. Incrementally increase the distance of your long paddle session by no more than 10 percent until you reach your target distance, which should be the distance you will be paddling in your next race. If you are aiming at an expedition-length race, however, make your sessions no longer than 12 hours. Unless you are a superelite paddler, any training session over this length will hurt more than it helps. Save the suffering for the race.

Strength. You can build strength by weighting your paddle. You don't need much weight to make this effective. Tape the weight to the paddle shaft where it joins the blade. I use a soft ankle weight, the type with a Velcro closure, but any small weight will do. Bear in mind that race-supplied paddles can be quite heavy, up to 4.5 pounds, so add weight accordingly.

Speed. Speed training in a boat is no different from biking or running. Speed intervals should represent up to 15 percent of your total weekly training time. When they first start paddling, most people cannot get their heart rates up to the levels they can in sports that use their legs. Once you have developed your paddling fitness, however, you should be able to do intervals at an intensity similar to those of running and biking.

Skills. Most of the muscles that can develop power in a paddle stroke are *not* in your arms. Instead, you should feel your abdominal, oblique, latissimus dorsi, erector spinae, trapezius, and deltoid muscles working to power your stroke. If your arms tire before your shoulders, you probably have too much arm flex and a low paddle stroke. To correct this, concentrate on delivering the power from your torso by twisting at the waist, with your arms as the connecting rods, not the pistons.

In a forward power stroke, allow your arms to bend only slightly. You can develop the basic elements of a good kayak stroke with the following drill.

1. Stand with your paddle resting on your shoulders behind your neck, with your hands placed in their normal paddling position. (*Note:* To find the correct hand position, hold the paddle with the center of the shaft resting on your head and your upper arms at right angles to your body, your elbows bent at 90 degrees.)

2. Keeping your hips facing forward, rotate your body so that the shaft is at 90 degrees from its starting position and you are facing to one side. Rotate back through your neutral position to 90 degrees on the other side. This is the motion your torso should perform whenever you paddle.

3. Without releasing your grip, hold the paddle out in front of you, with your arms straight and horizontal (elbows locked), and repeat the same rotation. Make sure that you don't rotate your arms at the shoulder and that you maintain a 90-degree angle between your chest and upper arm.

4. Repeat step 3, but drop each blade alternately as if you were dipping them in the water. Watch your elbows on each side to make sure your arms stay straight.

5. Finally, repeat step 4, but keep your head facing forward as you would while paddling. The paddle shaft should draw an imaginary arc over your imaginary kayak hull, as if you had a small dome tent pitched over it.

You can also try these additional drills.

• Paddle your kayak as you watch your elbow on each stroke, making sure it doesn't overflex. This will also help you rotate because your body will follow your head around as the blade passes the hull. Whenever you're not practicing skills, keep your head upright and facing forward at all times. This helps you maintain balance and lets you see where you are going!

• Try paddling with your eyes closed. This is more difficult than it sounds, but it will give you an appreciation of balance as well as heighten your kinesthetic senses.

• Try paddling with a tennis ball placed on a flat section of your deck. Ideally the ball should rock backward and forward with each stroke, but it shouldn't roll off to the side.

Once you develop your kayaking skills, your canoe and rafting strokes will follow relatively easily. Canoe strokes are longer than kayak strokes because you can angle your body with the paddle-side hip forward, which gives you greater reach. You can also lunge forward slightly at each stroke, although this can cause bobbing, which will slow you down.

Raft paddles are significantly longer than canoe paddles because you sit a lot higher in a raft than in a canoe. As a result, you can get a lot more leverage, which you need in big whitewater. Rafts are so buoyant that you can (and should) include a forward-backward lunge with your rotation, as this gives you a very long stroke without bobbing the raft.

Climbing

The rock-climbing skills used in adventure racing are somewhat peculiar to this sport. Races rarely include free climbing (climbing without ropes), due to safety concerns. More typically, race directors include fixed-rope ascents, Tyrolean traverses, and rappels. To the climbing purist this may sound insignificant, until you find yourself 3 days into a race, without sleep, and halfway up a 400-foot overhanging ascent while wearing a 25-pound pack.

The most important elements of adventure-race "climbing" are upper-body strength for ascending and traversing, and ascending technique.

Strength. The best physical training for climbing is, well, climbing. If you don't have access to ropes, cliffs, or an indoor climbing gym, you can get reasonable conditioning from doing pullups (chinups). This will help you build the grip strength and upper-body strength you need to complete a ropes section.

Skills. Use your skeleton and fully extended muscles to support yourself. For example, if you were hanging off a handhold, extending your arms and removing any flex would allow you to efficiently use *only* your handgrip strength, not your arm strength, to support your weight. Conversely, if you hold on with your arm flexed, you force the muscles of your arms to hold your weight. This is an entirely useless exercise, but quite common for neophyte climbers.

You can train by setting up a climbing rope from a tree, balcony, or other sturdy structure and then doing repetitions of ascending and rappelling. This will also give you the opportunity to practice passing knots and transferring between gear setups.

Endurance. You can work on your skills and endurance at the same time. Repeat your ascending and descending cycle to failure (until you can no longer complete a cycle). As you increase your fitness, you should be able to ascend an accumulated total of 100 feet or more at a time.

Speed. Your speed through a ropes course is heavily dependent on your skills and techniques. You can use your training rope setup to test your speed by timing how fast you can safely complete a cycle of ascent, knot pass, and rappel. As a guide, during a race well-trained athletes can ascend a rope at a rate of about 100 feet in 10 minutes, carrying a full pack.

Weight Training

Many single-sport athletes overtrain certain muscles and undertrain others, creating muscle imbalances that can lead to injuries and poor performance. Strength training provides a simple way to balance out these muscles.

For ultra-endurance activities such as adventure racing, you don't want to build large muscles, since you will pay a huge penalty trying to drag that extra bulk around the racecourse. Instead, aim for lean, all-around strength. To gain that type of strength, I recommend a *superset circuit* workout.

Below are descriptions of my favorite exercises for a body-balancing superset circuit workout. It's called a superset because you take no rest between exercises. Do only one set of each exercise, moving directly from one to another. Perform 15 to 20 repetitions quickly for power (about one repetition per second), not stopping until you've completely fatigued the muscle group you are targeting. To do that, choose a weight that's heavy enough that you can barely—and I mean *barely*—lift at the end of the set. Your *circuit* is the full group of exercises. You need only do two to three supersets per week, giving yourself at least one full day of rest between sessions.

It is important to use free weights, preferably dumbbells, to develop proprioception (nerve feedback reflexes) and balance. Always warm up to a light sweat and stretch before doing your superset. Leave time for a cooldown afterward.

Dumbbell flies. Lie with your back on a weight bench and your feet on the floor. Hold the dumbbells with your arms extended above your chest. Inhale as you lower the dumbbells out to your sides. Exhale as you raise them. This move targets your chest and arms.

Bent-over dumbbell rows. Stand with a dumbbell in each hand. Bend forward from your hips about 45 degrees, with your knees bent slightly. Start by lifting one dumbbell toward your chest, making sure you rotate your torso, twisting at the waist. Exhale as you raise your elbow and pull the dumbbell in toward your ribs, and inhale as you lower it. Lift the second dumbbell as you lower the first so that you mimic a kayak stroke, with lots of torso rotation. This exercise targets your abdomen, arms, shoulders, back, and neck.

Crunches. Lie on your back with your knees bent and feet on the floor. Hold a weight behind your head. Exhale as you curl your upper body up off the floor. Inhale as you lower. These target your abdominal muscles.

Modified squats. Start with your knees bent 90 degrees, your feet under your hips, and knees not beyond your toes. With a dumbbell in each hand, inhale as you straighten your legs and rise onto the balls of your feet. Then lift the dumbbells over your head and extend your arms as if you were lifting an object from the floor to a high shelf. Slowly lower the dumbbells and return to your starting position. This will work your legs, arms, shoulders, and chest.

Shoulder burn. Sit on a bench in a kayaking position, with your legs extended on the bench. Hold a broomstick, paddle, or weight bar and mimic a kayak stroke. This will strengthen your shoulders.

Leg curls. Leg curls are best done using ankle weights, but can also be done using a weight or cable machine. Start on your belly with your legs fully extended, and flex each one alternately to at least 90 degrees. This exercise will work the hamstrings (the backs of your thighs) and will help balance out your quadriceps (the fronts of your thighs).

Pullups (chinups). Hang from a high bar, so that your feet don't touch the floor. Exhale as you pull yourself up until your chin clears the bar. If you don't have the strength to do a pullup, ask a friend to provide assistance until you build enough arm strength to do one by yourself. It is easiest to face your fingers toward you (an underhand grip). Start that way, and once you can do 15 to 20 repetitions in a set, change your hand position so your knuckles are facing you instead (an overhand grip). Don't be tempted to add weight if you find pullups easy; that will add bulk to your frame. Instead, concentrate on adding speed to each repetition, which develops more useful power. This exercise develops your deltoids, forearm grip, latissimi dorsi, and biceps.

Periodization

Ah, and now for the true art of adventure training. How do you train frequently and hard enough for four or more sports, hone your speed, strength, endurance, and skills, sprinkle in the right amount of rest and recovery, and still somehow manage to find time for your family, personal, and professional life? It's actually all very possible, provided you are organized, disciplined, and efficient. Periodization, simply the science of breaking your training into periods, will allow you to get fit, recover, show up at the office, and find a few minutes each day to eat, feed the dog, sleep, and acknowledge your family.

Effective periodization requires a long-term plan. This plan could span months or even years, depending on your current state of fitness and your goal. The basic idea is that you intersperse each training session with a rest session and increase the load for each successive session in a systematic manner.

SAMPLE PERIODIZATION PLAN

Consult this graphic to design a periodized training plan.

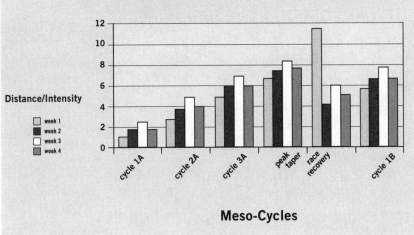

Sample Periodization Phase for 12-Hour Race

Distance/Intensity

- week 1
- week 2
- week 3
- week 4

Meso-Cycles

For periodization training to work, you must build in recovery cycles. For each *meso-cycle* of training (typically 4 weeks), you incorporate a recovery week that is shorter or less intense. This means that you increase your training level for 3 consecutive weeks, back off on the 4th week, and then start your next 4-week cycle at a level similar to that of week 3 of the prior meso-cycle.

You'll continue to build up your distance and intensity until the week before race day. Then you will taper your training during the final pre-race week. This will get you to the start line with a rested—but not comatose—mind and body. Above, you'll find a sample periodization plan. All of the training plans in "Sample Training Programs" on page 249 use a periodization approach.

Two-time Eco-Challenge winner Andrea Murray fuels up during the 1997 ESPN X-venture race in Baja.

> *"You can tell a lot about a fellow's character by his way of eating jelly beans."*
>
> —Ronald Reagan

10 FOODS FOR THOUGHT AND THOUGHTS ON FOOD

EVERYTHING YOU NEED TO KNOW ABOUT EATING FOR PERFORMANCE

Although the vast majority of people become quite attached to food and food quite attached to them, it's quite the opposite for adventure racers. Ultra-endurance athletes burn between 10,000 and 15,000 calories per day, depending on the environmental conditions while racing, but they only have the time and ability to eat 4,000 to 5,000 calories per day.

This calorie disparity leads to an array of interesting physiological effects, most of which are not particularly helpful to racing. Careful consideration of food choices, however, can ameliorate potential problems.

HOW *NOT* TO . . .

Eat While Racing

In the 1998 Raid Gauloises in Ecuador, we crossed the Andean Alps, from the headwaters of the Amazon to the Pacific coast, and summitted the 19,384-foot Cotopaxi, the world's highest active volcano. Almost half of the 9-day race was spent at altitudes of over 13,000 feet, and we suffered through the final 3-day paddling leg with virtually no food. Consequently, we almost lost the race in the final stages. We also lost an immense amount of body weight, 22 pounds in my case. Luckily for us, the second-place team also forgot their food, so, hungry and fatigued, we were still able to hold them off to the finish.

Fuel for Endurance

To go the distance, endurance athletes must obtain the bulk of their calories from carbohydrate, the sugar found in fruits, vegetables, starchy foods, and table sugar. Your muscles store sugar in the form of glycogen. Like your fat stores, your body accesses stored glycogen when blood-sugar levels begin to drop. Your muscles can only store up a limited amount of glycogen, about enough for a 20-mile run. When you do successive days of hard training and fail to eat enough carbohydrate to replenish your glycogen stores, the glycogen stores in your muscles run out—and you hit the wall.

How much carbohydrate is enough? This depends on the amount and intensity of training, but for multisport and other distance athletes, recent research suggests you aim for 70 percent of your daily calories. To give you an idea of what *not* to eat, a McDonald's Big Mac is 570 calories, with 49 percent of those calories from fat. Burger King onion rings are 600 calories (45 percent from fat), KFC breast is 400 calories (55 percent from fat) and Pizza Hut Meat Lover's medium slice is 543 calories (47 percent from fat).

To ensure you get 70 percent of your calories from healthier, lower-fat carbs, skip the doughnuts, candy bars, sodas, and fast food and get used to eating cereals, fresh fruit, and vegetables, and have them with lean meats. If you're on the go, Subway offers some very healthy sandwiches. Just avoid extra cheese, mayo, and oil. A Subway Club has 304 calories (14 percent fat) and is loaded with fresh ingredients and fiber.

Use this sample meal plan for a day to get an idea of what a 70 percent carbohydrates diet looks like.

Breakfast: 1 bowl of high-fiber cereal with 1 cup of skim milk or soy milk; 1 glass of orange juice; 1 banana

Midmorning snack: 1 apple; 1 cup of tea; 1 slice of toast with peanut butter

Lunch: 1 turkey breast sandwich with lettuce, tomato, Miracle Whip, salt, and pepper; 1 orange; 1 glass of iced tea

Afternoon snack: 1 toasted bagel with jelly; 1 cup of tea or coffee

Dinner: 1 small side salad with oil-and-vinegar dressing; 1 chicken breast, small fillet of fish, or lean steak; 1 cup of potatoes, rice, or pasta; 1 cup of steamed green vegetable (beans, broccoli, peas, and so on); 1 cup of fruit salad and ½ cup of frozen yogurt; 1 glass of wine or beer

The Role of Carbohydrates in the Body

Compared with fats and protein, carbohydrates function as the primary fuel for the body. Your body breaks down glucose and glycogen into energy for your muscles and other body cells. When you eat carbohydrates, your body converts them to glucose and usually either burns it right away or stores it in the muscles and liver for later use. If the glycogen stores in your muscles happen to be full, your body converts the carbohydrates to fat and stores it in your fat cells subcutaneously (under the skin) or intramuscularly (within the muscles).

During exercise the reverse happens. Your body generally burns blood glucose first during exercise. Blood glucose is extremely limited, enough to power only a few minutes of exercise. Your muscles also begin to burn up glycogen stores. You usually have enough stored glycogen to last through 18 to 20 miles of running. Once the glycogen stores become tapped, then your body begins to access fat from your fat cells. And if that storage depot runs low, the body will begin to burn protein stores (primarily muscle protein).

That's the simple explanation. Of course, it's a bit more complex in reality. Your body actually burns a mixture of energy stores simultaneously. This depends on the intensity of exercise, your fitness level, and your diet. For example, during rest and low-intensity exercise, your body will access a higher proportion of fat, along with glycogen and blood sugar. During high-intensity exercise, your body burns more glycogen and less fat. When we're at rest, fat provides 80 to 90 percent of our energy requirements, but this decreases as we start to exercise and as the intensity increases. During moderate exercise your body uses an equal amount of stored fat and carbohydrates for energy. As the duration of exercise extends beyond an hour and carbohydrate stores decrease, fat utilization increases. During prolonged exercise, up to 80 percent of the body's energy requirements come from stored fat. Your intensity and the duration of exercise, as well as your nutritional status, also affect the proportions of fat and carbohydrates you burn for energy.

As you become more fit, your metabolism shifts and you begin to burn a higher percentage of stored fat than untrained individuals. This is ideal, as you can go a lot longer by burning fat than you can by burning glycogen or blood sugar. Take the average college-age male's body as an example: his fat accounts for about 100,000 calories of potential energy, far in excess of the energy stored in the body as glycogen. There is almost enough energy in his fat to sustain a run from Denver to Los Angeles.

No matter what type of exercise you do, you never want to let yourself get to the point that your glycogen stores are completely exhausted and you begin to break down muscle protein. First, you need protein to build and repair your muscles. When your body begins to use it as an energy source, these important functions fall by the wayside. Second, you need some stored glycogen in order to burn fat. Lack of dietary carbohydrates leads to an oversupply of mobilized fat, leading in turn to an accumulation of acid by-products called ketone bodies (a condition known as ketosis). People who have severely bonked and continue to exercise have the telltale smell of ketones on their breath. In severe cases the kidneys and other organs shut down, and death may eventually result. Several people are hospitalized for ketosis each year at Hawaii's Ironman Triathlon.

All Carbohydrates Are Not Created Equal

I often hear athletes endlessly discussing which "-ose" (glucose, fructose, polycose) is the best for their sport. To understand the answer, we need to look at how each works as fuel in the body.

As the name suggests, carbohydrates are made up of carbon (carbo-) and water (-hydrate). There are three kinds of carbohydrates: monosaccharides, oligosaccharides, and polysaccharides. They derive their names based on the number of simple sugars that combine to make up the molecule. All this chemistry is not really important to us athletes; however, its action within the body is important.

The simplest carbohydrates are the monosaccharides ("mono" meaning one), such as glucose, fructose, and galactose. Glucose, also known as dextrose or blood sugar, forms naturally in the body as a result of digestion of more complex carbohydrates. Once absorbed by the small intestine, glucose can be used by the muscles for energy, stored as glycogen, or converted to fat for storage in fat cells. Fructose (fruit sugar) is abundant in fruits and honey and, because of its high level of sweetness, is often used as a sweetener in processed foods. Once you eat fructose, your liver slowly converts it to glucose and then releases it into the bloodstream. Galactose is only found in milk products and is converted by the body into glucose for use as energy.

The complex carbohydrates are the oligosaccharides, primarily the disaccharides (di- meaning two), which are formed from two monosaccharides. Common examples are sucrose (in natural sugars), lactose (milk), and maltose (cereals). Polysaccharides are made up of three or more simple sugar molecules, divided into plant (starch and fiber) and animal (glycogen). Although complex carbohydrates are, well, more complex, that doesn't mean they *necessarily* make their way from your mouth to your bloodstream any more slowly than simple carbohydrates. Many variables affect how quickly your body breaks down and uses the food you eat, which brings me to my next topic: the glycemic index.

The Glycemic Index

The glycemic index measures the speed at which your body converts carbohydrates into their basic structure and most useful form, glucose. On the glycemic index, pure glucose is assigned the number 100, since it is the food converted fastest. And all other sugars and foods have a lower number.

Glycemic index is important for athletes who want to regulate the speed at which glucose is released into their bloodstreams (via digestion) and is thus available to be used for energy. High-glycemic foods, such as candy (largely high-fructose corn syrup or glucose), enter the bloodstream very rapidly after ingestion. The downside to quick absorption is that your blood sugar swings to extremely high levels (hyperglycemia) and then, as the body tries to compensate, swings back to too low (hypoglycemia). On the other end of the scale, fat has an extremely low glycemic index, since it takes a very, very long time for the body to digest it and convert it to useful fuel. Fat is often used by sports nutrition formulators to slow the digestion of a particular food blend, but can cause gastric distress during high-intensity exercise.

For higher-intensity sports, such as running—which shuttles blood away from your gastrointestinal (GI) tract and to your working muscles—you need high-glycemic foods because they are quickly and easily digested. For ultralong endurance activity, however, you can get away with much lower glycemic index foods than you can for other sports. The lower intensity allows more blood to remain in the GI tract, allowing you to digest more complex foods more easily.

In fact, for extremely long races like the Eco-Challenge, the exercise intensity is so low that you can eat just about any food and your body will adequately process it and use it as energy for your working muscles. As a consequence, most ultradistance athletes going continuously over multiple days start to eat food that resembles meals, not unidentifiable processed mush. Energy bars can be quite nutritious, but they become unpalatable after a few hours, never mind days.

SAMPLE MENU FOR A MULTIDAY RACE

Here are some of my favorite foods to eat while racing.

Breakfast cereal bars
Cookies
Snickers
Crackers
Potato chips
Chee-tos

Beef jerky
Powdered meal-replacement
    drinks (such as Ensure)
Gourmet snack meals—lasagna,
    ravioli, Stroganoff, and
    so forth—in 8-ounce cans

Eating during Exercise

Most studies show that consuming carbohydrates during high-intensity, long-term aerobic exercise or ultra distances benefits performance. Carbohydrate consumption during exercise spares muscle glycogen and maintains a more optimal level of blood glucose. When you consume carbohydrates during exercise, you may be able to prolong your endurance by up to half an hour.

The easiest way to consume carbohydrates is by drinking a sports drink. This supplies both carbohydrates and fluid to help prevent dehydration, another of the endurance athlete's adversaries. Which sugar solution to consume is another bone of contention. Drink manufacturers would have you believe their particular blend of sugars and minerals has some special effect that opens the magic door to your energy system. In reality, any drink with simple sugars and a small amount of an electrolyte, such as salt, will work.

A small amount of sodium helps facilitate rehydration and gastric emptying. About ⅓ tablespoon of salt added to a quart of water is sufficient, and most sports drinks have a reasonable balance of the two. Sodium may also help prevent hyponatremia, a condition in which excess water absorption dilutes the blood and lowers its sodium concentration—with potentially fatal consequences. Up to 20 percent of Ironman finishers have been found to be hyponatremic, and some have even died from the condition.

The optimal concentration of carbohydrates in a drink varies from person to person and with environmental conditions. Under normal adventure-racing conditions, individuals can tolerate anything from a 5 percent to a 50 percent sugar solution. As conditions get hotter, it's important to consume increasingly more dilute drinks to offset dehydration and ensure you don't end up bloated (from slow gastric emptying). If you are exercising in extremely hot conditions, like those in the Ironman Triathlon in Kona, Hawaii, a solution with no more than a 5 percent concentration of carbohydrate will provide the best source of hydration. Even small amounts of simple sugars retard gastric emptying dramatically (and consequently restrict hydration). Some evidence shows, however, that maltodextrin solutions, such as SoBe Sports System, do not inhibit gastric emptying to the extent that drinks with glucose and other simple sugars do, since the carbohydrate exerts a lesser osmotic effect (the flow of fluids across cell membranes due to differing electrolyte concentrations on either side), facilitating hydration and carbohydrate replacement.

Although long-chain-carbohydrate drinks (such as those with maltodextrin) with a small amount of sodium are a good choice for fluid and fuel for most endurance events, in very cold climates or during multiday completions like Raid Gauloises, you need to also eat solid food. Bars, gels, and semiliquid replacements are convenient and easy to eat, up to a point. As the competition progresses, sweet foods become increasingly less palatable. At this point, more savory fare is in order. I've found that dehydrated meals, potato chips, jerky, and ramen noodles all work well.

Vitamins and Minerals

Sports-supplement manufacturers would like you to believe that it is impossible to obtain adequate nutrition through food alone. The medical establishment and the U.S. FDA, on the other hand, tell us that a balanced diet will meet all our dietary needs. Who can we believe? Considering that 80 percent of the world's athletic population does very well with no access to supplementation, one would tend to think that our medical community and regulatory bodies are correct.

The most pertinent question is why would we need supplements when humans have been functioning perfectly well for hundreds of

HOW TO...
Eat for Endurance

Select race foods that will last the distance and are lightweight, nutritionally sound, and palatable after a week or so on the go. I like to stash "transition foods," which are inappropriate to take on the trail but are tasty and nutritious. If you are doing a supported race, your support crew can provide you with cooked meals at transition areas, so the variety of foods you eat is much greater. One of my favorite types of transition foods is a gourmet meal in a can: lasagna, spaghetti Bolognese, ravioli, Irish stew, beef Stroganoff, chicken Kiev, and just about any other "real meal" I can find on the supermarket shelves. Canned goodies are too heavy to carry beyond the checkpoints. So for long bouts on the trail, we often use dehydrated hiking meals like Alpine Aire (www.alpineaire.com), which can be rehydrated by adding water and putting them in your pocket for 20 to 30 minutes. Meal-replacement powders such as Ensure, available from most supermarkets, are also nutritionally complete, simply require the addition of water, and can be shaken, not stirred, in a water bottle.

thousands of years on diets dramatically less complete than the diets we have access to today? Two billion Asians, who have traditionally been considered "small," exist on diets that provide 80 percent of their calories from rice, and yet their youth are now attaining a stature and build comparable to that of Europeans. Seven-foot-tall NBA basketball star Yao Ming is a classic example. African runners completely dominate endurance running on diets that most Americans would consider "chicken feed," with absolutely no supplementation.

Although we have access to the greatest variety of foods of any country in the world, what people choose to eat is another thing entirely. Sixteen percent of the American diet is provided by McDonald's— a frightening statistic if you consider the nutritional value of a typical McDonald's meal. If you discount fries, the average youth in this country gets only two fruit and vegetable servings each *week*. The recommended dietary allowance (RDA) is five a day, although many dietitians recommend nine. If you add in eating disorders (prevalent in gymnasts, wrestlers, ice-skaters, competitive rock climbers, ballet dancers, female runners, and so on) and the myriad of popular "health diets" that athletes often try, there may indeed be a requirement for athletes to take supplements.

Let me back up a little here. Let's suppose you eat a regular, healthy diet, one that meets the requirements of the RDA. In this case there is absolutely no peer-reviewed scientific evidence that you need vitamin and mineral supplements. Bear in mind that the RDA is specified for different age groups and pregnant women, but not for people with any sort of health disorder. If you are on a calorie-restricted diet (something I strongly recommend against if you are an endurance athlete), are a vegetarian, are lactose intolerant, have food allergies, or suffer from heart disease, then there are some specific supplements that you may need. It is best to see your doctor in these cases.

If you do take supplements and they make you feel better, then you may be compensating for a deficiency in your diet. Some common deficiencies include iron, zinc, and calcium in women, and vitamins C and E in general.

Finally, if you do supplement, save some money and choose the cheapest generic brand, since there is absolutely no chemical difference between, say, vitamin C derived from organic oranges grown in Florida and vitamin C synthesized in a huge factory in Detroit.

Hydration

Next to oxygen, water is the single most important ingredient for physical performance. To give you an idea of its importance, consider that you can survive at rest for 3 minutes without oxygen, 3 days without water, 3 weeks without food, and 3 years without sex. Okay, I made the sex part up, but you get the idea. For every 1 percent of body water you lose, you suffer a 5 percent decrease in aerobic performance. At about 5 percent dehydration (6 to 8 pounds of fluid for most fit people), your health is seriously compromised.

As you dehydrate, your resistance to heat and cold deteriorates. In a hot climate the body can no longer cool itself (via sweating and evapo-

INSIDE FACTS

Your body will absorb a cold fluid (41°F) more readily than a warm one, but this may also cause gastric distress. Obviously, in a warm environment a cold drink also helps lower the body's core temperature, but it may have disastrous effects in a very cold climate, possibly contributing to hypothermia.

rative cooling), the blood thickens, making the heart work harder, and electrolyte imbalances causes nerve and conduction problems, cramping, cardiac arrhythmia, disorientation, and blurred vision. If untreated, overheating (hyperthermia) eventually leads to heatstroke, heat injury, and death. Eva Oskarsen, from Swedish team Peak Performance, nearly died from hyperthermia during the 1997 ESPN X-Venture Race in Baja, Mexico. Every athlete in the race suffered some form of heat injury, as the conducted and reflected temperatures reached more than 200°F, boiling water in canteens and melting shoe adhesives. Eva was not adequately heat-acclimatized, and there was not enough water on the course to hydrate.

In a cold climate, dehydration also compromises the body's resistance to injury. Hypothermia (low core body temperature) is the major medical cause of withdrawal from adventure races (not bad feet, as many people believe). It's largely preventable with proper hydration and clothing choices (layering; ventilation; waterproof, breathable fabrics). A dehydrated body has lower resistance to hypothermia and cold injuries, such as frostnip and frostbite. People suffer from frostbite every year in the Alaskan Iditasport 100-mile race, a condition that is entirely preventable.

> *"When I woke up this morning my girlfriend asked me, 'Did you sleep good?' I said, 'No, I made a few mistakes.'"*
>
> —Steven Wright

11 | WHEN THE HELL ARE WE?

EVERYTHING YOU NEED TO KNOW ABOUT MANAGING YOUR SLEEP

Watching adventure racing on television would lead most observers to believe that the top teams don't sleep while they race. Nothing could be further from the truth.

Many rookie teams make the mistake of believing that they can put time and distance on other teams by skipping their shut-eye. While this may be true to an extent, the reality is that lack of sleep slows down your physical and mental processes. As you become increasingly tired, you lose the ability to make decisions and to operate at a useful athletic level.

The Stages of Sleep Deprivation

After about 48 hours without sleep, a person generally starts to have spontaneous narcoleptic episodes characterized by falling asleep at the most inopportune moments. In the 1995 ESPN X-Games adventure race in Maine, the top three teams all experienced serious sleep deprivation. By the mountain bike stage on day 5, my team, Eco-Internet, had only managed about 5 hours' sleep. Every one of us at some point fell asleep while mountain biking. Eventually we gave in and took a 10-minute "power nap," which felt like a solid hour of deep sleep.

After about 72 hours of sleep deprivation, it becomes virtually impossible to continue moving forward effectively or to make rational decisions. By 100 hours of sleep deprivation, the body shuts down so much that cognitive thought narrows to a dull glow in the cerebrum.

The Stages of Sleep

Quite a bit of research has focused on sleep and its effects on mental and physical function. Scientists have used recordings of brain activity, eye movement, and muscle activity to make up a sleep chart that breaks sleep into separate stages according to brain rhythms.

Sleep stages are sequentially defined as 1, 2, 3, and 4 and include graduations between REM (rapid eye movement) sleep and non-REM (NREM) sleep. Although the lines between sleep stages are somewhat fuzzy, the latter part of sleep, during stages 3 and 4 (slow-wave sleep, or SWS), are thought to be the most useful for recovery. During SWS your body recovers from physical stress, repairs tissues, and replaces energy stores. Because of this, you need even more SWS than usual after prolonged endurance exercise such as an adventure race.

You will experience four to six complete cycles of REM/NREM sleep during a complete night's rest. During adventure racing, however, you don't have the luxury of sleeping for 8 hours and repeatedly cycling through all of the stages. Rather, aim for at least one full cycle every 24 hours to continue effectively on the racecourse.

Sleep Strategy

My experience over the last 17 years of racing has resulted in a very rough rule of thumb for sleep while racing. For a race up to 3 days long, it is possible and effective to skip sleeping altogether, or at least get away with just a couple of 5- to 10-minute power naps. Once you are profoundly tired, after about 50 hours, most people find it extremely easy to fall asleep quickly (within a few seconds), making a 5- or 10-minute nap time well spent. The 5- or 10-minute losses in time on the racecourse are far outweighed by the mental and physical gains achieved later.

In races that last longer than 3 days but less than 5 days, you must accumulate at least an hour of sleep during each 24-hour period to maintain your speed and ability to think clearly. For races longer than 5 but less than 7 days, you'll need 2 to 3 hours of accumulated sleep during each 24-hour period. For races longer than 7 days, count on 3 to 4 hours of sleep for every 24-hour period. Each 24-hour period starts from the race start. Sleep deprivation is cumulative, and lack of sleep will catch up with you unless you keep your "sleep bank account" topped up.

A good example of my sleep bank theory is the 2001 Eco-Challenge in New Zealand. Team Pure NZ led into the third day of the race, largely by not sleeping and by maintaining a solid pace. On the first night, we were as far as 6 hours behind, since we slept for 3 solid hours in a shelter before the first transition. As the race progressed, we moved slowly up through the field, not because we were putting in more effort, but because our sleep strategy allowed us to maintain the same effort we started with, while the Kiwis' pace continued to slow from fatigue. By the fourth day, we hit the lead and Pure NZ was forced to sleep, allowing us to slip into the lead for a 21-minute win!

Your race tactics and the layout of the racecourse will determine how much and when to sleep during a race. A team should sleep in a nice, warm, dry, comfortable location, uninterrupted by noise, wind, rain, and other extraneous influences. You should also try to sleep in a solid block.

If the racecourse involves easy navigation and mild terrain, you can probably move forward effectively even while exceedingly sleep-deprived. On the flip side, even mild sleep deprivation may cause extreme danger in environments such as icefalls, crevasse-ridden glaciers, technical whitewater rivers, and precipitous mountain bike trails.

I recommend you err on the side of more sleep rather than less. Speed is heavily affected by lack of sleep, and you are better off moving faster after more sleep than slower with less.

An injured athlete is carried off the 2003 Raid Gauloises course.

> *"Dwell not upon thy weariness, thy strength shall be according to the measure of thy desire."*
>
> —*Arab proverb*

---

12 PHYSICAL MAINTENANCE

EVERYTHING YOU NEED TO KNOW ABOUT TAKING CARE OF YOUR BODY

Your body literally can get torn apart in races. Sore, blistered feet, traumatic injury, infections, heat injury, disease, and simply running out of steam all dramatically affect your (and your team's) performance. Interestingly, heat injury, either hypothermia (getting too cold) or hyperthermia (too hot), ranks as the number-one reason people drop out of adventure races. In fact, three out of four deaths in adventure sports can be attributed directly or indirectly to heat injury.

Staying Warm

During prolonged exposure to the cold, your body temperature can drop low enough to impair cognitive thought processes and physical functioning. In an environment where skill and decision making affect safety (such as in an adventure race), hypothermia can be lethal. For example, during a major international adventure race in Europe a few years ago, one of the competitors almost drowned in a canyon while swimming in near-freezing conditions. Rescuers were able to revive her, but she suffered permanent injury.

Ironically, as you get colder, you become progressively less able to recognize it. Eventually, you get so cold that you think you are hot, which can lead to a state known as "paradoxical undressing." Fortunately, if teammates quickly pick up on the signs of hypothermia and take action, they can arrest the downward spiral toward this deadly paradox. Signs of hypothermia include blue lips, unnaturally pale flesh, incoherence, inability to perform fine motor skills, lack of mental acuity, poor decision making, shivering, and shaking.

If a teammate is getting cold, take immediate action to prevent the condition from slowing you down and threatening his or her health. To warm someone, remove the cause of the cold, usually wind and moisture. Then warm him or her back up by covering his or her body with dry clothes, other dry items, or even your bodies. If for some reason the victim has reached a state of profound hypothermia (exhibiting incoherence, an inability to use fine motor skills, and a *lack* of shivering), get professional medical help as soon as possible. Warming someone in this state can be lethal if not done properly.

The ideal situation, of course, is to prevent hypothermia from occurring in the first place. Adventure athletes quite often end up cold because they are too focused on racing and not on their own maintenance (or that of their teammates). You can become hypothermic in seemingly benign conditions, even in the tropics, if the exposure is long enough. Evaporative cooling (as occurs, for instance, when skin is dampened while kayaking) can reduce skin-surface temperatures well below the ambient temperature. Conductive cooling (when you are in contact with a colder substance) leads to hypothermia even faster than evaporative cooling. The most common form of conductive cooling is submersion in water.

To prevent hypothermia, you must dress appropriately. Wear windproof gear, and possibly an insulating layer, in the case of evaporative cooling. If you will be submerged, you'll need waterproof insulation. This could be waterproof outerwear, a wet suit or dry suit, or a combination of thermal and wind- or waterproof layering.

Keeping Cool

Hyperthermia is even more dangerous than hypothermia. It is much harder to cool someone than to warm them. Also, the human body is much more resilient when in low temperatures than in high temperatures. When the human body overheats, it literally cooks itself, and the effects are irreversible.

Staying cool involves either removing yourself from the cause of the heat or providing a cooling source. It's toughest to do this in environments with heat *and* moisture. High humidity increases the heat index, which is the "real feel" of the heat. At 90 percent humidity, 90°F is equivalent to 120°F of dry temperature. As the environmental humidity increases, the effects of evaporative cooling decrease, until it becomes essentially ineffective.

The hottest environments inevitably have bright sunshine, or solar radiation. You can't remove the source of solar radiation, but you can hide from it quite effectively. Light-color clothing reflects a high percentage of the radiation (sunlight) that causes heating, greatly reducing the amount of energy you absorb, and thus your propensity to heat up in the sun.

Though it may seem counterintuitive, loose-fitting, long-sleeved shirts and pants are best because they allow air to flow to and from the skin. This is a principle the Bedouin desert nomads use with their flowing caftans, a complete cover-up that has proven extremely effective in the harshest desert climates. A wide-brimmed hat or cap with a legionnaire-style neck protector is also important, especially if you have dark hair, light skin, or follicular challenges (short or absent hair!).

The first signs of heat injury are quite confusing for athletes because they mirror the sensations experienced anyway during intense exercise. As core body temperature climbs, the skin flushes and sweats and the heart and breathing rates increase. In hyperthermia, these symptoms are abnormally accelerated and are often accompanied by other symptoms, such as dizziness and fatigue. Treatment of heat exhaustion involves removing the heat source, which usually means getting into the shade and resting, since physical exertion is the major contributor to increased body temperature. Cool drinks can rapidly lower core temperatures, and topical application of moisture with ventilation will promote evaporative cooling.

The first stage of heat injury is known as heat exhaustion. This significantly degrades athletic performance but is not an immediate threat to the person's health. If you don't take steps to treat heat exhaustion, however—especially in a race situation, where you are highly motivated to keep moving—heatstroke is a few short steps down the trail. During heatstroke, tissues, body organs, and the brain can become damaged. Progressive signs of heatstroke include an extreme elevation in body temperative (104°F and up), cessation of sweating, and hot, dry skin. Heatstroke is a medical emergency!

To treat heatstroke, immediately get the victim into the shade, remove excess clothing, and provide aggressive cooling methods. Use water spray, fanning, water immersion, ice packs, and alcohol rubs—the colder the better. One person on the team should seek medical assistance while the rest of the team tackles the cooling challenge.

Foot Injuries

Bad feet do not force a vast number of athletes out of races, but they do inflict unimaginable pain on an enormous number of people. Just about everyone will experience bad feet at some point if they regularly participate in long races, but it is possible to sidestep this problem with a little care and attention.

Just about all foot problems start with hot spots and blisters. Both are caused by pressure points, or friction between your skin and your shoes or socks. Wearing shoes that fit the size and shape of your feet and conditioning your feet with proper training (see chapter 3) will help prevent hot spots and blisters. Once you start your race, you can reduce the likelihood of foot problems by wearing high-quality wool or polyester (CoolMax) socks and frequent applying silicone-based lubricant, such as Hydropel, directly to your feet.

If your conditioning, lubrication, socks, and footwear fail to prevent those nasty blisters, then you can always go for the duct tape. The basic treatments are quite simple.

HOT SPOTS

These abnormally elevated areas of localized heat, redness, and soreness are the precursors to blisters and should be taken care of as soon as you feel the symptoms. Try first to locate and remove the source of the hot spot. Common offenders include tight laces, foreign objects in your shoes or socks, and poorly fitting footwear. If your shoes are the cause, you can use a knife to slit the shoe in the pressure area or cut a small

Ian's Adventure-Racing Wisdom

A herd of buffalo can only move as fast as the slowest buffalo. When the herd is hunted, the slowest and weakest ones at the back are killed first. This natural selection is good for the herd as a whole because the general speed and health of the group keeps improving by the regular killing of the weakest members.

In much the same way, the human brain can only operate as fast as the slowest brain cells. Adventure racing, as we know, kills brain cells. Naturally, the slowest and weakest brain cells are killed off first. In this way, regular participation in adventure races eliminates the weaker brain cells, making the brain a faster and more efficient machine. That's why you always feel smarter after an adventure race.

hole and enlarge it as necessary. If you make a hole, make sure you cover it with duct tape so it doesn't let more debris into your shoe and cause more problems. Next, clean off any lubricant on your foot with an alcohol swab. Then apply a small piece of duct tape, making sure you completely cover the hot spot with at least $\frac{1}{4}$ inch of overlap around it. Smooth out all wrinkles, slitting and overlapping the tape if you have to bend it around a toe.

BLISTERS

Your skin is made up of several layers, like an onion, and blisters form when the layers start rubbing together. Eventually the outer layers of skin will separate from those below, and the resulting cavity will fill with lymph fluid. In extreme cases, blisters can form on blisters, causing entire sheets of skin to separate and allowing blood vessels to rupture and form blood blisters.

Blisters are caused by a combination of heat, friction, and moisture. You can reduce heat with appropriate footwear. In general, highly breathable mesh is preferable to leather or waterproof shoes, unless you are in extremely cold conditions. Keeping feet dry in an adventure race is mostly a futile exercise (unless you are in the desert), so wear shoes and socks that drain and dry very fast. You can reduce friction with lubricants if you are in a wet environment, or with powders if you are in a dry environment.

Blister treatment starts by removing the source of the problem, then protecting the injury from further trauma. Take care not to irritate the area with additional materials, such as moleskin, tape, or bandages. Treat smaller blisters the same as hot spots. For blisters larger than about $\frac{3}{4}$ inch in diameter, do the following:

• Clean and wipe the area with alcohol.

• Sterilize a fine-pointed sharp object, such as a knife or needle, with an alcohol wipe or flame, making sure no soot accumulates on the implement's surface.

• Make two to four small holes in a line along one side of the blister. Small holes are less likely to cause the blister surface to tear away, and poking the holes along the side of the fluid sac helps it drain properly.

- Massage the fluid out of the sac, using your fingers, and dry the area once it is empty. Do not remove the outer layer of skin; this protects the tissue underneath.

- Check the blister periodically to make sure that the fluid keeps draining out and that the skin remains intact. If the holes you made keep resealing, you can make a wick to encourage drainage. Thread a piece of sterilized thread through the blister and leave the wick (thread) in place under some tape. The fluid will move along the fibers of the thread and keep the blister from re-forming.

- Do not drain the blister if it is filled with blood or if the fluid isn't clear. Doing so can cause infection.

- Infections can end your race if they are left unchecked. If your skin breaks from a ruptured blister, puncture wound, cut, or abrasion, clean and treat the wound site with an antiseptic and broad-spectrum antibiotic ointment. If the area becomes hot, red, raised, and sore, or if opaque fluid leaks out, you probably have an infection. If so, continue treatment as above. In the event that the infection becomes systemic, seek medical care.

Traumatic Injuries

Many athletes successfully complete an adventure race with surprisingly severe, yet not life-threatening injuries (see "Jane Hall and Her Broken Bits," page 182). If you are in remote wilderness with an injury that means you need to get out, you will need an ability to suffer, a strong will, a supportive team, and a little innovation. Lower-leg injuries are the most difficult to race through because a large proportion of a race is spent on your feet. Just about all foot problems, joint strains and sprains, and torn muscles, however, can be treated and shored up to provide serviceable limbs.

The first step is to stabilize the injury. You can do so with nonstretch adhesive tape (athletic tape or duct tape), bandages, and/or splints. If you have an injury above the waist (a dislocated shoulder or broken rib,

JANE HALL AND HER BROKEN BITS

Jane Hall was a bit of a wreck when she came in to the finish in Cairns at the Eco-Challenge Australia in 1997. After seeing her hugely swollen legs and an aching arm, the race medical staff whisked her off to the local hospital. Not getting any quick help in emergency room, Jane eventually walked back to the hotel and spent the next few days sightseeing with me and the rest of Team Pure Energy. Back in Sydney she wasn't improving fast enough and her doctor found she had second-degree tears in both knees and one ankle, and a broken arm. This was an old break that she admitted was the result of a mountain bike accident several weeks before the race. She didn't want to tell us before the event because she thought we wouldn't let her race. Tough woman!

for instance), immobilize the area and let someone else carry your pack. Lower limbs will still need to move, so an injury in this area requires some significant reinforcement. Again, ask teammates to carry some of your weight, and use some sort of crutch, such as a hiking pole, tree limb, or tent pole.

Soft-tissue injury (cartilage, ligaments, tendons), especially if there is heavy bleeding, can be quite serious, if not life threatening. Stem heavy bleeding by applying pressure directly to the wound with sterile gauze pads or folded clothing. If the wound is deep or if an artery has been severed, you may need to maintain pressure a long time (possibly hours) until the bleeding stops. Open wounds dramatically increase the likelihood of infection, which can result in serious, even life-threatening, health problems. Cover all wounds, and keep them clean at all times with liberal use of disinfectants and triple-antibiotic ointments. If infection sets in, you will be forced out of the race, especially if it becomes systemic and affects the whole body. Sure signs of this are dark streaks on your skin or tenderness in your lymphatic nodes, which are located in your crotch, armpits, and neck. Systemic infections should be treated with a prescribed antibiotic and under medical supervision.

Illness

Many races are held in exotic locations that are often teeming with exotic illnesses. Virtually every U.S. and European competitor in the 2000 Eco-Challenge in Sabah, Malaysia, contracted a virulent strain of leptospirosis, a bacterial disease spread from contact with the urine of infected animals (probably by swimming in a flooded river). Leptospirosis is a particularly vicious disease that causes nausea, headaches, fever, muscle aches, sensitivity to light, organ failure, hemorrhaging of the lungs, coma, and death, if not treated. Fortunately, an inexpensive and effective drug (doxycycline) can cure the illness.

The physical and mental stress of racing compromises the immune system, making illness more likely. You can take precautions to minimize illness, but not to eliminate it. Before the race, immunize yourself against known diseases. During the race, follow careful sanitation practices, such as treating your drinking water. Eat a complete diet, and take vitamin and mineral supplements as necessary. Though I usually don't recommend supplements during training and general life (see chapter 10), race time is the exception. Adventure racing taxes your body considerably more so than training. Also, during a race it is often difficult to eat balanced meals, especially if you are exercising continually for several days. Water-soluble vitamins in particular can be leached out of your system due to high volumes of perspiration and other fluid loss, making supplementation necessary. A complete vitamin/mineral supplement each day in a multiday race also helps to make up for the adventure racer's standard diet of candy bars and potato chips, which provides insufficient nutrients for tissue maintenance and repair and for fighting off foreign bugs.

Eco-Internet support crew member Angie Giustina organizes gear during the 1998 Raid Gauloises in Ecuador.

> *"When you face death, it's not the marks on your résumé you see, it's the faces of those you love."*
>
> —Beck Weathers

---

13 THE SPORTS STORE

EVERYTHING YOU NEED TO KNOW ABOUT APPAREL, FOOTWEAR, GEAR, AND EQUIPMENT

Adventure racing appeals to adventure seekers, adrenaline junkies, endurance athletes, and wilderness lovers. Above all, it satisfies the penchants of the most entrenched gear freaks. A committed adventure athlete can use gadgetry and technology of every conceivable shape and size. In this chapter, you'll find the lowdown you need to know to shop wisely for gear, apparel, and everything else you'll need at the sporting-goods store.

Apparel

Well-designed apparel protects you from the heat, cold, wet, and sun, thus allowing you to stay comfortable and safe in extreme environments. Modern, high-tech apparel companies use advanced fiber technologies to manufacture amazingly lightweight and comfortable clothing. This includes fabrics made from combinations of fibers in various weaves and knits that are tough, abrasion resistant, lightweight, highly breathable, vapor wicking, and virtually impervious to outside moisture. Clothing design incorporates paneling and cloth combinations that allow freedom of movement and ventilation without compromising the primary goal of environmental protection and control.

Base layers, those next to the skin, vary from ultralight (silk-weight) polyester blends, such as CoolMax, for cool conditions, to Supplex Nylon, which can also be worn as the outer (and only) layer in a hot environment. In colder climates you'll need to wear several lighter-weight layers rather than one big, heavy one. Such layering techniques help you move freely without feeling constricted by your clothing, and layers keep you warm, feel lighter, and provide an easy way to adjust your clothing for temperature variations. In really cold or wet conditions, you'll need a waterproof, breathable, and/or windproof shell as your outermost layer.

At the sporting-goods store, you'll find four types of layers.

1. Sun- or heat-protective layers

2. Wind- and moisture-protective (snow, sleet, rain, spray) layers

3. Insulation layers for warmth in cold conditions

4. Wicking base layers that prevent chafing and move moisture away from the skin

In the vast majority of cases, you should wear synthetic fibers, such as polyester and nylon.

Depending on which of seven climate zones (desert, tropical, forest, temperate, alpine, arctic, and maritime) you find yourself in, you'll need different combinations of the four primary apparel types.

DESERT

Clothing for hot climates should fit loosely to allow ventilation and be light in color to reflect solar radiation. Examples of effective warm-weather fabrics include Supplex Nylon and CoolMax. Though it may seem counterintuitive, wearing a light-color cotton hat in hot desert weather will actually reflect heat away from your head, as well as provide additional evaporative cooling for your head once the material becomes saturated with perspiration. Desert nights can be cool to cold, depending on the time of year, so you will also need warm layers.

I recommend the following apparel.

Pants: Long- or short-leg vented Supplex or ripstop nylon, such as Nike's ACG Runnable Short

Tops: Long-sleeved vented Supplex or ripstop nylon shirt, such as RailRiders Eco-Mesh Shirt

Base layers: Silk-weight long-sleeved top, such as Nike ACG Oregon Base Layer

Insulation: None

Shell: Light nylon windproof jacket, such as Nike ACG Oregon Shell with zip-off arms and hood

Hat: Cotton or polyester cap with neck protector, such as MontBell Stainless Mesh Cap

Socks: CoolMax ankle mesh, such as DeFeet Speede socks

Gloves: None

TROPICAL

Jungle environments are extremely harsh on apparel due to the extremes of heat, humidity, and dense undergrowth. Consequently, your clothing must be highly abrasion resistant, fast drying, and snagproof. It is extremely rare that more than one layer of clothing will be required in such high temperatures.

I recommend the following apparel.

Pants: Vented Supplex or ripstop nylon pants or shorts, such as Rail-Riders Eco-Mesh Pants

Tops: Long-sleeved vented polyester, Supplex, or ripstop nylon top, such as GoLite Ether Wind Shirt

Base layers: None

Insulation: None

Shell: Windproof, highly breathable nylon jacket, such as Nike ACG Oregon Shell jacket

Hat: Cotton or polyester cap, such as Pearl Izumi Mesh Hat

Socks: CoolMax low-cut mesh socks, such as DeFeet Aireator

Gloves: Light synthetic gloves to protect hands, such as SixSixOne Raji mountain bike glove

FORESTS AND TEMPERATE AREAS

Forests can exist in several climate zones, but always in areas where sufficient moisture and moderate temperatures can sustain high densities of trees. This may include subalpine, subarctic, temperate, and tropical climates. Forest environments require relatively tough garments with moisture-wicking capacity, lightweight thermal insulation, and outer shells.

I recommend the following apparel.

Pants: Long Lycra tights, such as Nike ACG Ultimate Athletic Trail Tight, nylon shorts, or nylon pants

Tops: Nylon, polyester, or Lycra top, such as Pearl Izumi Long Sleeve Endurance Top

Base layers: Silk-weight polyester or wool top and bottoms, such as MontBell Z-L.M.W. High Neck Shirt and Storm Cruiser waterproof jacket and pants

Insulation: 50- to 100-weight (measured in grams per square meter, g/m^2) polyester or wool fleece, or equivalent long-sleeved top, such as Nike ACG Composite Full-Zip Jacket

Shell: Waterproof/breathable shirt and pants, such as GoLite Ether Wind Shirt and Pants

Hat: Polyester cap, such as Nike Dri-FIT Feather Light Hat

Socks: CoolMax or wool crew socks, such as SmartWool Adventure Light Hiker

Gloves: Synthetic gloves to protect hands, such as Pearl Izumi Bomber Glove

HIGH ALPINE

High alpine environments, those higher than 8,000 feet, are subject to rapid changes in weather and temperature, varying from freezing to hot, with the possibility of thunderstorms and snow at any time of year. Peaks and exposed ridgelines have high winds, which significantly increase environmental exposure.

I recommend the following apparel.

Pants: Long Lycra tights, such as Pearl Izumi Therma Fleece Tight, nylon shorts, or nylon pants

Tops: See base layer.

Base layers: Silk- to lightweight polyester top, such as Nike ACG Oregon Aero LS Top

Insulation: 50- to 100-weight (g/m^2) polyester or wool fleece, or equivalent long-sleeved top, such as Mountain Hardwear Transition Long Sleeve Zip T

Shell: Waterproof/breathable jacket and pants, such as Epic Parka and full-zip pants

Hat: Lightweight thermal hat and cap, such as SmartWool Headliner

Socks: CoolMax or wool crew socks, such as SmartWool Hiking Sock

Gloves: Warm synthetic, wool, or fleece gloves with waterproof overmittens, such as Mountain Hardwear Torsion Gloves

ARCTIC WINTER

Subzero temperatures, deep snow, ice, and strong winds combine to make extremely tough conditions in arctic or subarctic winters. The primary concerns in extreme cold are frostbite and hypothermia. The highest risk of exposure is to your extremities, especially your fingers, toes, ears, and face. When in a cold environment, your body shunts blood away from your extremities and toward your core to protect your heart and organs. To ameliorate this effect, you'll need exceptionally warm gloves, footwear, and headgear.

I recommend the following apparel.

Pants: 50-weight (g/m²) long pants, such as Pearl Izumi Allegro Pant

Tops: 50-weight (g/m²) long-sleeved thermal top, such as Marmot Pre Cip Jacket

Base layers: Medium-weight thermal long-sleeved shirt and tights, such as Nike Sphere LS Half Zip Top

Insulation: 100-weight (g/m²) polyester or wool fleece or equivalent long-sleeved top, such as Nike ACG Hybrid Jacket

Shell: Waterproof/breathable jacket and pants, such as GoLite Reach jacket and Reed pants

Hat: Fleece hat, such as Fairydown Balaclava 100M

Socks: Wool expedition-weight socks and waterproof/breathable socks, such as DeFeet Woolie Boolie socks with SealSkinz Mid Thermal Merino outer socks

Gloves: Heavy fleece or wool mittens with waterproof/breathable shell, such as Mountain Hardwear Absolute Zero Mitt

AQUATIC

When paddling on rivers, on lakes, or in the ocean, the spray from the water can easily cause hypothermia if you are not dressed properly. Through an effect known as evaporative cooling, prolonged exposure to moisture combined with wind caused many teams to suffer hypothermia in the 2002 Eco-Challenge in Fiji, despite the country's location in the tropical South Pacific.

At a minimum you should include a spray jacket for warm paddling conditions, as evaporative cooling can quickly drain your body's heat if the wind picks up and you are continually soaked in spray. You'll also need a protective layer to prevent chafing. If conditions are truly inclement, you may need to wear a dry suit along with expedition-weight fleece, rubber booties, pogies (paddling mittens), and a thermal hat.

I recommend the following apparel.

Pants: Neoprene paddling shorts or padded bike shorts, such as the NRS HydroSkin Short

Tops: Long- or short-sleeved Lycra rash guard, such as Lotus Designs Core Skin Shirt

Base layers: Polyester long-sleeved top, such as Patagonia Silkweight Crew

Insulation: 50- to 100-weight (g/m^2) polyester or wool fleece, or equivalent long-sleeved top, such as SmartWool Aero LS Crew

Shell: Paddling jacket or dry top, such as Stohlquist Gore-Tex Con-Tour paddling jacket

Hat: Wide-brim soft hat, such as Sunday Afternoons Adventure Hat

Socks: CoolMax mesh crew (for preventing abrasion during portages), such as DeFeet Aireator socks

Gloves: Neoprene or synthetic gloves or pogies (paddling mitts), such as SixSixOne Nasty gloves and Stohlquist Yellow Jackets pogies

BIKE WEAR

Cycling has some very specific apparel requirements, due mainly to the propensity for crotch chafing and wind. Bike-specific apparel is not designed for extreme conditions, so you may need to double up with layers of other types of apparel, depending on the environment.

I recommend the following apparel.

Pants: Padded bike shorts, long Lycra tights, such as Pearl Izumi Microsensor 3D shorts, and Pearl Izumi Therma Fleece leg warmers

Tops: Short-sleeved three-quarter-zip Lycra cycling jersey, such as Pearl Izumi Originals Jersey, and arm warmers such as Pearl Izumi Therma Fleece arm warmers

Base layers: Long-sleeved polyester half- to three-quarter-zip shirt, such as Nike ACG Dri-FIT Half Zip Top

Insulation: Depends on conditions

Shell: Waterproof/breathable jacket, water-resistant/windproof pants with knee-length side zips, such as Nike ACG Oregon Shell Pant and Jacket

Hat: Skullcap or thin beanie, such as Pearl Izumi Microsensor Headband

Socks: Depends on conditions, but the Pearl Izumi AmFIB Shoe Cover is a good choice when you need more warmth.

Gloves: Synthetic or leather bike gloves, such as Pearl Izumi Pittard Therma Fleece Glove

Footwear

Your shoes cushion and protect your feet, provide traction, insulate your feet against the cold, and protect your feet from abrasion, cuts, and puncture wounds. Poor footwear can make your race experience miserable, and may eventually force you to drop out.

The three most important considerations for choosing shoes are fit, function (for the intended environment), and weight. Quite a few manufactures promote shoes specifically designed for adventure racing, such as Nike ACG Air Zoom Steens, Salomon Flagstaff, Montrail Kinabalu, and Brooks Trespass.

My favorite all-round shoe for adventure racing is the Salomon Flagstaff, although several, more specialized pairs of footwear may be necessary, depending on the race. In general, one shoe can do it all, but if you have the luxury of access to more than one, it is definitely beneficial to have the specialized equipment. Below, you'll find guidance for buying some of the more specialized types of shoes on the market, arranged by shoe type.

Trekking. Trekking includes trail running, scree running, bush bashing, jungle trekking, boulder hopping, canyoneering, and coastaleering, among other types of perambulatory forward progress (or backward, in the likely event you have to backtrack at some point). Your trekking shoes should not be too flimsy around the flex point in the upper, as this is a point of impact when running off-trail. A modest amount of reinforcement in this area (adjacent to the second joint of the first and fifth toes) and around the toebox can prevent a good deal of pain. In addition, the shoe should not be too high off the ground (usually seen in highly cushioned running shoes with generous midsoles), since this causes lateral instability. Good brands include Nike ACG, Salomon, Montrail, and HiTec.

Canyoneering. This is a sport popular in Europe, and is sometimes called canyoning. Most of the your time canyoneering is spent in water, swimming, scrambling, or rappelling (abseiling). Consequently, you need a shoe with an outsole that grips well in the wet and drains extremely fast. It is also useful to have ankle protection, since you often can't see where you are placing your feet and will tend to jam your feet between rocks. High-top shoes are nice if you have weak ankles. Good brands include Nike ACG, Salomon, Teva, and FiveTen.

Coastaleering. Also called coasteering, this sport involves traversing a coastline (ocean, lake, river, or other body of water) and staying at or within a specified distance from the shore, generally 3 to 7 feet vertically or 33 feet horizontally. Coastaleering shoes need good traction when wet. They must be fast draining and have a reasonable midsole, since you may spend a considerable amount of time jumping around on rocks. Good brands include Nike ACG, Salomon, Teva, and FiveTen.

Rafting, canoeing, and kayaking. The most critical features of a boating shoe are traction (for portaging), drainage, and a low profile

THE BEAUTY OF SANDALS

Sandals take the prize for drainage speed and are cool and lightweight. On the downside, they provide minimal protection and allow debris to lodge between the straps or sole and your foot. I recommend you have a pair of sandals ready for sections of the race where you are unlikely to smash your feet into anything and where you need to air your feet out (which is always a good idea in long races if you have the chance). I have used sandals in the desert and during long sailing and canoe/kayak legs. The company that made the original sports sandal, Teva, is absolutely the sandal king. Another brand worth considering is Nike ACG.

(minimal midsole, outsole, and padding) so that you can fit them in the tight space inside a kayak. If you'll be doing a combination of hiking and boating, a fast-draining running shoe may work better than an official water shoe. Whether or not to opt for a running shoe over a water shoe depends on how much time you will spend on your feet versus how much time you will spend in the boat. If you are primarily sea kayaking, then a low-profile aqua sock may work fine. If you will spend a lot of time on a river in a canoe and make multiple portages and long approaches, you probably need a running shoe. (See "The Right Paddling Shoe for the Right Conditions.")

Cycling. Cycling shoes should be lightweight (of course) and fast draining (for the inevitable stream crossings) and have good traction so you can adequately carry your bike in those interminable hike-a-bike sections race directors like to include as an element of torture. The ideal cycling shoe for adventure racing should be completely rigid when you are riding, since you want to transfer all your effort to the bike pedals, but flexible and cushioned for hiking. Unfortunately, these two requirements are at odds, so you will end up with a compromise. The best shoes currently on the market are rigid from the heel to the cleat at the ball of your foot and flexible in the forefoot. Good brands include Nike ACG, Sidi, and Pearl Izumi.

Ropes courses and climbing. You probably will never need official climbing shoes in adventure races, but you can choose your hiking shoes to maximize their usefulness in ropes sections. You will probably have to scramble on and around rocks to get to the climb site, so your shoes need good grip, preferably in all conditions, including water. Many big races put their rappels and ascents in or around waterfalls, so wet traction can be a big help. Good brands include Nike ACG, FiveTen, Teva, Salomon, Montrail, and HiTec.

FOOTWEAR ACCESSORIES

In addition to your shoes, you'll also want a few items that will make your footwear more effective. The first are custom footbeds. Also called insoles, these help spread the load evenly over the surface of your feet and provide additional cushioning, which reduces pressure points, hot spots, blisters, and the resulting damage from all of the above. Several

THE RIGHT PADDLING SHOE FOR THE RIGHT CONDITIONS

Consult this chart to find the right paddling shoe for your specific race.

Paddle Sport	Conditions	Footwear
Flat water	Beaches, grassy banks, easy water access	Bare feet, aqua socks, water sandals
Flat water	Rocks, steep banks, difficult water access	Hard-soled water shoes, trail shoes
Ocean paddling	Sand beaches, large bodies of open water	Aqua socks or water sandals
Ocean paddling	Beaches, rocky shore-lines, or coral reef	Hard-soled water shoes
Moving water	Fast-moving water, no portaging	Neoprene booties, water sandals
Whitewater	Class II+, minor portages	Hard-soled booties, water shoes
Whitewater	Class III+, major portages, difficult terrain	Water shoes, fast-draining trail shoes
Mixed paddling	Open and moving water, portaging, hiking	Fast-draining trail shoes

brands of footbeds are available from running and outdoor stores. My favorites include Superfeet in the United States and Formthotics from New Zealand (www.formthotics.co.nz).

In addition to footbeds, gaiters (tube-shaped pieces of material that can attach the top of your boots to the outside of your pants) will help prevent sticks, stones, and other annoying pieces of detritus from finding their way into your shoes. "Shoe shit" is more than just a nuisance; it can rapidly inflict small cuts and blisters. Ankle-length minigaiters are ideal for most conditions, and knee-high mountaineering gaiters are more appropriate for really tough conditions.

Finally, when in snowy or icy conditions, you'll want some extra traction. I recommend Kahtoolah shoe-traction systems for those occasions.

Paddle Stuff

In addition to your actual canoe, kayak, or raft (which you learned about in chapter 5), you also have an endless array of accessories that you can purchase. Some are useful, some are not. Below, you'll find some guidance on the most essential items.

SEATING

Sitting on your behind for long periods of time, especially when you are wet and can't move your legs around, can be an excruciatingly painful experience. Adding a seat can make your paddling encounter much more enjoyable, and it has a couple of side benefits. If made and installed properly, an add-on seat will be much more comfortable than the factory-installed, "hard" seat. The additional height of the extra padding also increases your leverage, allowing you to take more powerful strokes, and provides a better view for navigating.

One of the easiest and cheapest add-on seats is a fisherman's "bean bag," available from most outdoor stores in the North America for about $5. A fisherman's seat is a small round pad filled with polystyrene beads. It conforms to the shape of your anatomy (and that of the boat, making it a universal fit for any craft). The beauty of a fisherman's seat is that it is extremely light and can be used as a travel cushion or pillow in the event you have the opportunity to take a nap.

If you don't have access to a fisherman's seat, you can cut closed-cell foam sheets from a sleeping pad. Cut your foam seat pad at least $\frac{1}{2}$ inch thick, preferably a full inch. You can add a degree of comfort by cutting holes out for your ischial tuberosities (sit bones). To do this, sit on your pad in a kayaking position on a level hard surface for a few minutes. Stand up and quickly trace around the depression your buttocks made in the pad. You should end up with two circles 1 to 2 inches in diameter and 3 to 4 inches apart, depending on your physiology. Using a very sharp knife or razor blade, cut around your tracings so that each hole tapers gently in a cone shape to a concentrically smaller hole in the bottom of the pad. You will probably need to play around with the shape of the holes after using the pad for training. Just note where you have pressure points during a paddle, and shave off material as necessary.

The last option for seating is to buy a seat pad from a paddling or outdoor supplier. Off-the-shelf seat pads are usually closed-cell foam or inflatable and will be presized to suit most boats. Therm-a-rest makes quite a good one.

SPRAY SKIRTS

You'll need a spray skirt (also called a spray deck) to keep water from splashing into and swamping your kayak. You wear the top of the skirt (or deck) around your waist and attach the ends of the skirt to the

HOW *NOT* TO . . .
Sit in a Kayak

I first experienced pain while seated in a kayak during a 250-mile race down the Murray River in 1988. This was the first time I had subjected myself to such a long time sitting (almost 30 hours in an Olympic class K1 solo kayak). In the later stage of the race, I was in so much discomfort that I had to lie back on my deck and stretch my legs every 30 minutes. I finally resorted to cutting holes in my seat to try to relieve the pressure. Unfortunately, the pain was not just in my head. My legs and feet felt numb for almost a year after the race. I had rubbed the protective myelin sheath off the nerves to my legs as I twisted back and forth in my seat. These days I take great care to prepare and test my seating prior to a long kayak paddle and make sure I have a sheet of extra foam padding whenever I can't prefit my seat.

mouth of the kayak, completely covering up and sealing off the entrance to the boat.

You have two basic options from which to choose, one designed for whitewater and one for sea-kayak cockpits. Whitewater cockpits are slightly smaller than sea-kayak cockpits, and their spray skirts are usually tougher and tighter fitting to withstand more severe conditions and abuse. Sea-kayak spray skirts are made from lighter material and may have pockets, a waterproof zipper, and suspenders.

High-end paddling jackets and dry jackets are made with a "channel" that fits the body of a spray skirt and provides additional sealing against the elements. When selecting a sea-kayak spray skirt, look for sealed seams, strong elastic where it fits around the cockpit, and close-fitting material. Skirts that sag can funnel water into the hull, especially if the waist seam is not completely sealed. Additional useful features include mesh pockets, a waterproof entry zipper, suspenders, and an adjustable waist for a snug fit. A good example is the Wildwasser Pocket sea-kayak skirt (www.wildnet.com).

Spray skirts designed for whitewater should have very tight seals around the cockpit and your torso, since they have to withstand significant hydraulic forces when the kayak punches through waves. The best whitewater skirts include adjustable sealing elastic, abrasion-resistant material around the cockpit coaming (such as Kevlar fibers) and a high torso tube.

OTHER COOL STUFF

Other useful paddling accessories include:

- Suunto Orca deck compass (works globally and in heavy sea conditions)

- Wildwasser Overnighters dry bags (fit in tight places like sea-kayak bow and stern hatches)

- Deck Pilot for readily accessible food, equipment, and apparel storage

- Kayak cart for portaging

• 15-inch bilge pump

• Kite-surfing system—Wildwasser or Spirit (www.spiritsails.com) sailing kit for hands-free kayak sailing across or with the wind

Packs and Pieces

The largest packs required for multiday races that have an extensive gear list should not exceed 2,500 cubic inches in volume (preferably less). If you need a pack bigger than this, then you need to rethink your food, equipment, and apparel selections. A few important features to look for in an adventure-racing pack include:

• Comfortable harness system

• Water-resistant body material, with drain holes in the bottom panel

• Oversize buckles, closures, and pull tabs (for cold, gloved, or tired fingers)

• Wide waist belt with pockets on either side that are big enough to carry four energy bars each

• Lid pocket(s) that are easily accessible by another person, preferably two in different sizes, to keep items separate

• Folded and sewn hang loop for clipping on a carabiner (the folded hang loop prevents the carabiner gate from catching on the webbing)

• Easily adjustable sternum, shoulder, and waist straps

• Large external mesh pockets that expand when the pack is full. There should be at least two, preferably four (top, back, and sides). The back mesh pocket should be big enough to hold a bicycle or climbing helmet.

• Ice axe loop and pole loops (these should be secure enough to hold kayak or canoe paddles, hiking poles, or a snow shovel and/or ice axe)

• Integral hydration bladder holder(s) with oversize tube-access ports to prevent the bite valve from catching upon insertion or removal

• Water-bottle holders that are out of the way of your elbows but can be easily accessed without removing your pack (this can be in the side mesh pockets or specially made holders on the waist belt or pack body)

• Foolproof top closure for fumbling fingers

Examples of great packs include the Salomon Raid Race 300, Dana Designs Racer X, CamelBak Rally, Ultimate Directions Speed Demon, and GoLite Team Pack.

Bike Bits

Apart from the standard set of tools and spare parts for a bike, there are a few add-ons that can make life easier and more comfortable as you tenderize your rump on the trail.

Handlebar-mounted map holder. This is an essential if you want to know where you are going without taking your hands off your handlebars. Look for a model that rotates 360 degrees and that is large enough to hold a standard topographic map folded into four or six, about 12 × 8 inches. I recommend Nordenmark Bike Orienteering Map Holder, available in the United States from GO Orienteering (http://my.core.com/~gdt/Catalog.htm). To ensure that your maps stay dry, put them in an Aloksak waterproof bag before securing them onto the map holder.

Rear-mounted bike rack. Look for one that clamps around the seat post so you can use it with a full-suspension bike. Make sure the clamp is very solid so that the rack doesn't loosen or swing around behind you on technical trails. My pick: the Ascent Cross Rack, which can carry 25 pounds, available from most bike stores.

Seat post luggage rack. Look for a sturdy model that will allow you to take up to 20 pounds of weight off your back without the danger of breaking your rear wheel. Good brands include Topeka Beam Rack and Delta Post Haste Rack, both of which are available from Bike Nashbar (www.nashbar.com).

I use this to carry spare parts and tools. Use a large zip tie or cable tie to secure the bag in case its built-in straps fail, a fairly common occurrence in long races. My pick: Nashbar Handlebar Bag, available from Bike Nashbar.

Tow system. You'll find many types of tow systems, from a simple bungee (elastic) cord to complex telescoping systems. The most robust and simplest was developed by my teammate Mike Kloser. It's a car-radio aerial that threads onto a bolt fixed to the seat rail with a metal hose clamp. The aerial is lightweight and flexible and can be stowed along the top tube of the bike for transportation. The flexible extension behind the bike will prevent the tow cord from tangling in the rear wheel of the tow bike. Tie a short section of $\frac{1}{16}$- to $\frac{1}{8}$-inch-diameter cord or $\frac{1}{8}$- to $\frac{1}{6}$-inch-diameter bungee loop to the end of the aerial for the towee to hold on to.

Light systems. Good lighting is the single most important addition to a bike for fast and safe riding at night. It is well worth carrying the extra weight of batteries and spare lights for the speed you gain, as anyone who has suffered failed lights can tell you. There are many excellent brands of lights on the market, none of which is cheap, but they are significantly less expensive than a visit to the emergency room after crashing into that hidden rock/root/branch/dog you didn't see with your dim incandescent bulb. For fast riding in technical terrain, you need a minimum of 10 watts of halogen power—although I prefer 15 to 20 watts—focused in a spotlight (not a floodlight).

I prefer to carry the light on my helmet, and the battery on my back, so I can dismount without getting tangled in the cord. You can always face your head in the direction you want to ride, whereas your bike cannot, so a bar-mounted light will not illuminate the desired piece of ground. I also mount a small light powered by four AA batteries on my bars as a backup, and this works in a pinch if my main light fails. Rear lights are generally required for racing at night, and the best one I have found is the fully waterproof Guardian Light, available from Wildwasser. It's completely waterproof and very lightweight.

Helmet. My helmet is number one on my list of things to take riding, as I rate brain damage high on my list of things to avoid. If you have a cheap head, buy a cheap helmet; otherwise, pony up and buy the best available. Good helmets should be a perfect fit and provide excellent ventilation, unrestricted visibility, and a measure of sun protection. Of the more than two dozen helmets I have owned, my favorite by far is the Giro Pneumo, modeled after the one Lance Armstrong wears.

CO_2 inflators. The fastest way to inflate a flat tire is to use a CO_2 canister and valve adapter, an extremely handy aid for fast repairs. *Warning:* It is illegal to carry gas canisters onto airplanes, so ship them by land or source a supplier if you travel to a race.

Seat pad. If you are like me and have a bony behind, a seat pad can be a real asset over the long haul. The pad provides a little extra cush between the seat and your tush. You can also experiment with one of the ergonomic cutaway saddles. Your personal anatomy will determine which saddle works best for you. Good options include Nashbar Extra Gel Saddle Cover, Trico Sports Painkiller Saddle Cover, and QR Mr. Flitie Saddle Pad.

Bike computer. Find a model that is water-resistant and records speed and distance at a minimum. This will allow you to accurately locate your position from your map. Choose a cycle computer with big buttons and a big display so you can operate it with gloves on and at night. Most computers are not waterproof, but you can make them virtually hermetic by running a bead of silicone sealant around the joint of the case and where the wires enter the unit. You also want a unit that is intuitive for you to operate; otherwise, you will find yourself randomly stabbing at the buttons as you try to recall or reset the distance.

Mud guards. These help keep mud and grit out of moving parts and reduce spray, which can get in your eyes and mouth. Good brands include Headland Mudslide Front Mudguard and SKS X-3 X-Tra-Dry Fender, both available from Performance Bikes.

Rear stay chain-slap protector. This prevents damage to your rear right hand from chain impact during rough descents. These are available commercially but can be quickly and easily made from an old inner tube and three to four zip ties. Cut a length of inner tube and slit it lengthwise so it fits neatly over the stay. Secure with zip (cable) ties at each end and one or two places in between.

Bar ends. These allow you to ride in an extended position, and provide additional hand placements and more leverage for climbing. Good brands include Ascent ATB Bar Ends, Nashbar Mountain Bar Ends, Single Track Solutions Revolutions Bar Ends, and Performance Forte Carbon Stix Bar Ends, available from Bike Nashbar or Performance Bikes.

Bottle cages. Your cage should hold a full, large-size bike bottle through the most demanding terrain. Poorly designed cages will release a full bottle over rough ground and will end up breaking. If you are competing in a very arid environment, you may have to carry a hydration bladder in your pack. Otherwise, bike bottles are the most convenient way to stay hydrated. Good bottle cage brands include Pedros Milk Cage and Performance Quickdraw Carbon Fiber Bottle Cage.

Navigation Materials

Your map, compass, and altimeter are the standard required equipment for most races involving navigation. I always lose my compass, generally in the water, so I use a floating compass with a bright color, such as the Suunto MCB Amphibian. You should always keep your maps dry, or at least treat them to make them water-resistant. There is nothing more frustrating than pulling your map from the map case to find that the ink has run and the paper resembles cold Scottish oatmeal.

ILLUMINATION

Good lighting can greatly improve your speed at night. This allows you to see rapids on a river or distant features while navigating. Lights need to be water-resistant (or waterproof if you're in a very wet environment), have a high illumination (closely related to wattage or candlepower), and adequate endurance to last the night. LED technology has made great strides in prolonging the battery life of lights, but nothing comes close to halogen bulbs for truly bright lighting.

There are four basic choices in portable lighting for adventure races: traditional incandescent globes, high-power halogen, LED, and combination lights. The best solution currently available is a combination of LED and halogen technologies. The Petzl Myo 5 LED allows you to select an ultrabright halogen beam or three levels of LED brightness, a system that conserves valuable battery power.

Another consideration in light choice is the speed at which you travel. The faster you go, the brighter your light needs to be so you have time to react to the obstacles in your path. Biking at night creates the most demanding conditions, so you will want to choose at least a 12-watt halogen, preferably with options to select one or two lower power settings (JET Lites I³ is a good example of this system). Good options include Petzl Myo 5 LED (three brightness levels, halogen option, water-resistant, beam focus adjustment), Princeton Tec (www.prince tontec.com) Matrix (1,000-feet waterproof, three LEDs), Black Diamond (www.bdel.com) Ion (microlight, two-LED backup), and JET Lites (www.jetlites.com) Phantom "i" 8/10/12 W Halogen (water-resistant, three power options, up to 7 hours' burn time).

As for batteries, your best option is lithium dry-cell batteries, as they are about half the weight and have twice the burn time of standard alkaline batteries. They also cost about twice as much as alkaline batteries, but this makes them good value overall. Most high-quality bike lights use either nickel cadmium (NiCad) or NiMH (nickel metal hydride) rechargeable cells. The most common bike battery option is NiCad, which is a moderately priced, high-performance solution. NiMH has better storage capacity and performance than NiCad, but carries a commensurately high price tag. With batteries, you get what you pay for. The cheaper they are, the poorer their performance.

PART FOUR

Ian Adamson helps John
Jacoby with his climbing
gear during the 2000
Southern Traverse in
New Zealand.

"Coming together is a beginning, staying together is progress, and working together is success."

—Henry Ford

---

14 CAN'T WE ALL GET ALONG?

EVERYTHING YOU NEED TO KNOW ABOUT TEAMWORK AND COMMUNICATION

The biggest single thing that stops teams from finishing a race is not injuries, illness, equipment failure, hypothermia, worn-out feet, or fatigue. It's their inability to work together. Just about any problem a team encounters during a race can be surmounted, provided that the team is cohesive, focused, organized, motivated, and well-led.

Over the course of a week in a major adventure race, you will encounter a year's worth of life's experiences. The highs are higher, the lows are lower, and the mental, physical, emotional, cultural, and spiritual aspects of your life become richer and more poignant. As a consequence, small problems can become big problems, communication differences can become communication difficulties, and differing ideals can transmute into disturbing ideas. The elevated mental, physical, and emotional stresses that are part and parcel of adventure racing are exactly the things that make communication and teamwork so difficult.

Ian's Adventure-Racing Wisdom

Ask not what your team can do for you, but what you can do for your team.

Overcoming conflict and developing teamwork starts at the very beginning, the day your team forms.

Picking Good Teammates

With one exception, I have been racing with the same group of athletes for 10 years. My original teammates were from Australia and New Zealand. We have added new people to our squad, loosely named Eco-Internet since 1995, as needed. Various members have retired over time, but as the years have rolled on, we have gathered together a strong squad of like-minded and evenly matched individuals. The resulting team has had unparalleled success, based on a strong core group of athletes and a willingness for everyone to work together. The original core of Eco-Internet included Robert Nagle, John Howard, and me, with a dozen other athletes flowing into and out of the team, depending on circumstances. All these people remain great friends and on good terms, and we all race with and against each other quite happily.

Selecting teammates can be a difficult task. It takes time to get to know people and to figure out if they will interact well under the pressure. It's a lot like hiring someone for a job. You look at his or her résumé, interview him or her, and then see how he or she performs. As with job résumés, 80 percent of people embellish their accomplishments, so conduct a thorough check of race results and talk with other people who might know the potential teammate.

Just as you would when hiring someone to join a corporate team, you want to find individuals who are evenly matched physically, mentally, and emotionally. Obviously, a world-champion triathlete is unlikely to be a good fit with your team if everyone else is a midpack 10-K runner. Likewise, a first-time adventure athlete with no other endurance-race experience will not be a good fit if the rest of the team has been racing for several years.

Everyone must also have similar goals. Matching expectations is just as important as matching athletic ability and skills. It is frustrating and pointless if one person wants to win the race, whereas everyone else only wants to make the top 10 or merely finish.

Most important, you want people who will jell as a team. It is relatively easy to figure out if you like someone, but it is virtually impossible to foresee how he or she will perform under race conditions until you actually race together. Personalities can transform drastically under the pressure of a race, with sleep deprivation and physical, mental, and emotional stress thrown in. I have seen otherwise charming, levelheaded individuals transform into nasty, venom-spitting, selfish tyrants out on a racecourse. I've also seen them turn the charm and smiles back on at each checkpoint and transition area, or whenever the media were around. It is also quite possible for a formerly solid teammate to change over time as he or she gets comfortable with the team and starts to let ego and selfishness get in the way.

The most dangerous individuals are the ones who are charming and charismatic and can mask their weaknesses with personality and bravado. It may not be possible to determine if someone has these characteristics without prolonged evaluation, over months or even years of racing. Always check out the track record of potential teammates, and quiz people who have raced with them. If he or she hasn't raced consistently on the same teams, or his or her teammates change often, beware! It pays to be somewhat critical in your evaluation, as the ramifications of embedding a toxic individual in your team can be destructive.

To figure out how potential teammates might perform in an important race, engineer team training situations that are mentally, physically, and emotionally demanding. For example, devote a weekend to continuous training where sleep deprivation, long distances, and navigational challenges are combined. Start late on a Friday night and continue into Sunday morning, navigating through a course of running, biking, and paddling. Ideally, each team member should have the chance to take a leadership role in each of the disciplines, both at night and during the day. In addition to testing your team skills and interpersonal interactions, this gives you an opportunity to try out equipment, apparel, and food options.

Fixing Problem Teammates

What do you do when a teammate goes bad? Unfortunately, certain individuals have deeply ingrained behavioral characteristics that will be incompatible with the team or the team's expectations. People who are unfit, ill-prepared, unhealthy, selfish, self-centered, egotistical, lazy, discourteous, rude, or unwilling to contribute to the team, or who like to perform for the media, make poor teammates. If any of these traits surface, it is wise to take swift action to address them with the individual. Do so in a suitable environment as a complete team. This means somewhere you can talk face-to-face as a group, in an honest, open fashion. On the racecourse, through e-mail, and on the phone are poor forums for tackling such a thorny issue because feelings and intent can easily be misconstrued.

Confronting problem teammates is difficult and requires a careful, well-thought-out approach. Ask a neutral non-teammate to mediate, since the very characteristics that make a poor teammate will also make it difficult or impossible for him or her to own up to the problem.

Conflict Aversion

Communication is one of the foundations of good teamwork. This is primarily verbal (talking, not yelling!) between teammates, but it can also be written, visual, gestured, or physical. The primary rules for effective communication within a team are honesty, openness, and selflessness. Teammates need to be able to frankly discuss all issues, ideas, feelings, and problems and need to be able to do so unconstrained by fear of reprisal or an emotional response. To create open and honest communications, team members must agree to curtail any ill feelings or emotional reactions. In the end, each teammate should have the same goals and expectations, so the *only* motivation in any communication should be the team's goals. Team members should leave any personal agendas or grievances at the starting line, and put away any issues that arise during the race, until after the finish.

The stress and pressure of a race, fatigue, frayed nerves, and lack of sleep put people in a vulnerable emotional and mental state, so it is very easy to let things get out of hand. If you feel like you want to lash out or react to someone in a negative way, take a few deep breaths before saying anything and remind yourself that people are generally not motivated by malicious thoughts. Reacting to a perceived threat or poorly chosen words can easily result in an escalating dialogue that can spiral out of control, essentially a conflict situation. Conflict like this creates ill will and can destroy your team, your race, and possibly friendships.

If you sense a conflict escalating, you need to take immediate action to head it off. Sometimes a teammate becomes unmanageable, but regardless of his or her actions, no one else should react. Create an environment that absorbs the barbs and anger and deflects accusations and attacks in a positive way. I know it can be hard not to defend yourself when a teammate yells, "It's your fault. You led us into this mess, so you need to get us out!" Rather than react with "Well, if you weren't always harassing me and pushing so hard, we wouldn't be here," say something like "I know. I apologize. I am really doing the best I can. Perhaps you can help me with the navigation so we can get back on track as fast as possible."

The energy expended in conflict and argument wastes the time and precious reserves the team needs for rapid forward progress. Unsuccessful teams inevitably spend more time arguing than moving, and end up missing time cutoffs. If you find you are the one leveling the accusations, then you need to immediately check yourself and apologize. Swallow your pride and relinquish your ego, for the good of the team.

You can avoid escalating conflict by using a code word to warn each other of the approaching situation. Code words are useful because you don't want to let other teams, the race organization, or the media know you are not a perfect, harmonious group. Decide on the word before the start of the race and agree to use it when the team is in danger of conflict. Use words that are innocuous and preferably misleading to anyone who happens to hear what is going on. Our team has used words such as "Kiwi!" which sounds like we are urgently alerting the team to one of the rival teams (which in a way we are) and "Food fight!" which breaks the tension with some oblique humor.

You *must* resolve conflict quickly to prevent permanent damage to the morale and integrity of the team. If your team is in conflict and you are one of the participants, then purposefully and obviously disengage yourself from the situation. With any luck this will dissipate the argument. If this doesn't work, you need to take more direct action by breaking into

BEING KIND TO THE LOCALS

If you race in foreign countries, do yourself a huge favor and learn the local language and some of the local customs. Knowing how to say hello, thank you, and goodbye, as well as how to ask for basic essentials such as food, water, the bathroom, and directions, can save you a significant amount of time on the racecourse. Read travelers' guidebooks to bone up on the intricacies of local customs, what is likely to insult or compliment people, and how to avoid a faux pas that could land you in jail.

the dialogue with an assertive but level statement that describes what is happening. Establish a protocol or system to resolve conflict before you start the race.

Examples of effective conflict-breaking statements include:

• "GUYS! Stop! We need to focus on what is important."

• "STOP! We have a race to run/finish/win."

• "LISTEN UP! This is important. Unless we focus, we aren't going to get anywhere."

Deliver the message evenhandedly and with authority. You are essentially making yourself the leader and taking the opportunity to guide the team in a positive direction.

Leadership

Good teams are well-managed, but great teams are well-led. In any challenging or problematic situation, a first-class leader will be able to guide the team in the right direction. Good leaders have the poise, objectivity, and sensitivity to maneuver through the minefield of human emotions, thoughts, and feelings that affect a team's dynamics.

A group of extremely fit and talented athletes is useless unless the teammates work together, and this doesn't happen spontaneously. It takes leadership. One of the all-time great leaders in adventure racing was New Zealand's John Howard. John was a very accomplished athlete, but the quality that made him such a successful individual was his ability to lead. He could diffuse stress, head off conflict, motivate, and make good decisions on any team and at any time. As a result he won every major international adventure race, including three Eco-Challenges, three Raid Gauloises, two ESPN X-Games, the Southern Traverse, and the Elf Authentic Adventure.

Developing Synergy

Synergy happens when the power of the group exceeds the sum of its parts. An adventure-racing team that develops synergy moves faster and makes better decisions than the individual athletes could alone. Many people believe that a team is only as fast as its slowest member, but this is only true of bad teams. A good team that develops synergy should move considerably faster than the slowest teammate.

A basic example of synergy is a cycling pace line. The limiting force on any person riding a bike on flat ground is wind resistance. If four people ride so that a few bike lengths or more separate them, each of them has to overcome his or her own wind resistance. But if the team rides close together, one behind the other, only the front person has to overcome the wind resistance, and the three remaining riders can rest. By rotating the lead so that each person breaks the wind for a short time, the team can maintain a much higher speed than each rider could alone.

A more powerful form of synergy takes place when team members synchronize their motivation, mental energy, and emotional states. Obtaining this level of performance is something that can't be practiced, but it can be attained if every individual wants it badly enough. For this type of synergy to develop, every team member must:

• Agree to and support the team's goals

• Be highly motivated to perform

• Be physically and emotionally prepared for the challenge

• Be willing to relinquish ego

• Put the team ahead of himself or herself

• Be able to put aside personal differences and suppress emotional outbursts

TIPS FROM THE TOP

Below, you will find four towing tips from Michael Tobin, one of the strongest individual athletes in adventure racing and winner of the Eco-Challenge, Primal Quest, Balance Bar 24-Hour series, and X-Terra Triathlon world championships.

1. When towing a teammate on foot, use a line that is at least partially elastic to prevent jerking and potential friction between the tower and towee. Clip a mini carabiner to the lower back of the tower's pack and to the waist belt of the towee's pack. Facing a downhill, the towee can unclip from the waist belt and hand the line forward or stuff it into an outside pocket of the tower.

2. When towing a teammate on a bike, use a towline with significant stretch to absorb speed differences between the two (or more) bikes as they roll over varying terrain. Attach the line somewhere beyond the bicycle's rear wheel to prevent it from tangling in the rear wheel. I've seen lines extended rearward with fishing poles, car antennas, or plastic tubing secured to the seat rail or seat post. The towee should be able to grasp the line with both hands on the handlebars, using his or her fingers or a hook to secure it. When extended, the towline should allow 2 to 3 feet between the wheels of the two bikes.

3. When towing by boat, use a dynamic line or bungee, allowing a foot or two between the boats if you are in smooth water. Choppy conditions require greater length and more stretch to accommodate the surge as each boat moves with the waves. Ideally the front boat should tow from a point as close to the middle of the hull as possible to minimize being steered by the back boat. If the towline is attached to the stern of the front boat, any sideways movement by the back boat will pull it around, making steering extremely difficult.

4. Working efficiently with a towline requires good communication. Let the tower know when you're hooked in with a simple "I'm on." Also, let him or her know when you've unhooked. Since the towee can't see forward well, let him or her know of obstacles. After you jump over a log, don't take off running and expect the towee to still be on his or her feet. Check in with your partner occasionally; ask him or her, "How are you doing?" and "How's this pace?"

Michael Tobin

- Focus all his or her energy on moving forward

- See problems as challenges waiting to be solved

- See mistakes as an opportunity to learn, not to blame

- Want to develop synergy

Teamwork

Optimal teamwork does not always result in synergy, but it will give a team the ability to do some extraordinary things. The basic requirements for optimal teamwork are similar to those that allow the development of synergy. A great team working with flawless teamwork can quite easily win a race and, if it is lucky, can also develop synergy.

Soon-to-be winning team Eco-Internet transitions under the watchful eye of race director Mark Burnett during the 1996 Eco-Challenge in British Columbia.

"One who fears limits his activities. Failure is only the opportunity to more intelligently begin again."

—Henry Ford

---

15 HOW AND WHY THE BEST TEAMS WIN

LEARN THE TRICKS AND TECHNIQUES OF THE CHAMPIONS

Great teams and great adventure athletes seem to share a set of common traits that help them excel time and time again. For example, of the thousands of athletes who competed in Eco-Challenge between 1995 and 2002, 27 athletes have won the race, eight of them winning at least twice and four winning three times (see "The Winners' Circle" on page 220). The top athletes all are doing something right. They seem to possess a winning ingredient that others just haven't mastered.

Some teams perform well consistently, but never win. The French team Spie is a good example, having placed third, second, fifth, second, third, and sixth. The American team SCAR has consistently placed around 10th. This stratification in performance continues down

ECO-CHALLENGE TOP TEAMS

Since 1995 the same teams have tended to place in the top few places at the Eco-Challenge adventure race.

Year/Location	1st Place	2nd Place	3rd Place
1995, Utah	Eco-Internet (N.Z./U.S.),* Hewlett-Packard (France)	Benincasa/Nike/ACG (U.S.)	(tie) Southern Traverse (N.Z.), Swiss Army Brands (France/G.B.), Gold's Gym (France/U.S.)
1995, New England	Thredbo (Aus.)	TwinTeam (U.S.)	Eco-Internet (U.S./N.Z.)
1996, British Columbia	Eco-Internet/Reebok (N.Z./U.S.)	(tie) Hi-Tec Adventure (U.S.), Hewlett-Packard (France)	
1997, Australia	Eco-Internet (N.Z./U.S.)	Pure Energy (Aus.)	Canterbury (N.Z.)
1998, Morocco	Vail (U.S.)	Aussie (Aus.)	Cepos (Spain)
1999, Argentina	Greenpeace** (N.Z.)	Sierra Nevada (Spain)	Condor (Arg.)
2000, Sabah	Salomon/Eco-Internet (U.S.)	Spie (France)	AussieSpirit.com (Aus.)
2001, New Zealand	Salomon/Eco-Internet (U.S.)	PureNZ.com (N.Z.)	Spie (France)
2002, Fiji	Seagate.com (N.Z.)	GoLite/Balance Bar** (U.S.)	Air Pacific (Aus.)

*First across the line, unranked

**Team members of Eco-Internet

(Note: In 1998 Eco-Challenge stipulated each team must represent only one country, and all team members must meet strict nationality rules. This rule effectively broke up international teams like Eco-Internet, which chose to race the Raid Gauloises in 1998 rather than Eco-Challenge. In 1999 the core Eco-Internet team members raced under the New Zealand flag as Greenpeace.)

through the rankings, so that you see teams and athletes consistently performing at the same level year after year (see "Eco-Challenge Top Teams.")

What is it that makes a great team? Great athletes and great teams possess a strong combination of fitness, attitude, skills, and knowledge.

Of Brains and Brawn

In adventure racing, some unenlightened male athletes complain of having to "carry" the required female teammate. This is clearly not the case for the best teams. It's true that men generally are stronger and faster than women. Yet in adventure racing, such physiological differences play only a small role in the outcome of the race. Other factors, such as navigation skills and teamwork, often make the difference between first, second, third, and even last place. Women and men excel equally at such skills. Adventure racing places a stronger emphasis on communication skills, decision making, and team interaction than do solo sports, creating a much more level playing field for men and women.

A good illustration of the reduced differences can be seen from the results of the 1999 Eco-Challenge Argentina. Race rules required teams to be made up of both men and women. In any sport other than adventure racing, this makes complete sense, since virtually every athletic endeavor favors male physiology. Consequently, every team in the '99 race but one had three men and one woman. The exception was Team Atlas Snowshoes/Rubicon, which was made up of three women and one man—me. (See "The Battle of the Sexes," page 222, for the results of that race.) Nicknamed "the Super Chicks," our team was made up of some of the best American women in the sport, including Cathy Sassin and Rebecca Rusch.

The top 10 teams from the previous year's race were all represented, so we had our work cut out for us. The 1999 race was held in the lakes region of Patagonia, in central Argentina, renowned for its spectacular mountains and ferocious weather. Our maps revealed a 250-mile course through some seriously challenging terrain.

One person from each team was randomly selected by the race organization to paddle the team's two tandem sea kayaks to a start line

THE WINNERS' CIRCLE

Not surprisingly, the same athletes have tended to make up the winners' circle since 1996, as can be seen in this table.

Eco-Challenge Multiple Winners (Placings)

Multiple Winners	Country	1995 (UTAH)	1995 (N.E.)	1996	1997	1998	1999	2000	2001	2002	Points*
Andrea Murray	N.Z.	DNC	DNC	DNC	1st	DNC	1st	DNF	DNC	DNC	40
Sara Ballantyne	U.S.	DNC	DNC	DNF	19th	1st	DNC	DNC	1st	DNC	42
Robert Nagle	U.S.	(1)	3rd	1st	1st	DNC	DNC	DNC	DNC	DNC	58
Neil Jones	N.Z.	DNC	DNC	DNF	7th	DNC	1st	DNF	2nd	1st	73
Keith Murray	N.Z.	DNC	3rd	1st	1st	DNC	1st	DNF	DNC	DNC	78
John Howard	N.Z.	(1)	3rd	1st	1st	DNC	1st	DNF	DNC	DNC	78
Mike Kloser	U.S.	DNC	DNC	DNC	19th	1st	6th	1st	1st	2nd	96
Ian Adamson	U.S.	(1)	3rd	1st	2nd	DNC	4th	1st	1st	2nd	133

DNC—Did not compete, DNF—Did not finish, (1)—First across the line, unranked
*1st place = 20 points, 2nd place = 19 points, down to 20th place = 1 point

placed 200 yards from the shore of Lago Nuhuel Huapi. The remaining three people were split up and assembled along the edge of the lake. At the gun, those on shore swam to the boats to make a "wet entry" and head into the wild.

Eleven hours later we finished the kayak leg in fourth place, behind the world-class paddling teams of Australia and New Zealand. Only 30 minutes separated the six top teams, setting a pattern that remained for the rest of the race. For the next 4 days we swapped off the lead as teams Greenpeace, Halti, Sierra Nevada, and Condor followed closely.

The defining phase of the race occurred on day 3. A huge storm hit the course with 60-mile-per-hour gusts and blinding snow. We were trailing the leaders, team Greenpeace, by only a couple of hours. We both were caught in the blizzard as we paddled our inflatable kayaks through the whitewater of the Rio Manso. Teams immediately behind us were fortunate to find warm shelter and food in the transition area, but we suffered a sleepless night after having been blown backward up the river and freezing in the sparse shelter of a small rock.

During the final push up the 12,000-foot glaciers of Mount Tronador, the fresher teams, who had rested during the storm, quickly caught up and then passed us as we caught up on much-needed sleep. As little as an hour separated the six top teams as we summited Tronador. By the finish a day later, it was Greenpeace on the winners' podium, with Sierra Nevada 50 minutes later, local team Condor another hour back, and our "las Chicas" ("the goddesses") team holding on to fourth.

Without local knowledge and with the apparent "disadvantage" of having three women on our team, we still managed to beat two of the three previous winning Eco-Challenge teams, and proved beyond a doubt that women are not simply mandatory equipment in adventure racing.

Physical Ability

A surprisingly large proportion of competitors in long races simply don't have the fitness and skills needed to cope with the conditions. I call it the "nonswimmer in a triathlon syndrome." No one in their right mind would attempt a triathlon if he or she couldn't swim, and yet many people start long adventure races with little or no experience or training in climbing, whitewater kayaking, or wilderness navigation. U.S. team Outrageous Adventures made waves in the 2000 Eco-Challenge by swimming for 7 hours out to sea, when the team should have swum for 10 minutes to an obvious island. Japanese team East Wind was found on the wrong mountain range in the 1995 ESPN X-Games after having gone missing for 3 days in a section that should have taken no more than 12 hours. Mistakes such as these seem impossibly stupid to the casual observer, but are surprisingly easy to make if you lack navigation skills.

Fortunately, race organizers do a very good job of passing on information regarding the difficulty of the terrain and the skill level

THE BATTLE OF THE SEXES

Below, you'll find the results from the 1999 Eco-Challenge race in Argentina, when I competed with three women on team Atlas Showshoes/Rubicon.

Place	Team	Time (days:hours:minutes)	% behind 1st place
1	Greenpeace	5:00:33	0.00
2	Sierra Nevada	5:01:23	0.70
3	Condor	5:02:33	2.12
4	Atlas Snowshoes/ Rubicon	5:06:00	4.52

According to male and female world records for 500-mile and 1,000-K runs (also about 5 days), one would expect Atlas Snowshoes/Rubicon to be more than 20 percent behind Greenpeace. Yet the team was only just under 5 percent behind. The only reasonable explanation is that pure athleticism and strength are not the primary indicators of performance.

required for participants to stay safe. Unfortunately, many athletes seriously overestimate their own ability and end up in all sorts of trouble. To counteract this, race organizers often even require mandatory gear checks and ability testing.

One huge red flag is new gear. Really ignorant competitors arrive at the gear check with their equipment still in a new, unopened box. Having nice, shiny carabiners and a descender with the paint still intact is an immediate warning to the climbing staff that the owner may not know how to use it. In general, staff will take suspect people aside and give them a quick and dirty lesson on how not to die while on the ropes. Apart from the safety aspect of being competent in all the skills necessary for a race, familiarity will make you much faster.

When a race has open-ocean kayaking, you must practice by paddling on open ocean, and not on a river or your local reservoir. Likewise, you can't expect to learn self-arrest for mountaineering in Florida or white-water rafting in Kansas. I can't stress enough that anyone attempting a new skill should do so well in advance of the race.

Attitude

The old adage that winning teams have a winning attitude holds true for adventure racing as it does for most things in life. Mike Kloser is one of the most decorated endurance athletes in the world, with three Eco-Challenge wins, a world champion title in mountain biking, and numerous records and first places in winter multisport and triathlons. Now in his mid-forties, Mike is still winning at an international level, as he has for the past 20 years. The thing that defines Mike is his attitude. He sees nothing as an obstacle to winning a race, and he even has a phrase for coming second that helps him stay fired up: "Second place is the first loser."

It's not that Mike is unethical. In fact, he is one of the most sports-manlike athletes in adventure racing. The thing is, he believes he can win every race, and does everything in his power to do so. He trains and or-ganizes everything with the win in mind. In his view there is a solution to every problem and an answer to every challenge. This is his winning attitude, something that keeps him and his teammates winning.

Mike best displayed this winning attitude during the 2000 Salomon X-Adventure World Cup race in Utah. We had built a substantial lead on the first day and had become distracted when we chanced on the actor Don Johnson (of *Miami Vice* fame) having a barbecue on his ranch. Never too shy to ask for something, Mike strode up and scored us a few beers and sports drinks, which we downed as we bantered for 5 minutes with Don Johnson's guests.

By the final leg of the 30-hour race, we were 9 minutes down on the lead team, with only a 3-mile ride-and-tie (one horse between the three athletes) to the finish. Mike was so fired up he was jumping out of his skin, and kept saying we could still win. This seemed extremely unlikely, given that the time estimate for the leg was 30 minutes, but he was adamant.

The main challenge lay in the trail, which was a thin, winding single-track that snaked its way through a large grove of aspen trees. There was barely room for the horse, so we had to run right on its heels, bouncing off tree trunks as we raced around tight corners and jumped across streams and logs. Luckily for us, the run climbed for 2 miles before turning back downhill for the final mile to the finish. By the time we reached the top, we had the lead team in our sights. We didn't cross the line first, but we did gain back over 7 minutes, a testament to Mike's wining attitude. Without it, we would have sat back and accepted second place, rather than give it our best shot—and this was ultimately much more satisfying.

Organization

To move quickly through a racecourse, you must be organized. You must know where you are going, how long you can last between resupplies, what to take out on the course, the sports and order in the race, and what teammates will do what and when.

Organization is the responsibility of every person on the team, not just the team's manager or leader. It certainly helps to have someone with a complete understanding of the team and of the event, but the team manager shouldn't have to keep tabs on everyone else to ensure compliance. The team manager coordinates and communicates the event requirements, such as equipment, skills, and schedules. With this information, each person on the team needs to hold up his or her end.

Once on the racecourse, the same basic rules apply. It can be very useful to have a designated "equipment" person who carries a master list of the required gear and calls it out to the team in transition areas, but each individual needs to have his or her own gear organized in his or her own box. A hard-sided plastic box such as a Rubbermaid Action Packer, available from outdoor and hardware stores, is the best way to organize your personal race equipment. I have my box divided into four compartments, separated by three stiff cardboard or plastic panels. I designate one compartment for bike gear, one for climbing gear, one for paddling gear, and one for clothing. The equipment in each compartment will vary from race to race depending on the sports involved, and may include equipment for more than one discipline, such as mountaineering and hiking or skating and biking. I print and laminate the equipment lists from the race organization and then tape them to the inside of the lid, along with any other important race information. If I need additional equipment, such as ice axes, hiking poles, and navigational equipment, I tie transparent mesh to the underside of the box lid and store it there, where I can easily see the contents.

Maintenance

Check every piece of equipment and apparel before a race for wear and weak spots. This includes but is not limited to your climbing gear, bike, paddles, shoes, apparel, and pack. There is nothing more frustrating than a broken or blown-out chain, pack strap, or shoe during a race, especially because these occurrences are largely preventable.

An adventure team using the wind to move forward during the 2001 Expedition in the British Virgin Islands.

> *"Having once decided to achieve a certain task,
> achieve it at all costs of tedium and distaste. The gain
> in self-confidence of having accomplished a tiresome
> labor is immense."*
>
> —Arnold Bennett

---

16 SUPPORT CREWS

HOW TO GET ALONG WITH THOSE
WHO WORK BEHIND THE SCENES

Support crews are as indispensable to the team as the athletes on the racecourse. The support crew organizes, packs, unpacks, and transports race equipment and food. They also cook, clean, and provide moral, emotional, and motivational support.

Supporting is just as mentally and emotionally demanding as racing, and crews often operate on less sleep than the athletes. If you plan to compete as an athlete, understanding or even experiencing the work of a support crew will make you a better teammate and will make your support crew's job easier. Consequently, your race will go faster and easier.

At a minimum, a support crew moves the team's equipment and food around the course so that it is in place when the team arrives at each transition area. A top-notch support crew does a whole lot more, and can make the team's transition fast, efficient, and enjoyable. For big supported races, such as Primal Quest, Southern Traverse, or Raid the North Extreme, you should search out people who are well-organized, hard-working, levelheaded, good at making decisions, easygoing, positive, and adaptable. They should also be able to drive large vehicles, navigate roads in the wilderness, move heavy gear boxes, maintain and repair bikes and other race equipment, cook, clean, and motivate.

The best support crew members have a very good understanding of how you think and feel as an athlete. If your support crew members have competed in supported adventure races, they'll anticipate what you need while you're in the transition, often better than you can.

Here is a basic outline of the support crew's job, starting at the race's start line.

1. Pack all gear containers, food tubs, coolers, personal duffel bags, cooking equipment, bikes, kayaks, paddles, any stray items of clothing left by the athletes, and other loose items in the support van.

2. Locate the first transition area on the support crew maps, and plot a course there via the nearest bank, supermarket, outdoors store, and gas station.

3. Collect money from the bank, fill the vehicle with gas, and then purchase equipment and food en route to the first transition area.

4. Locate the transition area and secure the best available location to maximize efficiency for the transition once the team arrives.

5. Check in with the race organizers.

6. Unpack the vehicle, set up tents, shelter, tarpaulin, chairs, tables, stove, gear boxes, and extra personal bags, keeping a check on the time and estimated arrival time of the race team.

7. Start heating food options for the in-transition meal, and lay out food options for the next section of the racecourse.

8. Consult the support crew instructions and maps, and retrieve any additional information from the race organizers.

9. Prepare necessary gear, apparel, food, and water for each athlete for the next section of the course.

10. Prepare the medical kit to treat possible injuries, and tubs for washing feet, if necessary.

11. Prenavigate any new maps, using the course notes.

12. Scout the entry and exit points for the transition and any other parts of the course (abiding by the race rules).

13. Keep food warm and gear dry.

14. Once the team arrives, direct them to the gear and give them an overview of the upcoming course, explaining any pertinent information. Give the navigator(s) maps and instructions. Make clear what team members need and don't need so they can organize themselves.

15. Keep a couple of sets of laminated equipment lists, one list each for the requisite legs, mandatory gear, and other essential items, like food, maps, compass, and race passport. Read off each item required for the upcoming section as soon as the team is settled and listening, and again immediately before they leave. Make sure every person on the team acknowledges that he or she has each item as you read it off, preferably showing you the item.

16. Once the athletes leave, organize and repack everything into the support vehicle and drive like the wind to the next transition area, via the gas station, supermarket, and hardware store, for the inevitable random items now required.

17. Repeat steps 4 through 13, including cleaning and repairing bikes, clothes, and other equipment for the next section.

18. Repeat until the end of the race as you lose sleep and gain a peculiar odor and disheveled look.

It is extremely important as an athlete that you treat your support crew members well, as they perform a difficult job with little or no possibility of recognition. If you treat them with courtesy and respect, you will likely get a thorough, efficient effort in return. Understand that they are working under tough conditions with little sleep, just as you are, but with the additional stress of not knowing where you are or when you will show up.

Teams climb more than 14,000 feet from the start of the 1998 Raid Gauloises in Ecuador.

"Vision is the art of seeing things invisible."

—Jonathan Swift

17 | HOW TO FIND AND KEEP SPONSORSHIP

DISCOVER SUBTLE TRICKS
THAT WILL HELP PAY FOR YOUR ADVENTURE

Expedition-length racing costs between $30,000 and 50,000 a race, including the money needed to travel to exotic locations. Even a season of sprint races costs quite a bit, considering that three to four people have to travel several times a year around the country. Unless you are fabulously rich, you'll need sponsorship.

First, understand that sponsors want to get their money's worth. Any prospective sponsor is entering into a business deal with you to trade goods and/or hard cash for your services. Sponsors rarely enter into an agreement with a team or individual purely out of the goodness of their hearts, so turn on your business brain and come to grips with the idea that you are selling a product, which is you and your team.

There are only a few reasons a company would consider sponsoring an adventure athlete or adventure-racing team. The bottom line is that a for-profit business wants to find a way to increase earnings. You may be able to supply that need through brand exposure, either directly to their target market (with you as an ambassador at races) or through the print or television media. Of these, the most sought after and hardest to guarantee is television coverage to a wide audience. Only a handful of teams of the tens of thousands who race will be lucky enough to get this level of exposure, and even fewer will be successful in doing it with any regularity.

In addition to having a sound business approach to sponsorship, develop the best possible personal relationship with the people involved. When you approach prospective sponsors, try to understand how they think, by putting yourself in their shoes. If someone were soliciting you for money to race, what would you be thinking? Inevitably the answer is "What's in it for me?" You need to have that answer ready.

Most people think that a deep pocket will pay them to race in exchange for wearing a few logos and for naming rights, such as team Acme Widgets, with logos on equipment and apparel. These branding opportunities can be valuable, but Acme Widgets will be much more interested if you can promise to display their logos on television. The probability of this happening is depressingly low, unless you have a really good angle. For most teams the name/branding equation doesn't work.

If you watch the big events like Eco-Challenge on TV, you will notice that only a handful of teams are featured. Unless you win or have a team of movie stars, television personalities, or *Playboy* centerfolds, you are extremely unlikely to get your sponsor's logo-covered shirt on TV. This is where the creative angle comes in. Take a direct approach and simply ask the television producers what they are looking for. You will probably hear an answer that goes something like this: "We are looking for a human-interest story where the people involved are articulate and good-looking, and can create drama that the home viewer can relate to."

Featured teams during past years have included dysfunctional, argumentative disaster teams, feel-good "off-the-couch" success stories, three-women-and-one-man teams, perennial winners, well-known personalities, extremely young or old competitors, and physically challenged athletes. If you don't fall into these categories, you have to pull something else out of the hat to garner interest from a sponsor.

Fortunately, there are other ways you can provide value to your sponsor. Offer to provide images featuring their product and or branding and to prepare race reports and an interactive presentation once the race or race season is over. Make yourself visible (but not annoying) to your sponsor, giving the sponsor the idea that you are invested in the relationship, just as you would be in a friendship. Sponsors are not just big machines. Sponsors are people, and people want to feel liked and important. You can also give product feedback if the sponsor is in a relevant industry, make in-house or public appearances for the sponsor, or conduct workshops and lectures. The bottom line is you have to work for sponsorship, and finishing a race is not the work they are looking for.

Here is a top-10 list of requirements that will give you a potential start on obtaining (and keeping) sponsorship.

1. Prepare a business plan.

2. Build a team résumé, identifying your strengths.

3. Create a team Web site clearly outlining the team's offerings and highlighting any successes or past media coverage. It helps to have a section explaining the sport, since many people have never heard of "adventure racing." Many more have heard of Eco-Challenge, however, so use this as an example.

4. Invest in some serious and attractive business cards, as you will want to be seen as serious and attractive.

5. List potential sponsors and find out who in the organization deals with athletes.

6. If possible, obtain an introduction from a third party. Cold-calling is extremely unproductive and highly irritating to the company's athlete liaison. Most cold calls are eliminated on principle, so get their attention with something unique, like a letter in a pink envelope containing a race jersey (clean, of course) or some other small but memorable gift.

SAMPLE RACE BUDGET

Budgets vary enormously according to the location and complexity of a race. For the majority of races, however, you will have to consider a few major expenses, including entry fees, equipment, travel, accommodation, race food, meals, and sundries. The following is a sample budget for a team of three to comfortably do an out-of-state Balance Bar 24-hour race.

Item	Quantity	Amount	Total	Comment
Entry fee	1	$825	$825	2003 prices
Airfare	4	$400	$1,600	Two-week advance purchase
Travel	4	$100	$400	Parking, gas, tolls, and such
Van rental	3 days	$50	$150	Minivan or similar vehicle
Accommodations	4 rooms, 4 nights	$75	$300	Motel rooms pre- and postrace
Meals	20	$15	$300	Five meals pre- and postrace for four people
Race food	1	$100	$100	Including drinks
Equipment	1	$150	$150	Race-specific equipment, such as bike quick fills, spare tube, and such
Sundries	1	$175	$175	Someone always forgets something
TOTAL			$4,000	

7. Be persistent, but not annoying. Sponsors are in business and expect businesslike behavior. This means returning calls promptly and keeping deadlines and commitments. If they ask for a résumé, send it through the mail and via e-mail. Follow up with a phone call.

8. Make your sponsor your friend, and treat him or her like a friend. Even if you are the best athlete in the world, you will quickly be dismissed if you are unpleasant or difficult. Conversely, you can be an average performer but maintain sponsorship if you are genuinely liked and keep your end of the bargain. Most sponsored teams are not champions at racing; they are champions at being good sponsored athletes.

9. Overdeliver. If the sponsor asks for a finish-line photo with their product, give them a beautifully framed picture with your team,

IAN'S TOP TIPS FOR GETTING AND KEEPING SPONSORSHIP

These are some strategies that have helped my team earn sponsorship.

- Make friends with the athlete liaison in your target company. This is the person who makes recommendations, and quite often decisions, about who gets the money. If this person doesn't like you, you can either make friends or make like a tree (and leave).

- Overdeliver on any sponsor's requests. Make sure you respond quickly, and if asked for three, give four. The counter to this rule is not to promise more than you can deliver. If you say, "We are going to win Eco-Challenge and be shown on most of the coverage," you are kidding yourself and your sponsor. The best teams hope this is the case, but never believe it until the show has aired.

- Respond in a businesslike manner. This means being prompt, efficient, open, and honest. A sponsor-athlete relationship *is* a business relationship. Treat it like one (without compromising your friendship).

their logos, and the race banners prominently featured. It will only cost you $50, but they might reward you next year with another $5,000 or more in product.

10. Don't give up. It can take years to build a solid relationship with a sponsor, so be prepared to start small and grow your partnership with a view to the future.

One last option is to try to get a sports agent to work for you. Sports agents have great contacts, but they are also quite selective in taking athletes on, since they will only put effort into a team that they see as being a moneymaker. The same set of rules for sponsorship applies to an agent: You need to get their attention and sell yourself effectively.

ADVENTURE-RACING RESOURCES

Magazines and Web Sites about the Sport

Action Asia magazine: www.actionasia.com

Adventure Racing Newsgroup (the Adventure Racing Association): www.adventureracing.org

Adventure Sports magazine: www.asmagazine.com

Adventure World magazine: www.usara.com/adventure_world_magazine.htm

AR Extreme E-zine: www.arextreme.com

ARGear Web site—equipment and apparel for adventure racing: www.argear.com

Hooked on the Outdoors magazine: www.ruhooked.com

Inside Triathlon—online multisport journal: www.insidetri.com

United States Adventure Racing Association—for-profit company providing athlete services, publishers of *Adventure World* magazine: www.usara.com

World AR—Fitness and travel help, gear tests, Challenge School for Adventure Racing links: www.worldAR.com

Race and Event Web Sites

Active.com event resource guide: www.active.com

Adrenaline Rush, Ireland: www.asportsone.com

Arctic Team Challenge, Greenland: www.atc.gl

Balance Bar Adventure Race series (24-hour and sprint races), United States: www.balancebaradventure.com

California Sports Marketing, United States: www.csmevents.com

Coast to Coast, New Zealand: www.coasttocoast.co.nz

Corsica Raid, Corsica: www.corsicaraid.com

Cradle to Coast Ultra Challenge, Australia: www.threepeaks.org.au/tasultra/ctc

Desafio de los Volcanes, Chile and Argentina: www.desafiovolcanes.com

Extreme Adventure Hidalgo, Mexico: www.esmas.com

Eco-Challenge, international: www.ecochallenge.com

Expediçâo Mata Atlantica, Brazil: www.ema.com.br

Frontier Adventure Racing, Canada: www.raidthenorth.com

Gravity Play Sports, Colorado and Utah: www.gravityplay.com

Guilin Challenge, China: www.seyonasia.com/guilin/guilin.html

International Bimbache Extrem Raid, Canary Islands: www.meridianoraid.com/bimbache.html

Length of New Zealand Race: www.nzwildplaces.com/introduction.cfm

Mild Seven Outdoor Quest, Asia: www.msoq.com

Primal Quest, United States: www.ecoprimalquest.com

Odyssey Adventure Racing, United States: www.oarevents.com

Raid Gauloises, international: www.raidgauloises.com

Raid Ukatak, Canada: www.ukatak.com

Réunion d'Aventures, Reunion Islands: http://authentiqueaventure.com

Southern Traverse, New Zealand: www.southerntraverse.com

Terra Incognita, Croatia: www.adventurerace.hr

Tour d'Afrique, Africa: www.tourdafrique.com

Wild Onion and Wild Scallion Urban Adventure Race, United States: www.urbanadventureracing.com

X-adventure Raid Series, world cup: www.raidseries.com

Glossary

Abseil. See *Rappel.*

Air traffic controller (ATC). A ropes descending device originally manufactured by Black Diamond. The ATC is a development of the stitch plate and is also available in a variant called a tuber.

Amino acids. The building blocks of protein.

Antibot. A smooth plastic insert to a crampon that prevents the buildup of snow and ice.

Ascender. A type of mechanical controller used to climb ropes. Other types of mechanical ascenders include Jumars, Crolls, Triblocs, and Ropemans.

Azimuth. See *Bearing.*

Bailer. Container used to remove water from the bottom of a boat.

Bearing. A compass course used as a guide while navigating or as a tool to determine location on a map.

Bilge pump (kayak pump). A mechanical pump, usually hand-operated, that is used to empty water from the bottom of a boat (the bilge).

Bladder. A flexible reservoir used to store fluids for hydration while you're on the move. Bladders usually fit inside backpacks and have tube-and-valve systems to allow the water to be sucked by mouth, leaving hands free. The most recognized brand in hydration bladders is CamelBak.

Buoyancy vest. See *Personal flotation device.*

Bush walking. See *Trekking.*

Canoe. An open-decked boat propelled by single-bladed paddles. Canoes are often referred to as Canadian canoes outside North America.

Canyoneering (canyoning). A sport where you cross canyons on foot and by swimming, sometimes with the aid of ropes for rappelling.

Carabiner (biner, crab). A closable metal connector shaped like the link of a chain and used to secure climbing hardware. Carabiners are generally used in adventure races to attach ascending and descending devices to a climbing harness, or a climbing sling to a fixed anchor.

Checkpoint (passport control). Often abbreviated as CP or PC, checkpoints are locations on a racecourse that guide competitors through the intended route.

Climb heist. See *Prusik*.

Climbing sling. See *Sling*.

Coastaleering (coasteering). A sport that involves crossing the coastline of a large body of water. Coastaleering requires athletes to stay a minimum distance from the water and may include swimming, rock hopping, and beach running.

Crampons. Metal or hard-plastic spikes worn on the bottom of a shoe or boot to provide traction on hard snow or ice.

Cutoff time. A clock time specified in races at predetermined locations, after which teams are prevented from continuing. Cutoff times are used to keep the race field from spreading out too far, which can make it difficult to safely manage the course.

Daisy chain. A length of webbing with loops sewn in at regular intervals. Daisy chains are used to secure climbing equipment, such as ascenders, to a climbing harness.

Dark zone. An area or point on a racecourse where teams are not allowed to progress. Dark zones are designated in areas where movement at night may be dangerous, or are used by race directors to keep the race field close together.

Doubletrack. See *Singletrack*.

Dry bag. A waterproof bag used by boaters to keep equipment and apparel dry. Conventional dry bags are made with one end that can be rolled down and secured with buckles, creating a waterproof seal.

Dry suit. A waterproof garment with seals around the neck, wrists, and ankles. Dry suits are used for boating, swimming, and canyoneering in extremely cold conditions.

Duct tape (gaffer tape). Highly adhesive, strong, and flexible cloth-and-plastic tape. Adventure athletes use duct tape for fixing just about everything, from blisters to broken bike frames.

Equipment check (gear check). A section of a race where officials check team gear for compliance to race standards (prerace) or verify that the team has the gear (during the event).

Equipment drop. See *Gear drop.*

Etrie. A small ladder of between four and eight steps made from thin webbing and used to assist in "aid" climbing. Etries are sometimes required in adventure races as part of an ascending setup and are attached with carabiners to the ascenders.

Expedition-style race. An adventure race that takes the form of an expedition. Competing teams are required to carry all their equipment, apparel, and food for extended distances. Most expedition-style races require wilderness navigation and coed teams of three or four.

Figure eight. A piece of metal shaped like the figure "8" that is used for rappelling. The climbing rope is threaded through the figure eight and then attached to the climbing harness with a carabiner.

Foot loop. A lightweight climbing aid used as part of an ascending setup for fixed ropes. Foot loops are typically shaped like a step and made from $1/4$-inch-diameter cord and $1/2$-inch flat tape between the ascender and your foot.

Gaffer tape. See *Duct tape.*

Gaiter. A fabric cover that seals the opening between your shoe or boot and your leg, preventing dirt, rocks, vegetation, or snow from entering your footwear.

Gear check. See *Equipment check*.

Gear drop (equipment drop). A location on the racecourse where officials or the support crew leave gear to be collected by the team at a later time. Alternatively, it can be a location where teams leave gear for pickup.

Global positioning system (GPS). An electronic device used to accurately determine position on the Earth's surface. GPSs use radio signals to triangulate a position in three-dimensional space, displaying north-south, east-west, and altitude information. GPSs are rarely allowed for use as navigation aids in races, but are frequently required as an emergency positioning tool.

Glycemic index. A measure of how fast particular dietary carbohydrates are converted into blood sugar after ingestion. Carbohydrates with a high glycemic index (such as simple sugars) are converted quickly, and low glycemic index foods (such as raw foods high in fiber) are converted slowly.

Halogen bulb. A high-illumination light source used in powerful bike lights and headlamps. Halogen bulbs use a lot of energy and consequently require high-capacity batteries, which are quite heavy.

Hike-a-bike. The process of carrying your bike through unridable terrain.

Hiking. See *Trekking*.

Hot spots. Localized areas on the skin that become "hot" as blood is diverted to a site of irritation, often an indication of an impending blister, particularly on the feet.

Hyperthermia. Abnormally high body temperature.

Hyponatremia. A condition in which excess water absorption in the intestines dilutes the blood and lowers its sodium concentration.

Hypothermia. Abnormally low body temperature.

Jumar. See *Ascender.*

Kayak. An enclosed boat propelled with a double-bladed paddle. Kayaks are typically used in conditions where rough water can swamp an open boat. Sit-on-top kayaks are an exception to the "enclosed" definition, as there is no internal space for the paddler, who sits completely in the open on top of the boat.

Kayak pump. See *Bilge pump.*

Kite. A large aerofoil, similar to a paraglider canopy, used for sailing downwind or crosswind from a canoe or kayak. Most kites are adapted from kite-boarding equipment.

Le Mans start. A start in which the competitors do a short run to their bikes or boats.

Life jacket. See *Personal flotation device.*

Light-emitting diode (LED). A type of incandescent light that is very bright and has extremely low energy consumption. LEDs are the light of choice for most low to moderate lighting requirements for adventure races.

Lithium battery. A high-energy, low-weight battery used when weight is critical. Lithium batteries provide roughly double the electrical storage capacity at half the weight of regular alkaline batteries, and cost twice as much.

Logistics team. See *Support crew.*

Mandatory gear (mandatory equipment). Gear or equipment required by a race organization to be carried during designated parts of the course.

Mountaineering. The sport of climbing and traversing mountainous terrain on foot.

Mystery event. See *Special test.*

Navigation. The art of determining position, course, and distance traveled.

Orienteering. A timed cross-country event in which athletes or teams navigate using map and compass.

Passport (race passport). A document used in some races to verify the passage of a team through the race checkpoints and transition areas. Passports were originally introduced in the Raid Gauloises in 1989.

Passport control. See *Checkpoint.*

Personal flotation device (PFD, life jacket, buoyancy vest). A buoyant jacketlike garment used to keep a person's head above the surface of water.

Portage. A section of a paddling course where it is required or desirable to carry the boats rather than paddle them.

Prologue. A short event or race preceding the main race. Prologues are often used to determine race start order, familiarize athletes with unusual equipment, or acclimatize athletes to the race environment.

Prusik (prussic). A short section of climbing cord generally about $1/4$ inch in diameter that is tied in a loop between 24 and 48 inches in circumference and used as an automatic stop when wrapped around a climbing rope. A prusik made from a climbing sling is called a climb heist.

Race passport. See *Passport.*

Rappel (abseil). A controlled descent of a rock face, using a rope, a climbing harness, and a descending device such as an ATC (air traffic controller) or figure eight.

Recommended dietary allowance (RDA). The quantity of essential nutrients required to maintain the nutritional needs of healthy humans.

Ride-and-tie. See *Team biathlon.*

Rogaining. A style of orienteering that is time-limited rather than timed. Competitors are scored on the number of points accumulated in a set time, usually 6, 8, 12, or 24 hours. Score-O's are similar to rogaining events, but are much shorter, from 1 to 3 hours.

Sewn sling. See *Sling.*

Shortened course. A racecourse that is reduced in length because of safety concerns or to allow teams to finish within the predetermined time limits.

Shunt. A climbing device made by Petzl that is used as a mechanical prusik and typically required by European-based races, such as the Salomon X-Adventure.

Singletrack. A narrow path that is only wide enough for a single bike or person to use.

Skill testing. Prerace tests conducted by the race organization to verify that athletes have the required skills to safely complete the course.

Sling (climbing sling, sewn sling, tether). A loop of woven nylon or Spectra (high-strength Aramid fiber) tape used in rock climbing and ropes courses to secure a climber or climbing equipment.

Special test (mystery event, adventure skill). A section of a racecourse that require athletes to perform team tasks, unusual skills, cultural events, or unannounced sports.

Spray skirt (spray deck). A waterproof cover that seals the cockpit of a kayak or canoe from water. Spray decks are designed to seal around the boat's gunwale or cockpit coaming (the outer edge of the boat) and the paddler.

Sprint race. An adventure race of less than 6 hours.

Stage race. Any race broken into stages and in which the winning team has the shortest accumulated time over the combined stages. Typical stage race formats consist of: (1) several consecutive days of racing, with stages from 6 to 12 hours per day and a full night's rest between stages; (2) Consecutive stages lasting 6, 12, and 24 hours and completed over 4 days, with downtime between stages, depending on the speed of each team through the course; or (3) several days of near-continuous racing, with 1- to 4-hour stages and 15- to 30-minute stops between stages.

Support crew (logistics team). A team of one or more people who provide logistical support for the race team. Support crews transport and organize the race team's equipment and food between transition areas and provide moral support.

Team biathlon (ride-and-tie). A specialized sport in which athletes on a team share a reduced number of bikes, skates, boats, or horses. Team biathlon with teams of four, for example, could require each team to share one, two, or three bikes.

Tether. See *Sling*.

Tramping. See *Trekking*.

Transition area (TA). A point in a racecourse where teams can change equipment, apparel, and food, and possibly receive new maps and instructions.

Trekking (hiking, tramping, bush walking). Covering large distances on foot while carrying a backpack and equipment.

Throw bag. A length of buoyant rope stored in a small bag that is used for river rescues. A throw bag is constructed in such a way that the rope can be gripped at one end and uncoil as the bag is thrown toward the party being rescued. The bag itself is attached to a handle that can be held by the person in distress and is highly visible when floating in the water.

Towline. A thin cord used to tether a faster athlete(s) to a slower athlete(s) to increase the net speed of the team.

Tyrolean traverse. A method of crossing a deep chasm by using fixed ropes or cable. Tyrolean traverses are generally horizontal and require some strength and technique to negotiate efficiently. Tyroleans are often included in races as an adventure skill, rather than for practical reasons.

Universal Transverse Mercator (UTM). An international coordinate system used to specify positions on the Earth's surface. UTM grids are divided into 1,000-meter squares and generally have each square divided into increments of 1, 10, and 100 meters.

Unranked. The status of a team that is no longer included in the competition. An unranked team can usually continue the course but is ineligible for prize money or position in the final rankings.

V-sail. A small V-shaped sail used on canoes and kayaks in downwind or crosswind conditions. V-sails are mounted to the deck of a boat and may or may not have control lines.

Way point. A position on a map or racecourse that is used as an intermediate navigation point between checkpoints. It is not generally mandatory to find way points, but they may define an efficient, safe, or easy route.

Wet suit. A neoprene or synthetic fiber garment that preserves body heat when wet. Wetsuits are used for boating, swimming, and canyoneering.

Whitewater. Moving water in a creek or river that is colored white due to heavy turbulence and aeration. Whitewater is graded under an international classification between I and VI. Class I is easy, class II novice, class III intermediate, class IV advanced, class V expert, and class VI almost impossible.

Zip line (flying fox). A tight rope or cable with a downward slope used to cross an unsafe area or provide a shortcut through a racecourse. Zip lines are often included in races as an adventure skill, rather than for practical reasons.

Sample Training Programs

Use the basic structure of the following training programs to build a training schedule for your next adventure race. I've designed these programs with periodization in mind, to allow for rest, recovery, and build phases.

PROGRAM ONE

A 4-week training plan for a sprint race designed for recreational athletes

P1–sprint	Mon.	Tues.	Wed.	Thurs.	Fri.	Sat.	Sun.
Week 1	R–rec	R–spd	P–end	B–end	S–end	R/B–end/skl	P/S–str
Week 2	B–rec	B–spd	P–end	R–end	B–skl	P/S–end/skl	R/B–str
Week 3	P–rec	P–spd	R–end	B–end	R–skl	R/B/P–end	rst
Week 4	S–rec	R–rec	B–rec	P–rec	rst	race	rst

Sport key: **R**—run, **B**—bike, **P**—paddle, **S**—specialized sport, such as skate, ski, or climb

Training key: **str**—strength (hills, weights), **spd**—speed (intervals, threshold), **end**—endurance (long, slow distance), **skl**—skills, **rec**—recovery, easy session, **rst**—rest, **race**—your event

PROGRAM TWO

A 6-week training program for a sprint race designed for competitive athletes

P2–sprint	Mon.	Tues.	Wed.	Thurs.	Fri.	Sat.	Sun.
Week 1	R–rec	R–spd, P–end	B–end, R–rec	P–end, B–str	S–end/skl	R/B– end/skl	P/S– end/skl
Week 2	B–rec	B–spd, P–end	R–end, P–spd	R–str, B–rec	B–end/skl	P/S– end/skl	R/B–str
Week 3	P–rec	P–spd, R–end	R–spd, B–end	B–end, P–str	R–end/skl	R/B/P– end	rst
Week 4	R–rec	R–spd	B–end, P–spd	R–end, B–end	P–end/skl	R/B– end/skl	rst
Week 5	B–rec	B–spd	R–end	B–end	P–end	R/B/P/S– end	rst
Week 6	S–rec	R–rec	B–rec	P–rec	rst	race	rst

Sport key: **R**—run, **B**—bike, **P**—paddle, **S**—specialized sport, such as skate, ski, or climb

Training key: **str**—strength (hills, weights), **spd**—speed (intervals, threshold), **end**—endurance (long, slow distance), **skl**—skills, **rec**—recovery, easy session, **rst**—rest, **race**—your event

PROGRAM THREE

A 2-month training program for a weekend race designed for recreational athletes

P3–w/end	Mon.	Tues.	Wed.	Thurs.	Fri.	Sat.	Sun.
Week 1	R–rec	R–spd	P–end	B–end	S–end	R/B–end/skl	P/S–str
Week 2	B–rec	B–spd	P–end	R–end	B–skl	P/S–end/skl	R/B–str
Week 3	P–rec	P–spd	R–end	B–end	R–skl	R/B/P–end	rst
Week 4	S–rec	R–rec	B–rec	P–rec	rst	sprint race	rst
Week 5	R–rec	B–rec	P–rec	R–end	B–end	R/B–end/skl	P/S–str
Week 6	B–rec	B–spd	P–end	R–end	B–skl	P/S–end/skl	R/B–str
Week 7	P–rec	R–spd	B–end	P–end	R–skl	R/B/P–end	rst
Week 8	S–rec	R–rec	B–rec	P–rec	rst	race	rst

Sport key: **R**—run, **B**—bike, **P**—paddle, **S**—specialized sport, such as skate, ski, or climb

Training key: **str**—strength (hills, weights), **spd**—speed (intervals, threshold), **end**—endurance (long, slow distance), **skl**—skills, **rec**—recovery, easy session, **rst**—rest, **race**—your event

Program Four

A 3-month training program for a weekend race designed for competitive athletes

To train for a race longer than 48 hours, use the weekend training plan and make your sessions longer. When going longer, you have to reduce your intensity and increase your recovery time. If you train intelligently, you should be physically capable of stepping up to a multiday race.

P4–w/end	Mon.	Tues.	Wed.	Thurs.	Fri.	Sat.	Sun.
Week 1	R–rec	R–spd, P–end	B–end, R–rec	P–end, B–str	S–end/skl	R/B–end/skl	P/S–end/skl
Week 2	B–rec	B–spd, P–end	R–end, P–spd	R–str, B–rec	B–end/skl	P/S–end/skl	R/B–str
Week 3	P–rec	P–spd, R–end	R–spd, B–end	B–end, P–str	R–end/skl	R/B/P–end	rst
Week 4	R–rec	R–spd	B–end, P–spd	R–end, B–end	P–end/skl	R/B–end/skl	rst
Week 5	B–rec	B–spd	R–end	B–end	P–end	R/B/P/S–end	rst
Week 6	S–rec	R–rec	B–rec	P–rec	rst	Sprint race	rst

Sport key: R—run, B—bike, P—paddle, S—specialized sport, such as skate, ski, or climb

Training key: str—strength (hills, weights), spd—speed (intervals, threshold), end—endurance (long, slow distance), skl—skills, rec—recovery, easy session, rst—rest, race—your event

P4–w/end	Mon.	Tues.	Wed.	Thurs.	Fri.	Sat.	Sun.
Week 7	R–rec	R–spd, P–end	B–end, R–rec	P–end, B–str	S–end/skl	R/B–end/skl	P/S–end/skl
Week 8	B–rec	B–spd, P–end	R–end, P–spd	R–str, B–rec	B–end/skl	P/S–end/skl	R/B–str
Week 9	P–rec	P–spd, R–end	R–spd, B–end	B–end, P–str	R–end/skl	R/B/P–end	rst
Week 10	R–rec	R–spd	B–end, P–spd	R–end, B–end	P–end/skl	R/B–end/skl	rst
Week 11	B–rec	B–spd	R–end	B–end	P–end	R/B/P/S–end	rst
Week 12	S–rec	R–rec	B–rec	P–rec	rst	sprint race	rst

INDEX

Underscored references indicate boxed text.

Bicycle racks, 200
Bicycles. *See also* Cycling
  accessories for, 200–203
  boxes for, 65–67
  cable repair, 64
  carrying methods, 52–53
  cleaning of, 61–62
  computers for, 202
  equipment options, 56–57
  fit of, 44–45
  flat tire inflator, 202
  hand brakes on foreign, 46
  lighting for, 201
  lubrication of, 62
  maintenance of, 61–63
  mud guards for, 202
  packing and transporting, 65–67
  repair of, 63–65
  seat pads for, 202
  suspension styles, 56–57
  tips from an expert, 60
  tires for, 57–58
  types of, 56–57
Bike Nashbar products, 200, 202
BikePro bike bag, 65, 66
Bilge pump, defined, 240
Bilibilis, 134
Black Diamond light, 204
Bladders, hydration, 240
Bleeding, due to injury, 182
Blisters on feet
  causes of, 180
  keeping feet dry, 180
  treating, 180–81
Boating. *See* Canoeing; Kayaking
Boats. *See* Canoes; Kayaks
Bodyglide, 39
Body position, bicycle, 47
Bottle cages, for bicycles, 203
Boxes, bicycle, 65–66
Brakes, bicycle
  disc brakes, 59–60
  repair of, 64
  V-brakes, 60
Braking, bicycle
  on foreign bicycles, 46
  skills to hone, 45–46
Brooks Trespass shoes, 192
Brown, Frank, 5
Budget, sample, 234. *See also* Cost of racing
Bull, Dan, 6
Buoyancy vest, defined, 240

Burton, Richard, 3
Bush walking. *See* Trekking

C

Cables, bicycle, repair of, 64
Cabot, John, 3
Calories burned, in racing, 159
CAMDEX (Mexico), 17
CamelBak products
  hydration bladders, 240
  Rally pack, 200
Canadian canoes, 240
Canadian Mountain Guide system, 92
Cannondale Jeckel, 57
Canoeing
  clothing for, 190–91
  currents and, 85–88
  fitness training for, 150–53
  historic feat, 70
  loading and packing, 82–83
  paddles for, 74
  portaging, 78–79, 82
  sailing, 77–78
  shoes for, 193–94
  surfing, 84–85
  towing, 75–77, 77, 214
  wash riding, 75
  waves and, 83–85
  wind and, 80–81, 83
Canoe races, origins of, 5
Canoes
  accessories for, 198–99
  defined, 240
  gear bags for, 82–83
  paddles for, 72, 74
  perau outrigger, 139
  sails for, 77–78
  seating accessories, 196–97
  towlines for, 75–77
Canyon, as map feature, 118
Canyoneering
  defined, 241
  shoes for, 193
Canyoning. *See* Canyoneering
Carabiner, defined, 241
Carbohydrates
  in drinks, 165–66
  for endurance, 160–61
  kinds of, 163
  role in body, 161–63
  sample meal plan, 161

International Bimbache Extrem Raid
(Canary Islands)
description of, 29
as example of stage race, 17
International races
costs of, 22
descriptions of, 19–30
global compasses for, 109
illness and, 183
local customs and, 212
Interval training, for speed, 144
Ion light, 204
Ironman (Hawaii), 6–7

J

Jacoby, John, 86
Jenks, Cameron, 73
JET Lites bicycle lights, 204
Jones, Neil, 220
Jugs. *See* Ascenders
Jumar ascender, 93
Jumars. *See* Ascenders
Jumbo inflatable canoe, 71
Jumping obstacles, with bicycle, 47–48
Jungles, clothing for, 187–88

K

Kahtoolah shoe-traction systems, 196
Kayaking
clothing for, 190–91, 195
currents and, 85–88
fitness training for, 150–53
historic feat, 70
hypothermia and, 190
loading and packing, 82–83
in the ocean, 88–89
paddling tips from an expert, 86
painful seating story, 197
portaging, 78–79, 82
sailing, 77–78
shoes for, 193–94
surfing, 84–85, 89
towing, 75–77, 77, 214
wash riding, 75
waves and, 83–85, 84
whitewater race story, 73
wind and, 83, 84
Kayaks
accessories for, 196–99
defined, 244
paddles for, 72, 74

sails for, 77–78
seats for, 196–97, 197
spray skirts for, 197–98
towlines for, 75–77
types of, 70–71
Ketosis, 162–63
Kites, for sailing
defined, 244
fixed sails, 78
kite-board sails, 77–78
recommended brands, 199
Kloser, Mike, 6, 54, 60, 134, 201, 220, 223–24
Knoll, as map feature, 117

L

Lactose, 163
Ladders, for traverse, 100
Lake crossings, with bicycles, 48–49
Lassy, Ernest, 70
Layers, base, for
aquatic environments, 191
arctic winters, 190
cycling, 191
deserts, 187
forest environments, 188
high alpine areas, 189
Leadership, 212–13
LED, defined, 244
Leg curls, 156
Le Mans start, defined, 244
Length of New Zealand Race, 28
Leptospirosis, 183
Lewis and Clark, 2
Light-emitting diode (LED), 244
Lights and lighting
batteries for, 204
portable types, 203
Lindermann, Hannes, 70
Lithium battery, defined, 244
Livingstone, David, 3
Logistics teams. *See* Support crews
Lotus Design Core Skin Shirt, 191
Lubricants, foot
best products, 39
recipe for homemade, 39–40
Lubrication of bicycle components, 62
Luggage racks for bicycles, 200

M

Magazines about adventure racing, 237
Maintenance, bicycle, 61–63